Contents

To my wife Elissa and my son Charles

Foreword

We were more than pleased when Harrison Steeves asked us to write the foreword for this book; in fact, we are honored to do so. Throughout the following pages, the real Harry Steeves emerges to treat and delight us with his wit and humor, and more importantly, to introduce us to his innovative fly patterns. His wizardry at the vice comes through loud and clear. As the pages fly by, we are sure the readers, like us, will find themselves torn between putting the book down and rushing to the vice to tie one of Harry's new patterns or turning the next page in anticipation of what's to come.

Harry laughs when he thinks of the late Vincent Marinaro scoffing at the synthetic fly patterns in his fly boxes. But having spent many seasons with the old master, we can tell you that even Marinaro would be impressed with Harry's creativity. Marinaro has been credited with introducing us to the world of terrestrial insects and their value to us as fly tiers and fly fishermen and rightfully so, but Harry moves us light years ahead in fly design with his realistic and fascinating ideas for creating terrestrial patterns that literally crawl out of our fly boxes.

Harrison Steeves is more than a creative fly tier, he is a passionate and driven individual. He pushes forward with new insights in fly design and materials, but even more important is his sincere desire to share his ideas with others. We see Harry each year at most of the Fly Fishing Only Shows. He sits tying his patterns behind a chest-high table for all to see. The tabletop is covered with synthetic materials of all kinds and examples of his finished work. In front of the table his audience stands spellbound as they watch Harry work. He looks up as he puts a final whip-finish on his fly, and you can see a glint or sparkle in his eye, the Merlin in Harry at his best.

This is a book for all of us who endeavor to create and tie terrestrial imitations and the like. It gives us new insights and ideas to play with and it gets those creative juices flowing. But it's also a book that at times reads like a best-selling novel, capturing our attention and imagination as we find ourselves eagerly turning the pages as we become engrossed by its author's prose.

Harry, you've outdone yourself with this one! Thank you.

—Cathy & Barry Beck

Acknowledgments

Thanks to all those at Stackpole Books who were invaluable in the preparation of this book. Special thanks to Judith Schnell for her support and faith and to Amy Dimeler, whose aid in the preparation of the manuscript was invaluable.

Thanks also to all the people with whom I have traveled the roads to and from different streams. Your companionship and friendship over the years have been a joy. You have often turned a boring drive into a unique and unforgettable experience. On certain occasions the drive has been even better and more interesting than the fishing.

Finally, thanks to all those who have been kind enough to share the experiences fishing the patterns presented here.

Introduction

It's difficult for me to believe that the book *Terrestrials,* which I authored with Ed Koch, was published by Stackpole Books over eight years ago. There's been a lot of water pass by the waders, a bunch of fish taken, and a host of new patterns developed since then. Although some of what we considered cutting edge in the world of terrestrials back in 1995 has become established practice, much concerning the terrestrial mystique still remains. We still don't know why a trout will take a terrestrial pattern in the middle of a mayfly hatch. We still can't explain the trout's fascination with ants as an integral part of the diet. I still wonder why a cricket pattern is so effective, because I don't think that there are all that many crickets that fall into a trout stream. And why would any self-respecting trout eat something like a Los Alamos Ant pattern, which doesn't look like any terrestrial (or any other insect) that I have ever encountered? These are just a few of the things that we can't explain, but I gave up trying to explain trout behavior regarding dietary preferences a long time ago. We can speculate about these subjects all we want to, and sure, it's a lot of fun to think and argue about these things, but it really doesn't get us anywhere.

What is really amazing to me is the number of new terrestrial patterns that have been developed during this eight-year period. I really should go back through all the literature, particularly the more popular magazines, and catalogue these patterns, but I don't have the energy. This hasn't just occurred here in the United States. Every time I pick up one of the leading foreign fly-fishing magazines, I see descriptions and articles about new and unusual terrestrial patterns. It's almost as though we are experiencing a terrestrial renaissance! But why now?

One of the reasons, and maybe the most important one, may be that we now have a host of new materials available to incorporate into fly patterns. Something like closed-cell foam has been around for decades and has been used by many tiers, but other materials have only recently gained popularity. One has only to spend an hour or so in any well-stocked fly shop to get an idea of all the materials that have recently become available to the tier. Where did they all come from? That's a good question. I suspect the answer lies in the insatiable curiosity of most tiers and their propensity to haunt places like craft shops, needlepoint stores, and fabric shops. That and the fact that many tiers are somehow involved in the trade portion of the industry probably account for the majority of the new materials reaching the market. Something new will always put a few extra bucks in your pocket, so the profit motive cannot be discounted.

This "synthetic revolution" is certainly not limited to terrestrial patterns. More and more tiers are now incorporating these synthetic materials into caddis, mayfly, and stonefly patterns as well, and with phenomenal results. Many of these patterns would have been the envy of the "old-time" tiers, but only if they were willing to accept the use of synthetic materials rather than natural fur and feathers. There would of course be some who would not only balk at this heresy but would probably die of apoplexy if presented with something like a damselfly tied with only synthetic materials. A good example of this sort of purist would certainly be Vince Marinaro, who would undoubtedly have tried to strangle me if he had ever taken a peak into my fly box. Even today there are those who refuse to consider the various synthetics as valid tying materials. They still prefer to tie with natural materials. That is certainly their prerogative, but I believe that they are handicapping themselves. I have seen all sorts of patterns tied with synthetics that were absolutely beautiful renditions of the aquatic insects they represented. All of the new types of foam, synthetic dubbing, fibers, rubber legs, winging material, and many more man-made materials allow a freedom of expression to the tier that was not available a few decades ago. As the saying goes, "better fly fishing through chemistry."

Talented designers/tiers like John Betts, Phil Camera, Skip Morris, A. K. Best, Bob Popovics, and a host of others have produced patterns using synthetic materials that have taken a rightful place in the fly boxes of many. These patterns range from delicate mayfly imitations to wonderful creations for use in both warm-water and saltwater fly fishing. Their effectiveness is certainly not questionable. Thousands of fish have been taken on these patterns, and thousands more will be taken in the future. Although there are many patterns that are tied with only synthetic materials, there are many others that incorporate both synthetic and natural materials in their design. Here you have the best of both worlds because there are certainly natural materials for which there is no acceptable synthetic substitute. For example, I have yet to find any synthetic materials on the market that could serve as a substitute for peacock herl. Nor have I found any acceptable substitute for turkey feathers, marabou, or ostrich herl, all of which I use in many of my designs.

Chapter 1

Designing a Terrestrial Pattern

What sort of design represents a "good" terrestrial pattern? There is more than one answer to this question. One tier might define a good terrestrial pattern as an accurate imitation of some land-dwelling insect, whereas another believes that a good terrestrial pattern is more impressionistic than realistic. Bob Mead probably ties the most realistic terrestrial patterns of any of the modern fly designers, but you probably wouldn't want to fish with one of them. At least I can't conceive of anyone tying on one of his $800 praying mantis patterns and fishing it. You might want to fish one of his ladybugs, but that could run into money too. Another tier who produces beautifully realistic patterns is David Martin, but at $9 to $20 a pop, I don't think there are many folks who are going to sacrifice one of these to the fish gods. Maybe I'm wrong though, because there are probably those few to whom a 24-inch brown would be worth more than the cost of the fly. I don't believe, however, that there are that many anglers out there who are going to load up their fly boxes with patterns by either of these extremely talented tiers.

On the opposite side of the coin we have the impressionists who turn out patterns that resemble the original closely enough to fool a fish. Members of this school of design have been around a long time. McCafferty's Lacquered Ant, the Letort Hopper, and the Letort Cricket are examples of impressionistic patterns with which we are all familiar. Most of us have fished at least one of these patterns, and many of us have fly boxes crammed full of impressionistic patterns. Whitlock's Hopper, Lawson's Henry's Fork Hopper, fur ants, different cricket patterns, maybe a few examples of wasps and bees, Crowe Beetles, and inchworms are all common residents in many fly boxes. We fish them because they work, and they are inexpensive. When one compares the price of any of these with some of the saltwater and warm-water creations, the cost really isn't too bad.

We also have tiers who produce terrestrial patterns that do not fall into either of the preceding categories. These patterns really don't look like anything that walks, crawls, or flies, but they can be extremely effective. In many instances, they are more effective than any of the impressionistic patterns.

Take the Chernobyl Ant, for example. It doesn't look at all like an ant. It doesn't look like any terrestrial I've ever run into, but it is one of the most effective patterns developed in the last ten years. The development of this pattern is of interest because it was an evolutionary process. A number of anglers were involved, each in his own way, and the result was the development and naming of one of the most unusual and effective patterns to be produced within the last decade.

I knew that Larry Tullis of Orem, Utah, was somehow involved with this pattern, so I cornered him at a fly-fishing show and asked him to send me something about the development of the Chernobyl Ant. Here is what Larry had to say:

> The Chernobyl Ant is a great attractor fly that is a good imitator of cicadas, crickets, grasshoppers, and other terrestrial insects. Its development is (was) a collaborative effort by a number of individuals. I probably was the first to tie up a foam-body Cicada (from a foam beach sandal) for the Green River in the late 1970s, and I showed it to other Green River guides in the mid-1980s, but my foam Cicada looked little like the current Chernobyl Ant.
>
> The acknowledged originator, Mark Forslund, came up with the earliest version in the mid-1980s and called the hackled, black, closed-cell foam overbodied fly the Black Momba. Allen Wooley (Green River guide for Western Fly Fishers of Salt Lake City, Utah) added the rubber legs instead of the hackles, and the current version was born. Someone else whose name I can't remember actually dubbed the fly Chernobyl Ant (Mark would know). Emmett Heath, famous Green River guide, introduced the Chernobyl Ant to famous Jackson Hole angler Jack Dennis during a guided film

session on the Green River. The fly later won the prestigious Jackson Hole 1-Fly Contest (a contest organized and hosted by Jack Dennis Sports), and its fame quickly spread from there.

Well, that's the story of the Chernobyl Ant, and although Larry says that it is "a good imitator of cicadas, crickets, grasshoppers, and other terrestrial insects," I don't necessarily agree with him. It doesn't really look like any of these insects, but there are a great many patterns that are extremely effective and yet don't look like anything in particular. What's going on here?

Quite a few of my own patterns fall into this classification. Take the UFO, for example. I've never seen a terrestrial insect that even came close to looking like this thing, but I have caught hundreds of fish with it. What is the Madame X supposed to imitate? Nothing that I know of, and yet it is an incredibly effective pattern. What in blazes accounts for the effectiveness of these off-the-wall patterns? I don't really have a good answer for this question, and I'm not sure anyone else does either. Do they somehow trigger the aggressive tendencies of a fish (and I say fish, not trout, because many of these patterns are killers on smallmouth bass and panfish). Do they arouse the "curiosity" of the fish to the point that it feels as though it's just got to eat the thing? Do they trigger the aggressive tendencies of a fish to protect its turf and destroy the odd-looking intruder? Are they representative of a good hearty meal with a minimum expenditure of energy? If I could think like a fish, I would be able to answer these questions, but unfortunately, none of us has the ability to peek inside that tiny little brain and see just exactly what is going on. Personally, I think that all of these oddball patterns look like food, and a lot of food at that. What self-respecting trout is going to turn down one of these juicy offerings?

In the final analysis, what we have in terrestrial design are very realistic patterns, impressionistic patterns, and what I am going to term *imaginative* patterns. The same classification would probably work for any group of flies, aquatic as well as terrestrial. This is all well and good, but it doesn't tell you anything about how a tier comes up with an imaginative pattern. How does one go about designing one of these things? Frankly, I don't have a good answer for that question, but I can tell you a little about how it seems to happen.

First of all, in most instances I don't believe that anyone who designs a "new" fly is actually coming up with anything new. I think that most of the time something finally clicks in the cerebrum, and an idea begins to form. Now, what triggers that click could be almost anything. Sometimes it's watching someone else tie a fly, sometimes it's an article or a picture in a fly-fishing magazine, sometimes it's a comment made during a conversation. Whatever the trigger might be, that click sets off a series of reactions that sends us to the tying bench. Sometimes we manage to come up with something really interesting, sometimes the idea never really seems to work, and sometimes we discover that the idea is not really our idea at all! It never ceases to amaze me that so many "new ideas" in the world of the fly tier have been around for years. I remember that quite a few years back I woke up early one morning (real early) after I had spent the evening tying some size 22 and 24 Parachute Blue-Winged Olives. I struggled with the parachute post just like everyone else, and the results were not very satisfying. As I lay there in bed, something pulled that cerebral trigger, and an idea popped into my head that would just not wait for morning. So, careful not to disturb my wife, I got up and went downstairs to the tying bench to try out this new idea. Sure enough, it worked like a charm. It worked so well that I couldn't seem to stop and was busy cranking out the last one of about two dozen when my wife came down and reminded me that I did have to go to work that day.

A couple of weeks after that I was tying at a show in New Jersey and ran into Bob Lay and Al Beatty. I couldn't wait to show them this "new" technique, so I dragged Bob down to my tying bench, set a 24 hook in the vise, and showed off the new procedure. Bob got this funny look on his face, broke into a big grin, and said, "Hang on, I'll be back in a second."

When Bob came back to the bench, he presented me with a tape he and Al had recently done on tying techniques and said, "Take a look at this. We have that technique on our tape." Was I disappointed? Yes, a little bit, because I really thought that I had made a major discovery and was ready to share it with the world. This brought home to me the idea that there really may be nothing "new" in the world of fly tying.

On the other hand, sometimes someone comes up with what might truly be called a new idea or technique. It doesn't happen to me very often, but I do remember one event in particular. This also happened in New Jersey at a fly-fishing show (strange coincidence, or is there just something about New Jersey?). It was Sunday afternoon, things had reached an unbelievably slow point, and some of us were just sort of goofing off and not doing much of anything. As I recall, Ken Mead, Marty Bartholomew, A. K. Best, and a few others—including me-were having a contest to see who could tie the best GloBug. Imagine, all these good tiers sitting around with a bunch of egg yarn wasting time. Anyway, when this little contest was over, I was sitting idly at the vise, not thinking much about anything and playing with one of those little cutters that you plug the end of a cigar with. This thing doesn't cut the end off the cigar, but cuts a nice neat little circle out of the end. So there I was, playing with this cigar plugger, and I pushed the thing down on a piece of sheet foam sitting on the tying bench. Lo and behold, I had a nice little foam circle. Something clicked! I put a hook in the vise, attached tying thread and peacock herl to the hook shank, wound the peacock herl to the eye of the hook, and tied the disc down on top of the hook. Wings were added, and the Disc O'Beetle pattern was born. How long did this take? Maybe three minutes at the most, but I had a very nice beetle pattern, one that I thought would prove to be very effective and was a tier's dream. A. K. Best took one look at the beetle pattern and said, "Well, I'll be damned," and that was the general consensus of the other tiers.

Since then, the foam circle has become one of the major bits of ordinance in my fly-tying arsenal and has been incorporated in many of the new patterns presented here. And I believe that this idea of using a foam circle was perhaps a true "new" idea in the world of the tier. I cannot remember ever seeing anything about this in any fly-fishing magazines over the past twenty-five years, have never read anything about it in a book, and have never heard of anyone else using foam circles (until fairly recently). But does this make it a truly new idea or technique? Maybe someone else did it first and never bothered to write anything about it. They may have used them only for their own particular patterns and never publicized the technique. That's something I'll never know.

When it came to designing the Disc O'Beetle, it was nothing more than a little luck and some boredom. It happened so quickly that I am not sure how it happened. There was certainly not very much thought involved in the process. But this is the exception rather than the rule. Most new patterns take a good deal more time and effort than this, and they all seem to involve a period of what I would call "synthesis." That is to say, you think about it a lot before you ever sit down at the vise and start experimenting—and I do mean experimenting. On some patterns I tie quite a few prototypes before I'm pleased with the finished product. On my fly-tying desk are jars full of prototype patterns that for one reason or another have not lived up to my expectations, but I don't discard them—I fish with them. They might not be exactly what I have been looking for, but there really isn't anything wrong with them. They'll still catch fish, which don't seem to look at the pattern with the critical eye of the tier. And you know what? They work just fine. The problem is that I am not completely satisfied with the design, so they go into my fly boxes rather than to the general market. I also give a lot of these discards away, and so far no one has objected to their performance on the stream.

Designing any new pattern obviously takes time, effort, and a lot of thought, but when it comes to designing terrestrials, I feel pretty lucky. In many instances, what I am trying to do is to effectively imitate a natural insect. You have to do this for certain terrestrials such as Japanese beetles, hoppers, crickets, and any other insect that you are specifically trying to imitate. But, taking a page from one of Vince Marinaro's books, I learned long ago that sometimes a generalized pattern works just dandy. Marinaro's Jassid pattern is the perfect example of this. He realized that it was absolutely impossible to design a pattern for every single species of treehopper, leafhopper, froghopper, spittlebug, and planthopper that one might encounter along the banks of a trout stream. So Vince simply designed an all-purpose pattern, the Jassid, which worked fine back then and works fine now. Many of the terrestrial patterns on the market today fall into what I would call a generalized category. The Crowe Beetle is an excellent example of one, and so is the old fur ant. Many of the hopper patterns we see in fly shops have been around for years and represent wonderful generalized patterns. As such, they work well no matter where you might be fishing. But in certain instances, you might be better off designing a terrestrial pattern that more accurately resembles a local or regional insect. The Crystal Butt Hopper was designed with just this thought in mind and was tied to specifically resemble western hoppers rather than eastern ones. So what's the difference between the two? After collecting a bunch of western hoppers and giving them a very close examination, I found that they were not yellow. On most of them, the ventral portion of the abdomen was tan, olive, brown, or dull gray, but definitely not yellow. I'm certainly not the first to notice this. Take a look at Mike Lawson's Henry's Fork Hopper or Ed Schroeder's Parachute Hopper. My first thought was that this was why these two patterns were so deadly on western streams. I love Lawson's Henry's Fork Hopper and have caught a lot of fish with it, but it has its problems. The bullet head explodes after a few fish, and although it is still effective in this condition, I just don't like to fish it like this. And as much as I like Schroeder's Parachute Hopper, it gives me a lot of trouble, particularly on windy days, when it tends to twist the tippet into some pretty spectacular configurations. My answer was to design the Crystal Butt Hopper with a body the color of many western hoppers, but which would cast like a bullet, even in the wind. Because it is constructed almost entirely of foam, it also never needs dressing, floats low in the surface film, and looks a great deal like the natural. Strangely enough (or maybe not so strangely), it works just fine back here in the East as well, simply because most of our hoppers aren't yellow either! Surprised? You wouldn't be if you went out and collected a hatful of eastern hoppers. So why are so many hopper designs tied with yellow bodies? It all goes back to Vince Marinaro, who was so adamant about a hopper having a yellow body that I think he intimidated most of the designers of the time. From what I understand of the man, he didn't have any trouble intimidating people, so I'm not surprised.

In the final analysis, if you're going to design a terrestrial pattern (or any pattern for that matter), you can take one of three different approaches. You can design a realistic pattern, an impressionistic pattern, or what I call an imaginative pattern. An imaginative pattern would be one that doesn't really set out to imitate anything in particular, but looks like something that might be good to eat. The wonderful thing about these imaginative terrestrial patterns is that there just might be something out there that actually looks like the fly. You never know. Remember that there are so many different species of terrestrial insects, particularly beetles, that you just might have tied something that comes very close to being an impressionistic pattern of one. On the other hand, your imaginative pattern may look like nothing more to a fish than something that might be good to eat. If it's an effective pattern and routinely catches fish, do you really care if it imitates an insect or not? The Los Alamos Ant doesn't look like anything I've ever seen before, but it's a surprisingly effective fly, and I fish it all the time. I guess you could call any of these imaginative flies "food flies" if you wanted to.

Sometimes luck or fate plays an important role in designing a new fly pattern.

When the phone rang, I wasn't expecting it to be anyone wanting to go fishing, but I was pleasantly surprised to hear Ed Koch's voice on the line.

"What are you doing tomorrow?"

"Nothing really," I replied. "Why? Is something happening up your way?"

"You bet it is," said Ed. "We've got a major cicada hatch going on over on Clark's Creek, and the trout are going crazy. Is there any chance you can get up here within the next few days?" Did he really need to ask that question?

"Ed," I said, "I can be on the road first thing in the morning. I'll meet you at the Yellow Breeches Fly Shop at noon. Is that soon enough?"

"You bet. We'll have a blast," he said.

So the next morning I took off for Boiling Springs, Pennsylvania, arrived at the fly shop promptly at noon, and Ed was waiting for me. I loaded my gear in the back of Ed's car and headed for Clark's Creek with my anticipation level at maximum. When we arrived there, it was obvious that Ed had not been exaggerating. The noise was deafening! Anyone who has ever experienced a major cicada hatch knows exactly what I am talking about. These things are so loud that it seems almost surrealistic, and the constant drone rises and falls like the tides of the ocean. We were so excited that it was tough gearing up. You know what that's like. You miss one of the guides on the rod, you can't tie on a new section of tippet material, you forget to put on that extra pair of socks with your waders, you drop your sunglasses in the dirt, and a host of other mishaps seem to plague you. That's when it's time to take a deep breath, shut your eyes, calm down, and try to get it all back together again. We eventually did manage to get it all together, but it took some serious concentration.

I had tied up a dozen or so of my UFO patterns the night before, which makes a pretty good cicada imitation, particularly if it's tied with an orange underwrap on the body. I passed a few over to Ed; we each tied one on and headed for the stream.

Frankly, I had never seen anything quite like this. Every fish in the stream was on the prowl looking for the unlucky cicada that happened to land in the water. Caution was thrown to the winds as they cruised the gin-clear creek. Ed headed upstream and I headed down; there was plenty of water to cover and not another angler in sight. What happened after we parted was just short of spectacular for both of us. I have no idea how many fish came after the UFO pattern. Even the smaller fish tried to eat the thing, sometimes smacking it three or four times before giving up. At one point the foam body on one of the UFOs finally broke just behind the head and was hanging off the rear of the fly, so I cut the fly off, replaced it with an undamaged one, and continued to fish. You can only take this frantic action for so long, and I finally headed for the bank of the stream to take a break.

While I was sitting on the bank, I reached up and removed the damaged UFO from the fly patch on my vest, took out the terrestrial box, and started to put it away, but something about the fly caught my eye. When the foam body broke at the head, it flipped back over the rear of the fly and exposed the hook shank, which had been wrapped with peacock herl. This in itself was no revelation, but the silhouette of the hook shank intrigued me. It was decidedly wasplike, long and

> thin, and I figured that if I cut most of the loose foam away, I would have a nice fat little abdomen hanging off the rear. So, using my handy little scissors I cut away all of the damaged body except about a quarter of an inch. "An instant wasp imitation," I thought to myself, and tucked the modified UFO in the fly box for future reference.
>
> When I returned to Blacksburg, I headed for the tying desk, took the modified UFO out of the terrestrial box, and gave it a careful once-over. It did look a lot like a wasp, but with a little bit of work I figured it would look even better. The end result of half an hour of playing around at the vise was the Mud Dauber pattern, which is a much better imitation than the damaged UFO. Why a mud dauber, though, and not just a wasp? Well, mud daubers are a nice iridescent blue-black color, and because this pattern was tied with black foam, it was a much closer match for this species than for something like the common paper wasp.

In this situation, there is no question that luck played an important role in the design of the Mud Dauber pattern, which has proved to be very effective on many trout streams. But luck doesn't often play a major role in designing new terrestrial patterns. More often than not, it's hard work, imagination, and experience that counts. The two previously mentioned patterns, the Disc O'Beetle and the Mud Dauber, are certainly exceptions.

GENERIC PATTERNS

I'm sure that anyone who ties his own flies has noticed that once a tying technique has been devised and developed, that same technique often provides the basis for a host of different patterns. This should come as no surprise, because one has only to look at certain patterns to see that they have a great deal in common. For example, the traditional Catskill dry-fly patterns are all cut from the same cloth. In most instances, only the color (or material) of the body, hackle, and tail has been changed, while the style remains essentially the same. Another good example would be the Wulff series of hair-winged flies. Here again, the basic pattern remains the same for all; certain body colors have been changed, and the wings can be tied with either elk hair, deer hair, or calf tail, but they are all easily recognizable as one of Lee Wulff's creations. Over the years, many of these "genetically" closely related lines of fly patterns have been modified by the substitution of new materials, but the basic concept remains the same. Sometimes the patterns have been improved upon, and sometimes an "improvement" is questionable at best. You have to remember that most fly tiers are experimenters and will change, modify, refine, and tweak many patterns just to see what they can come up with. One good example would be the overall acceptance, use, and recognition of cul-de-canard feathers as a superior fly-tying material. Ten or fifteen years ago, it was virtually unheard of in the United States, but now it is used in tying everything from caddis to Cahills. The same holds true for the introduction of metal beads. Twenty years ago, you would not have found any nymphs in fly shops with bead heads, but now they're all over the place. Just about every known nymph pattern has been modified to include the bead head, which many people swear by as a terrific improvement. Personally, I don't much care for them, but I don't much care for nymph fishing anyway. On the other hand, a friend of mine, Dave Brandt, wouldn't be without them and fishes them in preference to just about anything else. I believe that Dave likes them because, although he is about average as a tier, his casting leaves something to be desired. Presenting a delicate cast with a small dry fly to a rising fish has always given him problems, so he has pretty much gone to nymph fishing within the past decade. That's fine, but it just doesn't work for me.

This common thread seen in patterns is easily recognized in much of what I do. If a material or tying technique gives a good result for one pattern, then I will often use it again as a basis for designing another pattern. My feeling is that if you are riding a good horse, you might as well continue to ride it. Sometimes a little modification is necessary, but if you look at many of the patterns in this book, the modifications are often minimal, and the generic technique is quite evident.

One final word about pattern design is necessary. I try to keep everything I design as simple as possible. The patterns presented in this book should prove to be no problem for the average tier, and I believe that simplicity is the key to any good pattern, terrestrial or otherwise. You should not have to labor at the tying bench. If you can't tie a respectable number of flies in an hour, then the pattern is too complicated.

Chapter 2

Materials

FOAM

Designing terrestrials in this day and age is certainly a great deal easier than it used to be. In the past, there were plenty of materials from which to choose, and there were plenty of effective terrestrial patterns that were designed. But in the last fifteen or so years, a smorgasbord of new materials has appeared that makes the job much easier. Deer and elk hair, wing quills, assorted yarns and threads, various feathers, and other natural materials are still used to design and tie extremely effective terrestrial patterns. I believe, however, that the designer who limits himself to only natural materials is operating under a severe handicap. With all the new and wonderful synthetic materials on the market, why limit yourself to only natural materials? I know that there are still purists who refuse to tie with anything except natural materials, but when it comes to terrestrial patterns, I think they are few and far between. Perhaps the ultimate purist was Vince Marinaro, who damned Don DuBois to hell for showing up on the Letort one day with a foam rubber beetle imitation. I really don't think there are too many Vince Marinaros left today. After all, why remain a dinosaur in the age of mammals?

So what are some of these modern-day materials we use for designing and tying terrestrial patterns? Perhaps the most useful—and the one that immediately comes to mind—is closed-cell foam. This really isn't a new material but has been around for years. I remember as a boy I used to buy foam-rubber crickets that were killers on bluegill, and that same pattern is still commercially produced. If you don't believe me, look in the Umpqua fly encyclopedia. There it is, and it hasn't changed one bit in the last five decades or so. Well, five decades ago you could get "sponge rubber" if you knew where to look, but you did have to search for it. In contrast, the modern types of closed-cell foam are easy to find. All you have to do is open up a fly-shop catalog, and there they are. If you don't want to deal with a fly shop, then go to Wal-Mart, K-Mart, or any craft shop, and you can find plenty of foam in different thicknesses and colors. About the only type of foam that can't be found in one of these craft stores is the soft 3/16- 1/8-inch-thick closed-cell sheet foam (advertised as Evasote or 1/8-inch Fly Foam). You still have to order this from fly shops, but it's relatively cheap, and a sheet of it will tie quite a few terrestrial patterns. You can even buy closed-cell foam that is precut into strips, but I prefer to cut it myself, because the precut strips are often not the correct size for the pattern I am working on.

A number of new foam products marketed under the name Locofoam and Locoskin have recently been introduced and have proved to be extremely useful for tying many different patterns. Locofoam is 1/16-inch-thick foam on which a metallic film has been applied, is available in approximately nineteen different color combinations, and can be used in any pattern that is ordinarily tied with 1/16-inch-thick closed-cell foam. (While this sheet foam, produced by Dance and Fibercraft, is advertised as being 2 millimeters thick, the thickness is quite variable. The average thickness is probably close to 1/16 inch.) I have found it to be an exceptional material because many of the color combinations match the natural iridescent or bright body colors of terrestrial insects. I now use it almost exclusively for most of my patterns and cannot help but think that this material has increased their effectiveness. The great majority of patterns given in this book are tied with Locofoam, but if the tier does not want to use this special type of foam, then 1/16-inch-thick closed-cell foam in the appropriate color can be substituted.

Locoskin has also proved to lend itself well for tying many patterns for both warm- and cold-water species of fish. It is a much thinner foam than Locofoam and is available in both single- and double-sided color combinations. In the single-sided form, one surface is covered with a metallic coating, and the other surface is coated with an adhesive and a protective paper backing. In the double-sided form, both surfaces are covered with a metallic coating. I have used both types in the development of certain patterns and am very pleased with the results.

Foam Preparation

Foam Discs

Many of my patterns require that foam be prepared in some way before tying with it. One of the most common methods I have devised is using circles cut from 1/16-inch-thick closed-cell foam. Cutting foam circles is relatively easy to do and was the subject of an article, "Circular Reasoning," by Boyd Pfeiffer in the Winter 1999 issue of *Fly Tyer.* I also discussed different methods in the article "Foamy Terrestrials," in the September 2000 issue of *Fly Fisherman.* All sorts of tubular material can be used to cut circles, but the easiest way to do it is to simply purchase a set of gasket punches. These sets will allow you to punch out foam discs from 1/8-inch diameter to 3/4-inch diameter with no trouble whatsoever. Once the punches have been sharpened, you can punch hundreds of discs without resharpening them. Foam punches can also be made from brass tubing of different diameters, which are available from most hobby shops. Old rifle cartridges can also be modified to cut foam circles. All one has to do is to cut off the base of the cartridge with a pipe-cutting tool and sharpen it with a case deburring tool, available from any reloading outfit. Another item that I have used to cut foam discs is a set of cork borers, which is available from any biological supply house (Carolina Biological Supply, Ward's). This is a rather neat set, although expensive. A set of twelve from Ward's lists for $36 and a set of six lists for $17, but they do a superb job and are easy to sharpen. They are made of nickel-plated brass, nest inside of each other, and are a nice compact unit. Of all of these, I prefer the set of gasket punches simply because I don't have to keep sharpening them. But then I cut hundreds of discs, whereas the average person would probably cut only what is necessary for his own purposes.

I also use a couple of sets of leather punches purchased from the Tandy Leather Company. These are excellent for punching out very small cylinders from the thick foam obtained from the soles of beach shoes or punching the smaller-diameter circles from 1/16-inch-thick sheet foam.

At one point the Kreinik Manufacturing Company was producing foam discs for fly tying, but I learned only recently that they are no longer going to produce these. Rainy Riding's company has picked up the idea and is now marketing foam discs in different sizes for those who do not want to cut their own. I would, however, recommend that anyone who is going to tie with foam discs manufacture or buy a set of cutters. The reason I recommend this is simple. Most of the time, if you buy precut discs, the size of the fly you are able to tie is determined by the size of the disc. If you're anything like me, the precut disc will never be exactly the right size for the fly you are contemplating tying!

Foam Triangles

In many of my patterns, I use foam triangles to form bodies and heads for flies, but trying to cut consistently sized foam triangles is a real problem without a template of some sort. The first template I ever made was from two of the heavier leaves from a feeler gauge, and it worked just fine. All you have to do is to pick up a set of feeler gauges from your local automotive supply shop and take it apart. Using two of the heavier leaves, a short bolt of the correct size to fit through the hole in the end of the leaves, two brass washers, a lock washer, and a wing nut, you can make a very respectable template. I also scribed marks every 1/8 inch along the leaves so that I would be able to duplicate the exact size of the foam triangle used for each pattern. The use of this sort of template is demonstrated on the tying tapes I did for Video Ventures a few years ago. This template works quite nicely, but I wanted something with which I could cut quite a few foam triangles within a minimal amount of time. I went to a friend of mine who is a machinist, told him what I wanted, and a week later he showed up with two dozen templates cut from 1/16-inch-thick aluminum sheeting. He happened to know another machinist who had access to a plasma cutter, and the guy was more than willing to set the thing up and run off a couple of dozen for me. These are beautiful, and they allow me to cut twenty-three triangles in just a few minutes. Most of these templates have been given to fly-tying friends of mine, so I have only four left. Needless to say, I guard them jealously.

Not so long ago, however, a friend and collaborator of mine, Blane Chocklett, ran into a fellow who cut us about a hundred more templates. These are a bit different from my originals. They are quite a bit larger and allow me to cut a whole range of different-size triangles. The larger triangles have proved very useful in designing and tying flies for both large- and smallmouth bass and other warm-water species.

Double-Thickness Foam

For quite a few patterns I use two sheets of 1/16-inch-thick foam glued together. My most frequent use for these 1/8-inch-thick sheets is to form what I have termed the *underbody* of certain patterns. It's a relatively simple matter to glue two sheets of foam together. All you need is a can of rubber cement and a little patience. I buy the large 1/16-inch-thick sheets of foam in different colors from craft stores (Michael's is one of my favorite places) or WalMart. I then trim and cut them with a paper cutter into 4-by-6-inch pieces and coat one side of each with rubber cement. I allow the rubber cement to dry and then stick them together. The bond is immediate and for all intents and purposes seems to be very durable. I can then cut strips, triangles, or circles from these foam pieces as the need arises. I might add that this same technique can be used to form the multicolored layered foam used in patterns like the Chernobyl Ant, Club Sandwich, and the different hopper patterns that have appeared recently. Besides being easy to do, it's much cheaper to make your own layered foam than to buy it, plus you can make it in any colors you desire.

When using this foam for underbodies, I will refer to it in the tying directions as "manufactured" foam.

Foam Cylinders

You can buy closed-cell foam in cylinders of different diameters, which I find extremely useful for certain patterns. A few years back, these were available from only a single source, but now they are marketed by a number of supply houses. To my knowledge, the first to supply these foam cylinders was the Dale Clemens Shop in Allentown, Pennsylvania, which markets them under the name Livebody foam. Rainy Riding has also marketed cylindrical foam for a number of years that has a somewhat different texture from that offered by Dale Clemens. Her company also markets foam cylinders in multiple colors, which might be useful when tying certain patterns, but which I find to be a little too fragile for my purposes. Another item her company markets is a foam cylinder in fluorescent colors, but the colors appear to have been sprayed on the foam, and I question their durability. I would much prefer that the color be actually incorporated into the foam, but what the heck—if that's all that is available, you might as well use it. Another good source for foam cylinders, multicolored and layered foam, and other foam products is Bill Skilton's USA-Flies, PO Box 64, Boiling Springs, PA 17007-0064.

Special Foam

There are times when I simply cannot find the correct color of foam to use in certain patterns. For example, I was recently designing a horse fly pattern, which sounds pretty easy to do, and it is if you can find the correct shape and color of foam for the eyes. The particular horse fly I had in mind was one that landed on my leg. I let it sit there long enough to take a good close look at it, but not long enough for it to do any damage. As a matter of fact, right before it was ready to bite me, I gave it a gentle swat, stunned it, and dumped it in a bottle of alcohol so I could take a close look at it. The body and head of the fly were tan, the wings formed a distinct delta shape over the back, and the legs were light to dark tan. This was easy enough to duplicate with standard materials, but the eyes were huge and brilliant green. I had nothing that would even come close to approximating the eyes of this insect. So what do you do in a situation like this?

The answer is simple. Take a trip to your local WalMart, K-Mart, Roses, Ben Franklin, Target, or any other store that carries inexpensive foam beach or shower shoes. Head for the shoe section, and hold on to your wallet. There you will find beach shoes (flip-flops) in both solid and multilayered colors and ranging in price from a buck or so to about $4 for the more expensive ones. These stores are a veritable foam mecca when it comes to colors. You of course buy the largest sizes available in the colors you want, because they will cost the same regardless of size. On my last trip to the local WalMart, I found a pair of beach shoes that are just the right color for the eyes of the Horse Fly pattern and also picked up another four pair in different colors. The total cost of the five pair of beach shoes was less than $20, and I will use them for a long time.

For lack of a better term, I will simply refer to foam obtained from beach shoes as *special foam*. I use most of this special foam for tying ant patterns and for the eyes on certain terrestrial patterns, both of which require the use of a foam cylinder. I simply take a cork borer or a leather punch of the correct diameter and cut cylinders from the soles of the beach shoes. It's as easy and as simple as that, and you get hundreds of cylinders from a pair of beach shoes.

OTHER MATERIALS

There are so many other materials, both synthetic and natural, that are available for tying terrestrial (and other) patterns that it is simply not possible to include all of them in this book. Other authors have devoted a great deal of time and energy to material compendiums, and I see no reason to duplicate their efforts. Suffice it to say that just about anything can be used when designing and tying terrestrial patterns. All one needs is a bit of imagination. Here are a few of the materials that I find to be most useful for my purposes.

Peacock Herl

Of the natural materials available, I seem to use a tremendous amount of peacock herl. A few years back, I ordered a bundle of peacock herl from one of the major suppliers, not realizing just how much was in that bundle

(I had read the figures incorrectly). When it arrived, I went into a state of shock at how much there was and thought to myself, "What have I done? I can tie with this stuff for years." But I was dead wrong. I believe that bundle of peacock herl lasted only two years—maybe a little bit longer, but not much. It was quality material though, and since then I have judged all peacock herl by that particular batch. Most of what's available now is pretty bad stuff, lots of "shorts" and broken barbs, brittle and just not up to snuff. When I pick through a batch of peacock herl, I always take my time, examine it carefully, and if it doesn't meet my criteria, I reject it. When I find a good batch, though, I have a tendency to go overboard and buy it all.

Hair

Other natural materials I use a great deal of are elk and deer hair, and again, I am very picky about the quality. Over the years I have come to prefer elk rather than deer hair for most of my patterns for a number of reasons. Elk hair ties down without "flaring," it's a lot tougher, it spins beautifully in a dubbing loop, and it trims up nicely. On occasion I use moose mane or moose body hair for special applications. I also use peccary (or javelina) body hair, for which on some patterns there is no substitute. It's tough, beautifully marked, and gives me exactly the effect I am looking for. I might mention that the best source for javelina I have found so far is English Angling Trappings. What I have bought from them over the years is of top quality.

Feathers

Turkey wing and tail quills are indispensable. I also use mallard duck wing quills on a few patterns. Although there are now some pretty good synthetic winging substitutes on the market, I still prefer turkey for such things as wing cases for hoppers. I might mention that when using these, there is a little trick to tying them in. I've seen quite a few people struggle with a section of turkey quill, trying to get the thing to tie in correctly. When I point out how to prepare the feather and how to tie it in, they are amazed at how easy it is. The first thing I do is spray the feather heavily with a matte finish artist's fixative. This is what artists who work in charcoal or pastels use to spray the finished product to keep the medium from smearing. It is available in any art supply or craft shop. I spray both the back and front of the feather until it is saturated and then hang it up to dry. The easiest way to do this is to clip off the end of the feather, insert a stiff wire (florist's wire is excellent) into the base of the feather, and bend the other end of the wire into a J shape. You can then hang it over a string or wire, and any excess liquid will drain off the end of the feather. One word of advice though: Spray the feather outside, not in the house! The solvent in the spray fixative is not particularly good for you, and the smell, which I find rather pleasant, will probably send your spouse up the wall. One other thing I do is prepare a lot of feathers at the same time. There's nothing worse than running out of prepared feathers in the middle of winter when it's 10 degrees below zero outside and the only alternative is to prepare stuff in the basement. You might be asking for a divorce. Once the wing or tail feathers are dry, I stick them in a Tupperware container, put the lid on tightly, and store them until I need one.

Cutting a section from the quill is easily accomplished. You can simply separate the width of the section you need using a needle, and then cut it from the stem of the feather. One extremely useful little tool I have for doing this is an adjustable draftsman's compass, on which I have replaced the lead with a needle. You then have a compass with two nice sharp points, and the adjustable wheel allows you to set the compass at whatever width quill wing is desired. All you have to do is insert both of the points through the feather, slide them to the edge of the feather, and *voila:* a wing of perfect width. Using the edge of the first separation as a guide, you can then separate the next section and continue right on up the feather. You wind up with turkey quill wings all the same width.

When tying in a quill wing section, there are only two things to keep in mind. First, tie in the thin tip section of the wing quill, not the heavy butt section. Second, the shiny side of the wing quill goes down when you tie it in, and the feather will fold over naturally. If you remember these two tips, you'll never have any problems.

Synthetic Materials

Winging Material

There are so many different materials on the market with which one can tie wings that it boggles the mind. I have used many of the metallic braids available from both Kreinik Manufacturing Company and Gudebrod for this purpose and find both of excellent quality. There are all types of polypropylene yarns, Antron yarns, plastic canvas yarns, and acrylic yarns that are marketed under quite a few different trade names. In addition to these, there are all sorts of other synthetic materials, which go by trade names such as Fluorofiber, Kinky Fiber, Zing, and Lord only knows what else. This plethora of trade names is terribly confusing because many of these products appear to be the same. My advice is simply to find one you like and stay with it. On many of my patterns I prefer a relatively stiff winging material and find that Krystal Flash, Kinky Fiber, and Ultra Hair (Super Hair) work better than anything else.

Dubbing

Most of the dubbing I use is very fine. I prefer Kreinik silk dubbing for most purposes but am not sure if they still manufacture it. I have plenty of it, though, and because I only use small quantities, I don't think I am in danger of running out. For my purposes, any fine synthetic dubbing will do the job nicely. One of the best is marketed by Umpqua Feather Merchants under the trade name Superfine Dry Fly Dubbing.

I tend to stay away from coarse synthetic dubbing because it does not pack down the way I want it to. Besides the synthetic dubbing, I have frequently used fur dubbing, but only that which is extremely fine, such as rabbit. The only problem I have with commercially available rabbit dubbing is that the guard hairs are blended in with the underfur, which makes it a touch too coarse for my taste. Rather than buy rabbit dubbing, I have taken to purchasing Zonker strips and making my own with the guard hairs removed.

Ribbons and Braids

My favorite ribbons and braids are those manufactured by Gudebrod and Kreinik, and I use both of them. Both can be used as winging material, wing cases for beetles, underbody wrap, braided bodies for certain patterns, and for many other applications. Of the two manufacturers, Kreinik makes the most variety of colors and sizes. Would you expect anything less from a company whose primary interest is the embroidery and needlepoint market? Rather than try to locate the Kreinik materials through your local fly shop, I suggest you visit the local needlepoint store, where you can probably find exactly what you are looking for.

Leg Material

Many of my patterns are tied with legs, and I have used quite a few different materials for this purpose. On the larger terrestrial and warm-water patterns, I prefer rubber legs of one type or another. Round rubber legs are available in at least three different sizes and quite a few colors, and these work admirably. Rubber Silli-Legs also work well; these are available in a whole spectrum of colors and color combinations. Either of these rubber leg types is readily available through fly-tying shops. Not long ago, however, I made the revolutionary discovery that Silli-Legs are exactly the same thing that jig skirts are made of. Since then, I tend to buy all of these through some place like the local tackle shop, WalMart, or Bass Pro Shops. There is one place I know of which must have thirty different types of jig skirts, and I think I've bought them all—at least it seems that way. The extremely small, round rubber legs that are marketed as nymph legs look good on small terrestrial imitations such as beetles and spiders, but they are sometimes difficult to work with.

On certain patterns I have used black Krystal Flash (ants), black nylon paintbrush bristles (a lifetime supply for less than a buck), and moose body hair or moose mane. Virtually anything that is relatively stiff and the right color will work just fine, so don't be afraid to experiment with different materials.

Chapter 3

Fishing Terrestrials

Because the great majority of patterns in this book are terrestrial patterns, it seems only right that I say a few words about how to fish them. In the book *Terrestrials,* which I coauthored with Ed Koch, I went into some detail on this subject, but a little review might help those who are not familiar with certain techniques.

There is no magic to fishing a terrestrial pattern, although at times the results may seem to be magic. There are no rivers I have fished in the United States where terrestrial patterns did not work, and there are no set rules as to which pattern to use on any given river. Unless there is a noticeable hatch of terrestrial insects, such as flying ants or Japanese beetles, most terrestrial patterns seem to work well. Some patterns work better on certain rivers than others, or at least they seem to. Certain patterns seem to work anywhere, and these are the patterns I will try first when fishing unfamiliar water. I have confidence in these patterns because they have produced well in the past, and I expect them to produce wherever I might be fishing.

EQUIPMENT

When it comes to equipment for fishing terrestrial patterns, you don't need anything special in the way of a fly rod. Whatever you've been fishing your local waters with will probably work nicely, so there's no reason to run out and buy the newest model on the market. Over the years I've developed quite a collection of fly rods, and although I use most of them from time to time, I do have certain prejudices. On small streams I prefer something in the 7- to 7 1/2-foot length, 4-weight, and I frequently overline it with a 5-weight line. The reason I use a heavier line than called for is simple. When you are making casts of 20 to 25 feet, the rod loads up nicely with the heavier line, and your accuracy is much improved. On smaller streams I also use a 9-foot leader. I've found that there is no reason to go to anything longer than this, and most devotees of small-stream fishing seem to agree with me. On larger water I have tried just about everything in the 8- to 9-foot range and from 3- to 5-weight. Right now I use both an 8 1/2-foot, 5-weight rod and an 8 1/2-foot, 4-weight rod for most of my "big river" fishing back east. When out west, I prefer a 9-foot, 5-weight rod, and I go to a 6-weight if the wind is up.

Leader length and tippet size can be critical. You certainly don't want to fish a big terrestrial pattern on a 16-foot leader with 4 feet of 6X tippet. That's a disaster waiting to happen, and your break-off rate will skyrocket. When fishing these larger patterns, I usually use a leader between 10 and 12 feet long with a few feet of 4X, 5X, and sometimes even 3X tippet. I really don't worry very much about tippet size when I am fishing the larger terrestrial patterns. It's been my experience that any trout that takes it into his head to gobble up one of these things is not paying very much attention to the size of the tippet. On the other hand, there have been plenty of occasions when I've gone to 16-foot leaders and 6X or 7X tippet when fishing the really small terrestrial patterns. The reason is simple. Most of the time when I fish these patterns, it's because I am fishing flat water and casting to spooky, selective fish that have often been pounded by previous anglers. Certain of the eastern and western spring creeks immediately come to mind, but I've found out something rather interesting over the years. In many of these "spooky fish" situations, a large terrestrial pattern works better than a small one, but it's hard to convince someone of that. On numerous occasions, some of my friends and I have had incredible days on heavily fished spring creeks and freestone streams casting size 8 to 10 terrestrial patterns like the LA Ant and the UFO and using 5X and 4X tippets.

WHICH PATTERN TO CHOOSE

OK, so now you've got your rod length, line weight, leader length, and tippet size figured out. What's next? Simple: You put on a terrestrial pattern and fish it, right? Well, no, not exactly. As I said previously, some streams, particularly tailwaters, are not really streams where terrestrials are the answer, although they can be very effective on these rivers at times. One example, Colorado's Frying Pan River, immediately comes to mind. It is simply not what I would call a terrestrial river. Most of the people who fish the Pan fish nymphs (the Copper John is a favorite), midge larvae or emergers, mysis shrimp imitations, or patterns for the different caddis and mayfly hatches encountered here. The reason is simple: These are the predominant food items on the trout's menu in the Frying Pan, so you fish the imitations. On the other hand, I've had some spectacular days on the Frying Pan fishing a size 18 fluorescent orange ant when no one else seemed to be doing much at all. Go figure! The same holds true for New Mexico's San Juan River, where I often fish a size 19 Firefly or a size 16 to 18 fluorescent orange ant. Some of the guys at the Scott Rod Company in Montrose, Colorado, have told me that on this river, the size 8 UFO is often their first choice, but I've never tried it there myself. On the East Coast, we also have tailwaters where you would not normally consider terrestrial patterns to be major producers. But given the chance, these patterns can give phenomenal results. What I am getting around to saying is that you may not consider certain rivers to be the type where a terrestrial pattern would give results. If you think that way, you're making a big mistake. You should try terrestrial patterns everywhere—not just on spring creeks and freestone streams with lots of streamside vegetation such as trees and shrubs. Take a look at the Henry's Fork of the Snake River, for example. Many people never consider fishing a terrestrial pattern there (they refuse to listen to the fly-shop owners), but beetle and ant patterns are deadly. As you walk into the Railroad Ranch section from the top, there is only one tree on the left about a quarter mile downstream, but no self-respecting terrestrial would live there because it serves as an outdoor privy for quite a few fishermen. But the high grass along the bank? Well, that's a different story. Its loaded with all sorts of terrestrial insects and the guy who refuses to fish these patterns on Henry's Fork is losing out. In my experience, most westerners just don't fish many terrestrial patterns. To them, a terrestrial means a hopper (usually Schroeder's Parachute Hopper or Lawson's Henry's Fork Hopper), and it's fished only during the latter part of the summer during hopper season. I'll occasionally run across someone fishing a cricket pattern or a Crowe Beetle, but for the most part, if they are fishing a terrestrial pattern, it will be a black fur ant, and they have gone to it because the fish were refusing everything else cast to them. All I can say is that an ant or a beetle would have been the *first* thing I tried, not the last.

I'm not sure it's much different back east though. Most of the people I meet who are new to the sport just don't think about fishing terrestrial patterns, and I have a hard time convincing them as to their effectiveness. It's bad enough trying to convince someone who's been fly fishing for thirty years that a fluorescent orange ant is a killer pattern or that something like the Turbo Wasp is deadly on Henry's Fork. Try telling someone who has only been at it for a few years the same thing, and you are immediately branded a liar, a thief, and accused of sucking eggs or smoking some illegal substance. Why? Because what they know is what they have read in the fly-fishing magazines, and to them anything that isn't in print appears to be bogus.

And you know something else? Most fly fishers are hesitant to try anything new in the way of terrestrial patterns, and I can't figure out why. My Lord, they've bought every sort of bead head, cone head, and all other types of weighted nymph and streamer patterns on the market. They've bought all sorts of strange creations that really don't resemble much at all, but they've been told how effective these patterns are, and yes, they do catch fish with them. When it comes to nymphs, streamers, saltwater patterns, and many different caddis and mayfly patterns, they are willing to try it all. But terrestrials? No way. If it ain't an old-fashioned hopper, beetle, or ant pattern, they simply will not try it (unless one of their more adventuresome buddies buys a few and proceeds to bring the river to its knees). Crickets? To most people there is only one cricket pattern, and that's the Letort Cricket. Any other pattern is not worth trying.

For those adventuresome souls who buy and fish the new foam terrestrial patterns, the rewards can be tremendous. I believe that more and more fly fishers are beginning to catch on to them. The trick, though, is not so much buying them as it is fishing them. By that I mean don't let them sit in your fly box untouched. Take one out, tie it to your tippet, and fish the thing. Don't be hesitant about it. But when you fish it, where you fish it, and how you fish it are going to have a great deal to do with your success rate.

WHEN TO FISH A TERRESTRIAL PATTERN

Just exactly when do you fish a terrestrial pattern, foam or otherwise? That's a question that is frequently asked, and my answer is simply "all the time." I am immediately reminded of something that happened one year on the Madison River.

Not far above Slide Inn and on the opposite side of the Madison River, there used to be a marvelous pool, just loaded with big browns and rainbows. At the head of the pool was a pretty fast chute that gradually tailed out into a deep run. This in turn became a relatively flat pool, which became shallower toward the tailout, at which point the water was only a few inches deep. The left bank of the pool (when facing upstream) was a gravel bar, whereas the right bank had large rocks along the middle section, high grass toward the bottom portion, and overhanging shrubs and small trees in the upper stretch. There were fish scattered all through the pool, but it seemed to me that they tended to concentrate in the middle and lower sections. I used to love to watch people walk up to this pool and fish it. Most anglers would wander over from the main channel, see all those big fish holding in the pool, and try a few casts. The results were abysmal. After a few perfunctory casts with a big weighted nymph and a strike indicator the size of a navel orange, the only thing you could see in the pool were the trails of big fish heading for cover. It was not an easy pool to fish, but a friend of mine, Miller Williams, and I broke the code.

It was the middle of July. Miller and I had wandered up to this pool and immediately gone to our knees when we saw what riches the water held. The first thing we saw was that the only way to fish the pool was to sit on your butt and slowly work your way into position, using the steep gravel bank on the left as a background screen. We would have been happier if we had been dressed in desert camo, but we figured khaki would probably work fine, which it did. The next step was pretty obvious. We were not going to get away with a 4X tippet, a big nymph, and a huge strike indicator—not with these fish. We rebuilt our leaders to somewhere between 14 and 16 feet long, with a 3-foot section of either 6X or 7X tippet. Then the question was, "What fly do we use?"

For some reason, probably because it had worked well in similar circumstances, I picked out a size 18 fluorescent orange ant. Miller tied on a size 19 Firefly, and we crawled into position. You had to be careful when casting—the high gravel bank behind us limited the arc of the rod, but we managed well enough. What a morning we had! If a fish refused the Firefly pattern, it would probably take the ant. We also discovered that if you sunk the ant, nine times out of ten a fish would suck it right in. What made this sunken ant technique so effective was that we could easily see it in the water and watch a fish take it. We also discovered that we could only fish this pool from early in the morning until about 10:30 A.M., when the sun came up over the mountains and began to shine directly in our eyes.

What's the point of this anecdote? Well, we had been going up to this pool every morning and fishing until the sun came over the mountains, and every morning there had been a guide with his clients over on the main section of the Madison. He'd drift them down to one of his favorite places; they would get out of the boat and throw weighted nymphs into deep holding water. They didn't do badly, but they hadn't had near the success that Miller and I had on this backwater section. About the third day I was fishing this run by myself, Miller having opted for something else. The guide came floating down the river as usual, anchored the boat in the same place, got his clients into position, and started them out with the usual nymph rig. Then he came walking over to where I was hunkered down on the bank, fast to a nice brown of about 19 inches. After I landed and released the fish, he spoke.

"You guys have been pretty impressive," he started out. "I've been watching you for three days now. Most people just walk on by this place, but you seem to have it all figured out. Mind if I ask what you are using?"

"Not at all," I answered. "I'm using either this little beetle pattern or a small orange ant."

"So you're fishing terrestrial patterns?" he said.

"Yeah," I answered, "I fish them all the time."

"Isn't it a little early for terrestrials?"

I looked at my watch. "I don't think so," I said, "It's past 10:30."

"No," he said. "I mean early in the year, not early in the day."

"Well," I answered, "I don't know about that. I've been fishing them steadily for more than three months with pretty good success."

"You really mean that?" he said. "We don't even think about fishing terrestrials out here until about August," and he walked away shaking his head.

But I was telling him the truth. I fish them all the time, from early in the spring until late in the fall, but during this span of seven or more months, there are times when I am very selective about fishing them.

FISHING TERRESTRIAL PATTERNS DURING A HATCH

If there is a heavy hatch of one of the aquatic insects going on, I'm just like everyone else. I'll fish the hatch, doing my best to match the insect that is coming off with something from my collection of nymphs, emergers, or drys. But there are plenty of times when I get frustrated during a hatch, just as others do, and frantically paw through my fly boxes trying anything and everything I have that might just match what the trout are feeding on. It's during those times that I have to kick back, take a deep breath, clear my mind, and calm down, and it's at that point that I'll open up the box of terrestrials. Does it work? You bet it does. Even during a heavy hatch of aquatic insects, there is magic in a well-presented ant, beetle, or some other terrestrial pattern. Let me give you an example. Most of us like to fish a Trico hatch or spinner fall, but it can get old after a while. You get tired of all the refusals, tired of not being able to see your fly, tired of making a gazillion casts, and frustrated with your lack of success. Well, so do I, but there is an answer to the problem.

The Little Lehigh River in Allentown, Pennsylvania, is intriguing. It's a freestone spring creek, and although I have only fished it a few times, I certainly plan on fishing it more in the future, particularly because one of my sons, Owen, now lives in Easton, which is a short drive away. My introduction to this spring creek was during the month of August when the Tricos were coming off en masse. Ed Koch and I decided to drive up and fish the stream with three of the local gurus: Dave Norwood, Lincoln Palmer, and Bob Miller (author of *Tricos*). We arrived at the stream, met the other three guys, and drove on down to a section where Bob said the Tricos would be thick. I was certainly not disappointed. They were so thick that the trees along the stream bank appeared to have a light mist surrounding them.

Bob took a look and said, "This is nothing. If they were really thick, you'd have a hard time seeing the trees."

Well, it looked pretty good to me. Besides, I was in the presence of the Trico king, and I planned on making the most of it. I had plenty of Trico imitations in my midge box, but because Bob was there I thought, "Hmmmmm. Let's see if I can scrounge a few flies." I was sure that my imitations would work fine, but the ones that Bob ties are truly works of art. They are tiny little 24s, tied with immaculately split tails, lovely little dubbed bodies, and teeny hen-feather wings. I had watched Bob tie these at numerous shows and had vowed to get a few from him some day. I had no intention of trying to tie the things myself.

"Hey Bob," I said. "Would you part with a few of those little Tricos of yours?" I was prepared to grovel if necessary, but didn't have to. He handed over half a dozen with no hesitation. I tucked five of them into the midge box and tied the sixth to the end of my 14-foot leader. I was using about 4 feet of 6X tippet and figured that would be fine to start with. I could always go to 7X if I had to.

Bob was nice enough to give me first crack at a lovely stretch of water where the fish were rising to Trico spinners. I waded in, and he stepped into the stream about 30 yards below me. I cast to the first fish. Then made another cast. Fifteen or so casts later, the fish was still feeding and ignoring my fly. "OK," I thought to myself, "that fish just isn't interested. Time to try for another one." The second fish wasn't interested either. Neither was the third, the fourth, or the fifth fish. After casting to a dozen or more fish with no luck at all, I waded over and sat down on the bank. There was only one solution to the problem, and that was to break down and tie on a terrestrial pattern, preferably a beetle. Why a beetle? The answer was simple enough. Quite a few years back, Ed Koch and I had discovered that a beetle was a deadly pattern during a Trico hatch. It was the obvious choice.

I cut the leader back, added 3 feet of 5X tippet, and tied on a size 14 Firefly. The next fish I cast to took the Firefly on the first cast. I proceeded to take a half dozen or more fish, and finally Bob yelled upstream to me, "What are you using?"

"You don't want to know," I yelled back.

"It's one of those damn terrestrial patterns isn't it?" Bob said.

"Yes," I admitted, "it's a size 14 Firefly."

"Sumbitch," I heard him say, "I might have known."

I worked on upstream, taking a fish here and there, and by the time I ran into Dave a few hundred yards upstream, I think I had taken more than two dozen trout on the Firefly pattern. At times I was tempted to go back to one of Bob's beautiful little Trico patterns, but when you're in the zone, you might as well stay there.

This is only one example of going to a terrestrial pattern during a blanket hatch of aquatic insects. There have been many times when I have fished a fluorescent orange ant during a "sulfur" hatch, a small beetle during a hatch of blue-winged olives, or the Turbo Wasp during a caddis hatch. At other times I have gone completely away from the smaller terrestrials and fished a large terrestrial pattern during a major hatch. A good example of fishing a large terrestrial pattern during a hatch is given following the description of the UFO pattern.

FISHING TO STRUCTURE

You now know that you can fish terrestrial patterns pretty much all the time, not just during the peak summer months, and that they work well even during major hatches of aquatic insects. So what else is there? Actually, quite a lot, and it applies to many fly patterns, not just to foam terrestrial patterns. First of all, I use many of these large patterns as "searching patterns," casting them to good holding water when no hatch is in progress. In order to do this, you have to learn to read a stream, and to really do it well you have to know a river or stream intimately. The best example I can think of is Virginia's

Smith River, which I probably know better than any other river. I've fished this water for so many years that I know exactly where trout are located, which sections are top producers, where to spend a lot of time, and which water to pass by. I've watched others who did not know the river waste hours casting to what I consider sterile water and wading through sections that I know hold many fish. I've also watched fly fishers stand in one place for hours at a time making cast after cast. I cannot imagine what they are thinking. You simply cannot fish a river once or twice and get to know anything about it, but you can learn to read the water and to recognize good holding lies. Once you learn to do this, then casting a good searching pattern to these places will often prove productive, and the searching pattern can be anything from an Elk Hair Caddis to a Chernobyl Ant.

FISHING TO THE BANK

A wonderful technique for fishing any large fly (particularly terrestrials), and one that I have used effectively for many years, is to fish the fly close to the bank. On any stream with heavy streamside vegetation and good cover along the bank, this is a deadly technique. It's surprising how many large fish will stay right next to the bank, but when you think about it, why shouldn't they? Terrestrial insects are constantly falling into the water; the bank is frequently undercut, offering wonderful cover; and it's a natural holding area.

One of the things I have noticed is that many people seem to disregard the banks of a stream, preferring to pound the deeper runs, the riffle water, and the midstream structures. Although there is nothing wrong with this, they are overlooking what I believe to be the best part of many streams: the cover along the bank. I don't understand why people cannot get used to the idea of casting toward the banks of a stream. Maybe it's because they are scared they will hang the cast up in the cover along the bank. Maybe it's because they think the water along the bank is too shallow to hold a big fish. Maybe it's because they can't see fish holding in this part of the stream. I can certainly understand the desire not to lose a fly in a tree or a bush along the bank, but if the cast is well done and does manage to slip under the bankside cover, you might be into the fish of a lifetime. So what if you lose a fly? There have been many times when I have been more than willing to sacrifice a fly to the trees on the chance of taking a nice fish. One thing I will not do is wade over and retrieve a hung-up fly immediately. No way! I'll simply break the fly off with as little disturbance as possible, rebuild the leader if necessary, tie on another fly, and try it again. There have been many times when I have seen someone hang up a fly, march over to the offending tree, shrub, or grass clump, and retrieve it. That, to my way of thinking, is a big mistake. If there happens to be a good fish holding in the vicinity, you can kiss it good-bye. I'd much rather disturb the area as little as possible, lose the fly if I have to, and try it again. But then I tie my own flies, so losing one is no big deal. I imagine that those who pay a couple of bucks for a fly want that fly back, but they should be willing to pay a few bucks for a good fish. After all, they've paid a pile of money for equipment, travel, food, lodging, and maybe guide fees, so the loss of a few flies shouldn't worry them all that much.

If you fish one stream a great deal, you should take a little time, wade over to the bank on occasion, and check the depth of the water. It's surprising how deceptive water depth along the bank appears to be from 30 or 40 feet away. Most of the time it looks mighty shallow—too shallow for any self-respecting big fish—but that's often not the case at all. There have been plenty of times when I have waded over to the bank of a stream and was surprised to find that what looked like no more than 6 or 8 inches of water was actually deeper than a foot. Not only that, but there was plenty of cover on the bottom, where even a large fish would feel very comfortable. The water depth and bottom structure along the stream bank, coupled with the protective nature of overhanging vegetation and the presence of undercut banks, make it an ideal holding area for fish. If nothing is hatching, no fish are actively working, and the stream seems to be dead, then I will spend the majority of my time fishing along the bank, blind casting to what looks like good holding water with a large searching pattern. The results are often explosive to say the least.

Frequently, however, you do encounter fish feeding randomly along the bank of a stream. This can really get the old ventricles pumping, because fishing to them often requires some pretty accurate casting. You have to figure out how to get the fly under the foliage, whatever that may be, and to the fish without messing up the whole scenario. My advice in a situation like this is to think it through. The worst thing you can do is to just start casting. Currents along a bank are frequently tricky, so you have to figure out the stream hydraulics before you do anything. There are always little obstacles in the way: a twig, a few blades of grass hanging down in the water just above the fish, a rock that might be in the way. All of these play a role in what you have to do to take the fish.

How well I remember the three browns on Armstrong's Spring Creek outside Livingston, Montana. I had been sitting on the bank for about fifteen minutes watching these three fish feed and trying to figure out just what to do to take at least one of them. The problem was fairly complicated. They were all under a log, which was about 6 inches in diameter, and just above a brush pile on the far side of the stream. They were spaced roughly 2 feet apart along the length of the log, which hung at about a 15-degree angle off the bank. All you could see was half the head of each fish, but that was more than enough to tell me that they were well worth casting to. The water along the far bank created a stream hydraulic when it hit the log that pushed anything floating by about an inch away from the log. I knew this because I had been sitting there watching little bits of flotsam go down the bank, hit the log where it was stuck in the bank, and then travel right down in front of the log about 2 inches from the noses of these fish. If one of the fish decided that a particular item looked appetizing, it simply nosed up and took it. You never saw more than about one-third of the fish when this happened, the rear two-thirds remaining safely under cover.

The only way to get a fly to these fish, the way I figured it, was to cast a good 6 to 8 feet above them and as close to the bank as possible. Then you would have to throw a whole bunch of stack mends, putting as much slack in the line as possible so the fly would drift naturally through the hydraulic created in front of the log. I would like to say that I did it just right on the first cast. I didn't. As a matter of fact, it took a number of casts to get it just right, but when I did, the second fish in line came from under the log and sucked in the fly. Yep, it was a fish worth taking, all right.

I went back to the bank and waited about ten minutes until the other two fish were back on station and feeding. To make a long story short, I did manage to take the other two fish, and they were just as nice as the first, but it took about half an hour to do it.

After I had hooked and released the last fish, I went back up the bank and sat on the fisherman's bench. A few minutes later, one of the local guides who had been upstream with a couple of clients joined me on the bench. I had been watching them for some time, and I'll tell you, this guide was good! His clients were from Japan, neither spoke a word of English, and yet he had them into fish using nothing more than sign language and excellent rapport. Frankly, I was impressed.

We chatted for a few minutes, and I complimented him on his guiding ability.

"You're doing a hell of a job with those clients," I told him.

"Thanks," he replied. "It's been an interesting morning. They are so enthusiastic that it's actually been fairly easy." He stuck out his hand, "James Mark's my name. What's yours?"

I introduced myself to him and we chatted for a few more minutes. Finally he said, "I saw you take those fish from under that log. Pretty good trick! Would you mind if I ask what you took them on?"

"Not at all," I replied, and showed him the little orange ant tied to the end of the tippet.

"Well, that figures," he said. "More people should learn to fish stuff like that. I fish ants a lot here, but I can't get many clients to use them because they have a hard time seeing them."

"You don't have any problem seeing this one," I said, "and I fish it all the time. It's one of my favorite patterns."

I think I gave him a few of those orange ants, but I don't really remember. If I didn't, I should have.

This is only one example of a time when careful planning while casting to fish along a bank paid off. My advice in any situation like this is to think it through before you do anything. One bad cast, one hang-up, one little mistake can leave you frustrated beyond belief. So take your time, and put the odds in your favor.

Chapter 4

Ants

When it comes to tying ants, foam is hard to beat. True, there are certain ant patterns I tie and fish that are tied in the traditional manner (dubbed bodies), but these are ant patterns for which no colors are as yet available in foam. The fluorescent orange ant is a perfect example of this because there is no fluorescent orange foam that is commercially available.

I also use epoxy for all of my sinking ant patterns (the TransparANT and the AttractANT).

For all other ant patterns, I now use foam as the major component. It is such an easy medium to work with that I just don't see any sense in working with anything else. The patterns are highly effective, extremely durable, easy and quick to tie, and cheap. What more could you ask for? For example, the Hot Spot Ant pattern can be tied in about three minutes by the average tier, and when I really get cranking on this pattern, I can do one in fewer than two minutes. As for the cost for this pattern, I guess each one would run about 12¢, and the great majority of the cost would be the hook. Compare that with the cost of the McMurray Ant, which is usually only good for a few fish before the body begins to disintegrate.

Foam for ant bodies can be cut as strips from sheets of either 1/16- or 1/8-inch-thick foam, punched out of 1/16-inch-thick foam to form circles or ovals, or bought as cylinders from suppliers such as Dale Clemens Shop in Allentown, Pennsylvania, or Bill Skilton's shop in Boiling Springs, Pennsylvania. With the exception of fluorescent colors, there is an entire spectrum of colors to choose from, but black, tan, and brown will probably remain the colors of choice for most tiers. I would recommend, however, that you also try red, yellow, and orange foam. On certain days, these colors will prove highly effective, and I always keep a supply of brightly colored foam ants in my fly box for just such days. One brightly colored pattern, the Cow Killer Ant, is for me an American Express pattern. I "don't leave home without it."

I have recently discovered a good source for foam in all sorts of nifty colors and color combinations, including fluorescent orange. It isn't commercially available—at least not in the sense that you can buy it in fly shops—

but it is readily available. The foam I am talking about comes from the soles of flip-flops (shower shoes or beach sandals). I punch cylinders from this foam to make ants in all sorts of different colors and discuss how this is done later in this section.

I should mention that there is one source of fluorescent foam cylinders—Rainy Riding's shop in Ogden, Utah—but I have never been really pleased with this foam. Although it is fluorescent, the fluorescent color is applied to the foam as a coating and over time will begin to flake off.

AttractANT

Hook:	Tiemco 101, size 16, or equivalent. Do not use a down-eye hook. The epoxy used to coat the head has a nasty habit of flowing downhill into the eye.
Thread:	Gudebrod 6/0 or 8/0 or equivalent, color as desired.
Abdomen:	Tying thread, color of choice.
Body bead:	Glass milliner's bead, color to contrast with or complement the color of the thread.
Head:	Tying thread, color to match or contrast with the color of the abdomen.
Legs:	Hackle; color at the discretion of the tier.

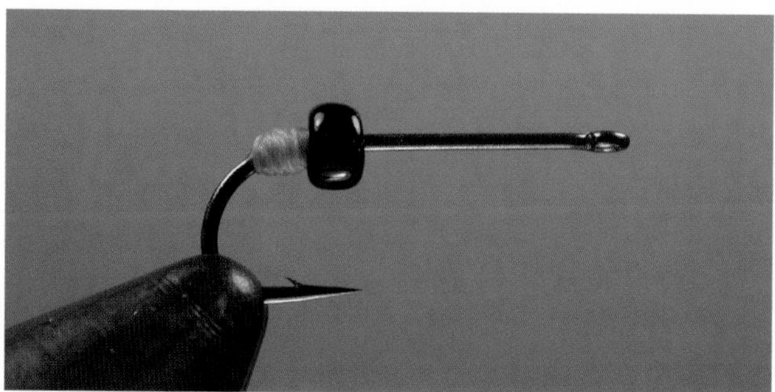

1. Slip the glass bead over the point and barb of the hook and up the shank. Then wind a ball of tying thread at the rear of the hook. Make the thread ball large enough so that the glass bead will not slip back over it. Whip-finish, and remove the thread.

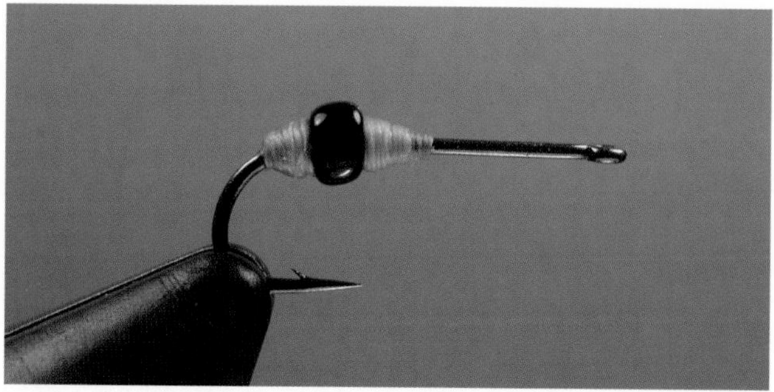

2. Push the glass bead into the front of the rear ball of thread and wind another thread wrap in front of the glass bead to hold it in place. Both the rear and front thread wraps should be large enough to come almost to the top of the glass bead. The easiest way to do this is to first make the rear thread wrap just large enough to prevent the bead from slipping over it, do the front wrap, and then come back and complete the rear wrap. The front thread wrap must be whip-finished before doing the thread wrap for the head.

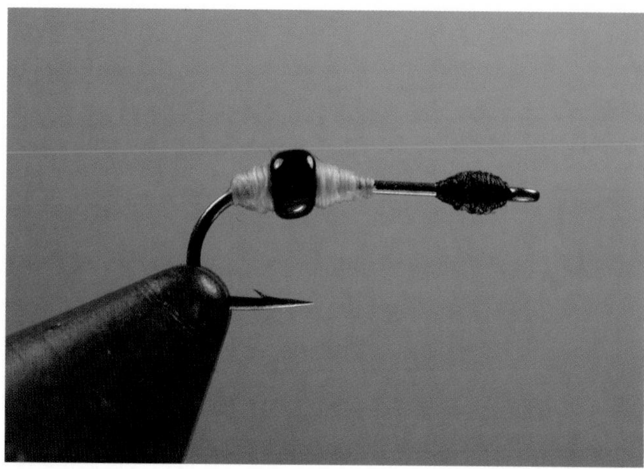

3. Form the head by tying a ball of thread just behind the eye of the hook. The size of the thread wrap for the head should be smaller than that for the abdomen of the ant. *It is imperative that a portion of the hook shank be left bare between the abdomen and the head. If this is not done, the epoxy used to coat these two areas will flow together.*

4. Mix a small amount of five-minute epoxy, and while rotating the vise, apply it to both the abdomen and head of the fly. For this step, a *true* rotary vise is almost mandatory. When the epoxy has set up, remove the fly from the vise, and place it on a magnetic strip, where it is allowed to cure for at least one hour.

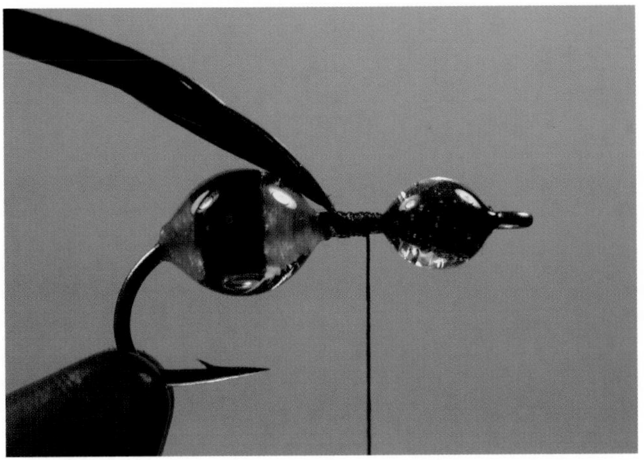

5. Once the epoxy has cured, return the fly to the vise, wind the bare portion of the shank with tying thread, and tie in the hackle.

6. Give the hackle a couple of wraps to form the legs, tie it down, cut away the excess hackle, and whip-finish.

There are some tricks to tying this fly that are worth knowing. First, the front of the rear thread wrap is formed as a cone-shaped wrap so that the body bead will fit solidly on the cone and be in line with the hook shank. In other words, you are centering the hole in the bead on the cone-shaped wrap. The wrap in front of the body bead is then formed in a pyramidal shape, with the base of the pyramid butting up against the front of the bead. Once these two wraps are done, the rear wrap is finished by filling in the small gap between the thread and the bead with more thread wraps. I know this sounds complicated, but once you've done a few of these ants, the procedure becomes simple and easy to do.

If you plan on tying a lot of these ants, it helps to have some sort of device to rotate the vise for you as you apply the epoxy. I've rigged up my rod-finishing motor to my Renzetti vise so that it rotates the vise for me. This works perfectly. The motor turns at 5 rpm, which is just the right speed for applying the epoxy to the body and the head. This also gives me a good break between flies. I can get up from the bench, go to the bathroom, get something to drink, or just stand there and look out the window while the motor does all the work for me.

I use Post-It notes for mixing the epoxy. The size doesn't matter, and they are cheap. For mixing and applying the epoxy, a fine sewing needle chucked into a small pin vise works beautifully. The needle is going to have to be cleaned periodically, and a 35-mm film canister packed with coarse steel wool works well for this. Take the film canister, pack it tightly with coarse steel wool, cut a small hole in the lid, and you have a handy-dandy needle cleaner. Just jam the needle down into the steel wool, give it a few turns, and it's clean. ■

EZC Carpenter Ant

Hook:	Tiemco 100, size 14, or equivalent.
Thread:	Gudebrod 6/0 or equivalent, black.
Body disc:	1/4-inch-diameter disc cut from 1/16-inch-thick black foam.
Head disc:	3/16-inch-diameter disc cut from 1/16-inch-thick black foam.
Midbody wrap:	Peacock herl.
Legs:	Black Krystal Flash.
EZC spot:	1/8-inch foam disc punched from 1/16-inch-thick closed-cell foam: yellow, chartreuse, or red.

It is necessary to attach the EZC spot to the top of the body disc before tying this pattern and to trim it to approximately half its original height. Place a very small amount of Zap-A-Gap near the edge of the body disc, and use a fine pair of forceps to place the EZC spot in position. Once the bond has set, trim the EZC spot to about one-half its original thickness with a sharp pair of scissors. I usually prep at least a dozen bodies before tying these ants. The color of the EZC spot is at the discretion of the tier. I normally tie these ants with EZC spots in all three colors because certain colors will show up better under different light conditions.

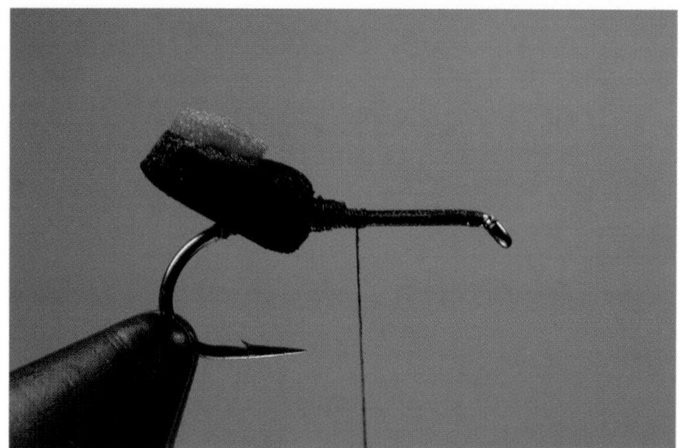

1. Wrap the shank of the hook with the tying thread from front to rear and then forward again to a point on the shank in line with the point of the hook. Tie in the front of the body disc at this point.

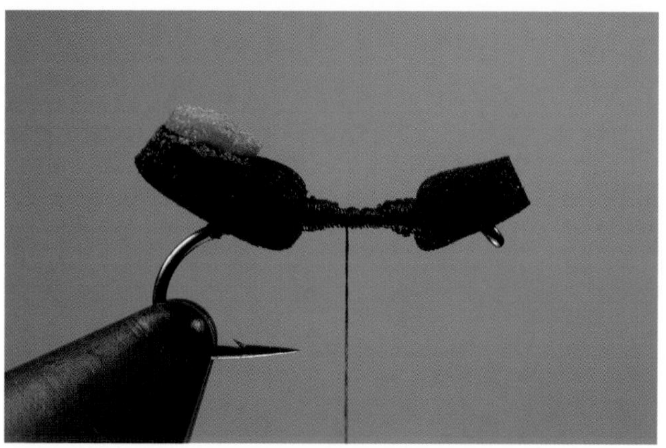

2. Wrap the tying thread forward to a point about $^{1}/_{6}$ inch behind the eye of the hook, and tie in the rear of the head disc. The head disc should extend just over the front of the eye of the hook.

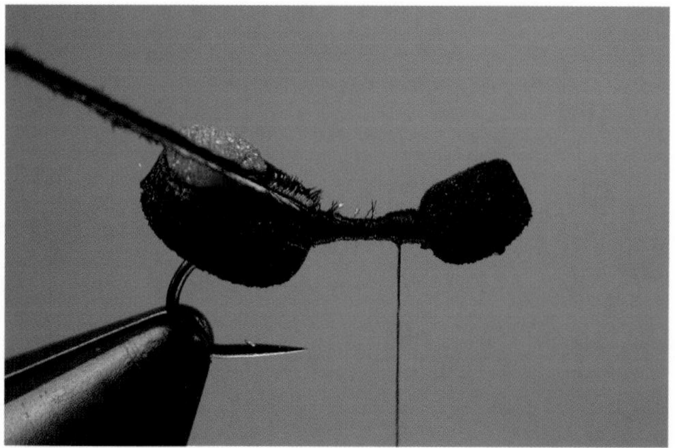

3. Wrap the thread rearward again to the point at which the body disc was tied in, and tie in two or three strands of peacock herl. Wrap the thread forward to the head disc.

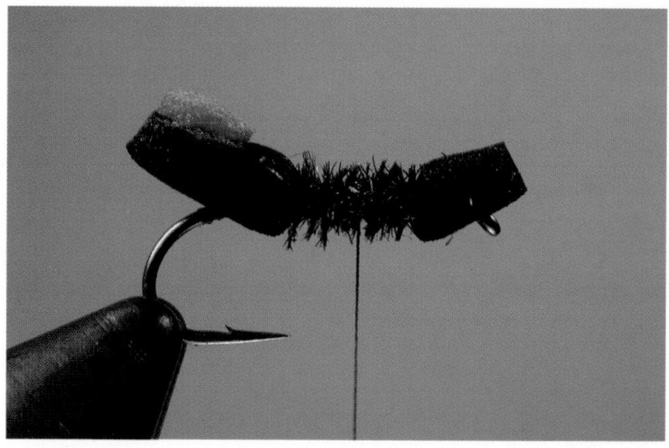

4. Wrap the peacock herl forward to the rear of the head disc and tie it off. Trim away any excess herl (it doesn't take much herl to do this, so save what is left over for other ants). Wrap the thread rearward to the middle of the herl body wrap.

5. Using a figure-eight wrap, tie in four to six strands of Krystal Flash for the legs, and trim them to the proper length. Whip-finish, and remove the thread.

This pattern has rapidly become one of my favorites for a number of reasons. It floats like a dream, you can see it, and—best of all—it has proved to be highly effective. Although I usually tie it in a size 14, I also tie it in smaller sizes by varying the size of the discs used to form the body. With a little practice, it is possible to tie this ant in a size 18, but your fingers begin to get in the way as the size of the hook and the disc size decrease. In a size 18, I also eliminate the EZC foam disc for the spot on the top of the abdomen. ■

Cow Killer Ant

Hook:	Tiemco 100, size 12, or equivalent.
Thread:	Gudebrod 6/0 or equivalent, black.
Abdomen:	5/16-inch-diameter disc cut from 1/16-inch-thick Locofoam. I prefer the Pearl Yellow, Pearl Orange, and Metallic Red Locofoam for the abdomen of these ants.
Center wrap:	Two to four strands of peacock herl.
Legs:	Six to eight black Krystal Flash fibers.
Head:	1/4-inch-diameter disc cut from 1/16-inch-thick Northern Lights Locofoam.

The Cow Killer Ant is tied in exactly the same manner as the EZC Carpenter Ant. The only difference between the two patterns is the size.

Why the name "Cow Killer" for this pattern? Quite a few people have asked me about this, so I feel it does need a little bit of an explanation. When I was a kid living in Alabama, we used to frequently encounter these large brightly colored "ants" that could give you a really nasty bite. We were told that they were so potent that if they bit a cow, the cow would die, hence the name "Cow Killer." At least that was what we were told by those older and wiser than ourselves. Years later I found out that they aren't ants at all but a species of wingless wasp referred to as "velvet wasps." One never bit me nor my buddies, so I can't attest to the toxicity of the venom.

The fact that these insects are not widely distributed and that they can give something a nasty bite raises a few questions. They don't occur along any trout stream I have ever fished, so they certainly aren't part of the trout's everyday grocery cart. So with these facts in mind, why even bother to tie something like this as a fly pattern for trout? The answer is simple: They are relatively large, they are brightly colored, and they look like food. Besides that, they work.

The first time I ever fished this pattern was on the Madison River, and the results had me talking to myself. I had located a small channel off the main river just below Slide Inn and was sneaking up through the tail of a pool to the faster water at the head when I saw a nice rise. Then another, and another. That pool was full of nice fish, and they were rising freely, all the way up to the faster water at the head. For about 20 yards there were fish strung out all over the place: some in the center, others behind underwater structure, and still others along both banks. They were feeding, but what they were feeding on was certainly not obvious, at least not to me. Whatever prompted me to tie on one of these Cow Killer Ants, I'll never know. Maybe it was the fact that I had never fished the pattern before (I had tied it just before leaving Virginia), so I had no idea as to whether it would be effective. It didn't take long to find out. Those trout jumped all over the thing. Red, yellow, or orange—it didn't seem to make any difference to them, and they took it with a vengeance.

I tried it on other western streams that summer and since then have fished it extensively on many of our eastern waters as well. In most instances, it produces as well as any other terrestrial pattern, but there are those times when it will outfish every other pattern. As a result, it has taken a prominent position in the fly box.

I have also had quite a few other anglers tell me that they too have found the Cow Killer Ant to be very effective.

The Cow Killer was a killer again this year in the Catskills. Just ask Richard Frank. He has become a convert and just wrote me a couple of weeks ago to find a source for the cutters. I caught fish with every one of the flies that I tied. I am looking forward to doing more of them this winter, especially the Los Alamos Ant.

—Earl Grossman

The first week in June 2000, a group of us met to fish the Catskills and stayed on Willowemoc Creek. The fishing was proving a little difficult in the creek, which is not surprising because the fish have seen just about every fly in creation. One of the guys, Richard Frank, had received a box of flies from Harrison Steeves, and we all marveled at the unusual foam creations. Richard decided to try some of these flies to see if he could raise some of the sulky browns. He had strikes on virtually every fly that he tried, but the biggest trout was a monster brown that rose to the Cow Killer. He lost the fly and the fish, but it left me determined to learn to tie some of these foam patterns over the winter.

At a fly-fishing show, I purchased two of Harrison's videos and began tying his flies, beginning with the Cow Killer. I tied up six size 10s and six size 12s. My first opportunity to try these out was the first week in June 2001, back at the same spot in the Catskills. When we arrived, Willowemoc Creek was chocolate brown as a result of recent rains and didn't look very promising. Figuring that I wanted something bright and noticeable, I tied on a Cow Killer as the first fly of the trip. I had many rises to the fly and caught a number of nice browns. When I left the water, the group of guys I was with asked for and received Cow Killers to try themselves. The results were astonishing. It was as if the entire section of dark brown water suddenly turned on. Everyone was getting strikes and landing fish on the Cow Killer.

Over the next couple of days as the waters cleared, the Cow Killer fished very well and continued to provoke strikes all through the week. When the week was over, I found that only two Cow Killers remained from the dozen I had tied. I fished my last two Cow Killers on my home streams and ponds in New Hampshire and caught fish regularly with them, even in situations when I could get no action on any other pattern. This winter I will be tying the Cow Killer again as it has earned a regular spot in my fly boxes. I will be tying two dozen this time so as to be prepared to pass some on to folks who witness its success and want to try it.

—Earl Grossman

Your Cow Killer has been one of the most effective patterns for fussy browns in smooth, clear water on the Willowemoc. Last year I had to borrow a few from Earl Grossman. This year I'll bring my own, and lots of them.

—Richard Frank

All of these other anglers are from the East, and I have the distinct impression that they are using the pattern on smaller waters, such as mountain freestone streams or spring creeks. The trouble is I can't get any of them to tell me exactly where they are fishing. Seems as though everyone has become a bit hesitant about giving out information like this. OK, I can live with that—I do pretty much the same thing. I'm not about to give away secrets either, particularly concerning small streams that hold large trout—no way! ■

Hot Spot Ant

Hook: Tiemco 100, sizes 16 to 20, or equivalent.

Thread: Gudebrod 6/0, or equivalent, color to match that of the body.

Body: Livebody foam. This foam, which is in the form of round cylinders, is available from Dale Clemens Shop and from Bill Skilton's USA-Flies in a wide variety of colors and diameters. I use black, cinnamon brown, and mottled black-gray-white almost exclusively. If you wish to experiment with different colors, however, try the yellow, red, light dun, and green. For this pattern I use either the 1/16-inch- or the 1/8-inch-diameter foam, depending on the size of the ant I wish to tie. If you want to tie extremely small ants, the foam is available in 1/32-inch-diameter cylinders, but only in white. It is, however, an easy matter to color the white foam using Pantone markers.

Hackle: For tying ants of all types, I use nothing but high-quality saddle hackle of the appropriate color to match that of the body. Black for black-bodied ants, brown or furnace for cinnamon-bodied ants, and grizzly for the black-gray-white–bodied ants. With one good saddle hackle, it is possible to tie a dozen or more ants.

Hot spot: E-Z Shape Sparkle Body, yellow or red.

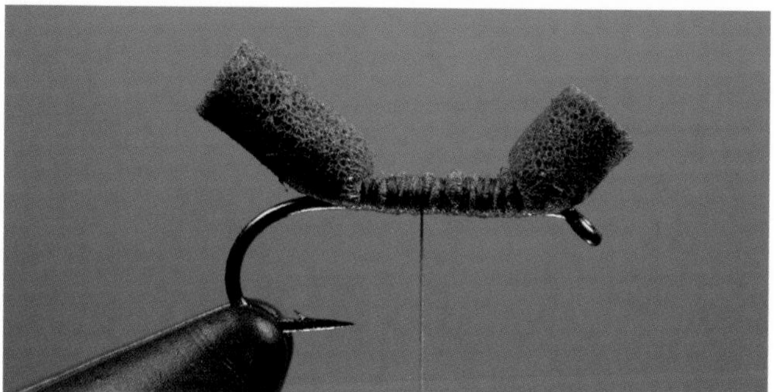

1. Attach the thread to the hook shank well behind the eye of the hook, and cover the middle of the hook shank with a thread wrap. There is no need to wrap the entire shank of the hook with thread. Tie in the Livebody foam at the front of the thread wrap, and continue tying it down rearward to the end of the thread wrap on the hook shank. The front portion of the Livebody foam should extend over the eye of the hook. Trim the Livebody foam at the rear of the hook so that the abdomen of the ant extends a little past the hook bend.

2. Wrap the thread forward a little, and tie in the hackle.

3. Wrap the thread forward again, wrap the hackle forward two or three turns, tie it off, and trim. Whip-finish, and remove the thread.

4. Place a small drop of the E-Z Shape Sparkle Body on the top of the head, and allow it to dry for a few hours.

This is an incredibly easy pattern to tie. Anyone should be able to turn out at least a dozen or more in an hour. It's also cheap and much more durable than the McMurray Ant, while still having all the appeal of this popular pattern.

I have fished this pattern from Virginia to Montana, and it hasn't failed me yet. Sometimes (as with any pattern) one size or one color works better than any other, but it's just a matter of trying them out until you hit on the correct combination. On occasion I have had good luck with this ant tied in yellow or red and hackled with black hackle. If one of the brighter colors of foam is used, there is no need to add the Hot Spot, because these will show up even under low-light conditions.

I had heard for years about the San Juan River and the great fishing. You can only listen to stories like this for so long, and then you simply have to go and see for yourself. So, I pointed the van west, took the southern route, and a couple of days later arrived at the fabled Abe's Motel and campground on the San Juan. I knew nothing about the river and was too tired to fish that evening, so I bought my license, paid for a camping spot, poured a good stiff drink, washed the trail dust out of my mouth, and hit the sack.

Early the next morning I drove up the river, turned in to one of the access points, parked the van, and began to gear up. About that time another guy pulled in, and we struck up a conversation. It turned out he was from Arkansas, had fished the San Juan extensively, and was willing to share his information with me. So we geared up and took off for the river. When we hit the river, there wasn't another soul to be seen. I was flabbergasted!

"Where," I asked him, "are all the fishermen? For years I've heard about how crowded this place is, but no one is here!"

"Wait a couple of hours." He grinned. "We're early. By then there'll be fifty or more folks standing right here."

He was right. At 10:00, the river was a zoo. His estimate fell short by half again as much. There were fishermen everywhere and drift boats passing by at an alarming rate. It was, more than anything else, a party atmosphere. Frankly, I had never seen anything like it, even back on what we considered "crowded" eastern streams. Guys were standing in the stream drinking a beer with one hand and flogging the water with the other. The distinct odor of a certain illegal plant drifted by on occasion. I took a seat on the point of an island, rubbed my eyes to make sure that I wasn't seeing things, and just watched for a while. After about thirty minutes of sitting there with my jaw dropped down to my knees, something in my peripheral vision finally registered—a rise! Turning to my left, I began to look up this backwater. There were fish rising all over the place, and it wasn't really a backwater. It turned out that it was a channel coming off the main river, and it was packed with fish: big fish, feeding fish, and not another soul in sight. So I sort of quietly began to move up this channel and out of sight of the main river where the circus was going on.

Once I was out of sight of the main river, I knotted a size 20, cinnamon-brown Hot Spot Ant to the 6X tippet and began to stalk one of the risers. A few casts later and a 20-inch rainbow was in the net. The action lasted for more than two hours, and in that time I never saw another angler in this channel. If a fish wouldn't take the ant, it would take a size 19 Firefly, so I alternated patterns as I worked my way up this amazing little channel. Every now and then another angler would pass by the spot where this channel emptied into the main river, but not one of them chose to fish it. Why? I have no idea. It was private, the fish were on the take, but none of them ever saw me playing a fish. If an angler went by while I had a fish on, I simply dropped the rod tip and broke the fish off. Sneaky? You bet it was sneaky, but it insured my privacy on this spectacular little section of the San Juan.

Since I first tied this pattern more than three years ago, it has rapidly become one of my favorite ant imitations. It's easy to tie, the hot spot makes it easy to see, and trout readily accept it. It is also a very durable pattern—much more so than one might expect. ■

Flip-Flop Ants

Hook: I use two different hooks for these ants, the Tiemco 100 and the 102Y, or the equivalent. Both work well for this pattern.

Body: A foam cylinder punched from the sole of a flip-flop shower shoe. The size of the cylinder is determined by the size of the ant you wish to tie. The easiest way to punch the cylinders from the sole of the flip-flop is to use a set of cork borers, which can be obtained from any biological supply house (Ward's or Carolina Biological Supply are both good sources). As I recall, you can buy a set of twelve that will have just about any size you need. You can also buy brass tubing in different sizes from hobby shops that can be sharpened and used as punches. I would offer a word of advice about using sharpened brass cylinders, however. Wrap some tape around the dull end to remind you which end fits in your hand. If you don't, you just might cut a plug out of your palm rather than the sole of the flip-flop.

Hackle: Good-quality saddle hackle, color at the discretion of the tier.

The Flip-Flop Ant is tied in exactly the same manner as the Hot Spot Ant. What makes this ant so appealing is the tremendous number of different color combinations available from beach shoes. You can buy all sorts of different color combinations from stores like WalMart, K-Mart, Target, and many others. I even see beach shoes sold in grocery stores and drugstores. I'm afraid I have spent way more than I should have on different-colored beach shoes, but I just can't seem to pass up a pair that looks as though it would tie a great-looking ant. Many of the colors found in foam beach shoes are not available in sheet foam (at least not yet). Fluorescent orange, hot pink, yellow-green, blue-green, magenta, and other off-the-wall colors are readily available in foam of this type. I have two suggestions to offer, however, when shopping for beach shoes. First, buy the largest sizes you can find in the colors you want. You will pay the same price regardless of size. Second, take your wallet. If you are like me, you'll spend way more than you plan to. One other thing I might mention is that if you run across a particularly appealing color, such as fluorescent orange, you should buy more than one pair. You may never find that particular color again! ■

Los Alamos Ant

Hook:	Tiemco 5212, size 10, or equivalent.
Thread:	Gudebrod 6/0, or equivalent, color of choice.
Underbody wrap:	Three or four strands of peacock herl.
Rear legs:	Two medium- or small-size round rubber legs or two Silli-Legs, color as desired.
Body:	Two triangular pieces of foam, colors of choice. For a size 10 hook, the triangle should be about 1 inch long and 3/8 inch wide at the base. Adjust the size of the triangle accordingly for larger or smaller hook sizes. I usually use Locofoam to tie these ants, but any 1/16-inch-thick sheet foam can be used.
Front legs:	Round rubber leg material, medium or small size, or Silli-Legs, color to match that of the rear legs.
Eyes:	Fabric applique paint or E-Z Shape Sparkle Body.

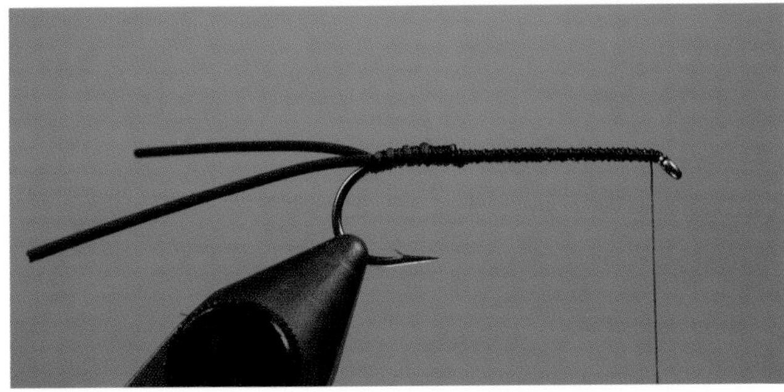

1. Attach the thread to the hook shank, and wrap it all the way to the bend of the hook. Tie in the two rear legs on opposite sides of the hook shank. Cut them approximately the same length as the hook shank or a little longer if desired. Wrap the thread forward to the eye of the hook.

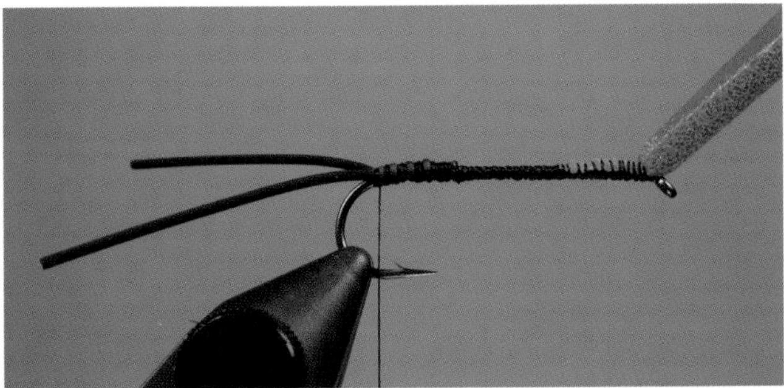

2. Tie in the tip of one of the foam body pieces so that the base of the triangle will be pointing forward. On a size 10 hook, about one-sixth of the triangle should be tied down. This triangle will eventually be folded backward over the hook shank—check it at this time to make sure that it's long enough to extend to or slightly beyond the hook bend. If it isn't long enough, unwrap the thread and tie it in again. A little practice will show you the correct length. Wrap the thread all the way back to the rear of the hook shank.

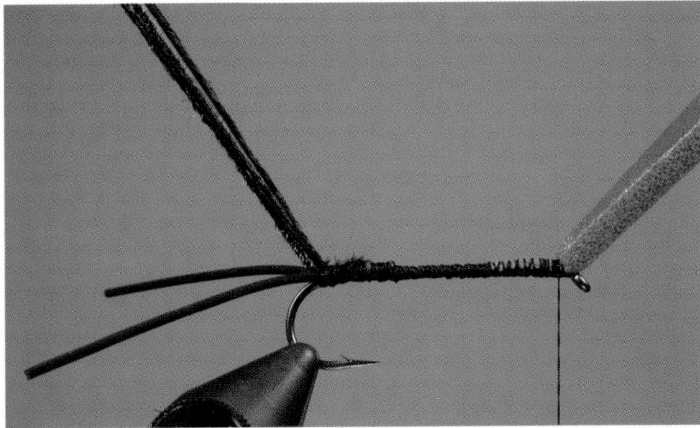

3. Tie in four or five strands of peacock herl, and wrap the thread forward to the eye of the hook.

4. Wrap the peacock herl forward to the eye of the hook, and tie it off. Trim the excess, and wrap the thread backward through the herl to a point even with the point of the hook.

5. Fold the foam backward over the hook shank, and tie it down. The point where it is tied down should be even with the point of the hook.

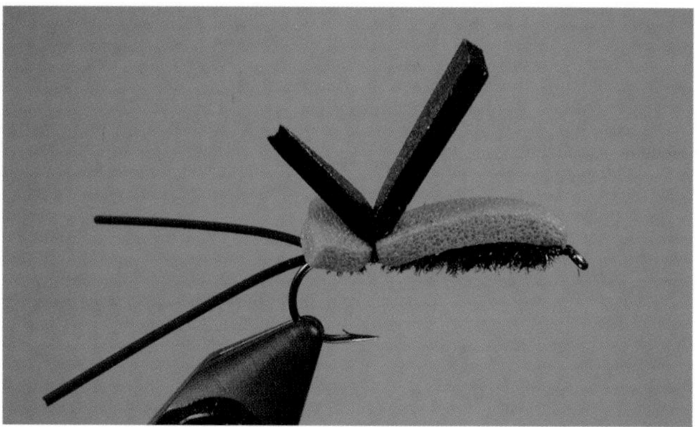

6. Tie in the second piece of triangular body foam at the same point with the tip projecting rearward. The tip of this triangle will automatically point upward to form a "tail." The base of the triangle should point forward and be even with or extend slightly over the rear of the eye of the hook. Whip-finish, cut, and remove the thread.

7. Reattach the thread over the first triangle at about 3/16 inch back from the eye of the hook.

8. Now fold the second piece of foam forward, and tie it down in the same place. This will form the "head" of the finished fly.

9. Tie in a single rubber leg on the lateral margins of the fly at this same point. A portion should point forward and a portion rearward to form two legs on either side of the fly. Whip-finish, and remove the thread.

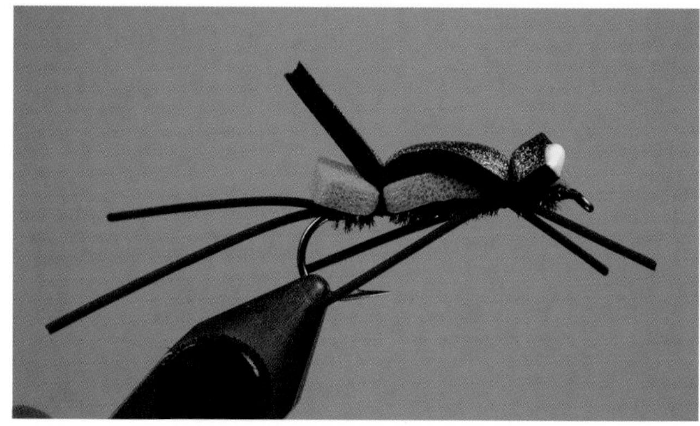

10. Add eyes by putting a drop of liquid applique or E-Z Shape Sparkle Body on both sides of the forward-projecting portion of the top triangle. If desired, the appliqué can be put on the upright "tail" to give the fly better visibility. Let the "eyes" dry overnight before using.

About six years ago I walked into the old Blue Ribbon Fly Shop, located a few miles downstream from Raynolds Pass Bridge on the Madison, thinking I would spend an hour or so shooting the breeze with George Tanfield. George was a schoolteacher from New Jersey who spent each summer running the shop for Craig Mathews, and I always stopped by when in the neighborhood. After we had thrown the usual insults at each other, I wandered around the shop for a while, checking out new goodies (or at least goodies I hadn't seen before) and eventually stopped over at the fly bins. There, to my horror, I discovered a couple of dozen of the ugliest, strangest-looking critters I had ever seen. Huge, black, closed-cell foam bodies, with a big red wad of yarn stuck on top, rubber legs going in every direction. It was called a Chernobyl Ant, and it was the damnedest thing I had seen in a long time.

"George," I called across the shop, "what are these things?"

"Which ones?" said George.

"These Chernobyl Ants. They've got to be a joke," I said.

"No joke," replied George. "At least I don't think it's a joke. But you're right; I've never seen anything like 'em either. I don't know whose idea it was to order the things, or even how they ran across them. But, I'll tell you one thing, they're probably going to be right there in those bins for the next ten years."

"I think you're right, George," I said. "Who in their right mind would buy one of those awful-looking things? You really have no idea where they came from or who came up with this pattern?"

"Nope," said George. "Don't know a thing about them, other than when I die they'll probably still be around the shop."

"George, old buddy," I said. "I wish you luck. If I were you, I think I'd go ahead and put 'em in a yard sale next week. If you're lucky, you might be able to get rid of some of them. On the other hand, you might have to actually pay someone to take 'em off your hands."

Yeah, we got a good laugh out of that first shipment of Chernobyl Ants. Have two guys ever have been more wrong about a fly pattern? I doubt it, because the Chernobyl Ant just happened to become one of the hottest patterns around, and there are probably tens of thousands of the things sold every year. I have seen people fishing them from Montana to Tennessee, and I've heard plenty of stories about how effective this pattern is for just about everything. It's been used to win fly-fishing contests, and it has given rise to an entire colony of clones and look-alikes, which is the normal progression for any really successful pattern. I have to admit, I wish I had thought of and designed this pattern, but I didn't.

But about a year after George and I had our laughs over the Chernobyl Ant, I was playing around with some triangles cut from 1/16-inch-thick foam. I was designing some terrestrial patterns with them, messing around with different sizes of triangles, different sizes of hooks, and different ways of tying the triangles on the hooks. One of the things that I came up with sort of reminded me of that goofy-looking fly the Chernobyl Ant, and figuring that the United States should have its own radioactive member of the *Formicidae,* I coined the name Los Alamos Ant. One of the noticeable things about this pattern was that the tail of the fly stuck up nicely above the body. A splash of some brightly colored material applied to this upright tail made the fly visible at any distance.

When I first tied this pattern, it was the middle of the winter, so I didn't think much about it at the time. I tied up some in different colors, all the same size, and stuck them in a box in the old fishing vest, figuring that I would fool around with them sometime that spring. Well, early spring rolled around, and I got a call from Dave Lewis, who lives in Harrisonburg, Virginia (and, by the way, builds a mighty sweet fly rod). He invited me up to fish a private section of water on Mossy Creek, and of course I gladly accepted. It was early spring and still pretty chilly, but I figured anything to get on the stream again.

I met Dave early in the afternoon, and we proceeded to fish this section of Mossy Creek, but with little success. We took a few fish, missed a few fish, sat in the sun, shot the breeze, and generally didn't take the fishing too seriously. But at one point, something happened, and the memory of this event burrowed its way into my brain and stuck there.

Dave had gone upstream. I had gone down and was just standing on the bank, not doing much more than watching the water go by. I opened up my terrestrial box to pick out a beetle pattern, but for some reason picked out one of the Los Alamos Ants instead. I think that I just wanted to see how the thing would cast and ride in the water more than anything else. I tied it to the tippet, cast it out about 20 feet, and was just sort of playing around with the fly, not paying much attention to anything other than the way it looked in the water. After a few minutes, I let it drift downstream, through a chute leading into the next pool, and let it hang there in the faster water.

"Interesting," I was thinking to myself. "The way the foam sticks up in the front makes the thing bounce around and sort of pop in the current. Throws up a bit of spray too, sort of like a bass bug."

A 14-inch brown thought it was pretty interesting too! He came out of nowhere, slammed the fly, and hooked himself. I never even had to raise the rod tip. That was a nice surprise, but what really piqued my curiosity was that he hit the fly when it was hopping and splashing all over the place. Was it just a fluke, or was there something about skipping and hopping this pattern across the current that would prove useful in the future?

The answer to that question came that summer on my annual trip to the Catskills with the usual fishing group. This bunch of guys includes some of the best fishermen I know—Cliff Rexrode, Urbie Nash, Steve Hiner, and Pete Bromley in particular. We always do the

West Branch of the Delaware, the Willowemoc, and the Beaverkill, as well as a few other streams, and we always have a good time. But this trip proved to be a testing ground for the Los Alamos Ant.

We fished it everywhere. We fished different colors, we fished it on a dead drift, we skipped it across current and across flat pools, we fooled around with the thing until I had just about run out of them. What we discovered was that the blasted thing was deadly. In most cases, color didn't seem to matter because each of us would be fishing a different color and we would all be catching about the same number of fish. What each of us noticed independently, however, was how deadly the fly was when you gave it a little action, skipping it along as though the thing was a bass popper.

"Cliff," I yelled downstream, "come up here and look at this."

Cliff's voice floated back upstream. "What is it?"

We were fishing a section of the Willowemoc that has always produced some very nice fish, but today we had absolutely hammered the fish using the Los Alamos Ant. It was also on this day that the name became shortened to the LA Ant. Lots of folks at fly-fishing shows have asked me why I call it the Los Angeles Ant, and I have to tell them the right name. Although, having spent a little time in Los Angeles and seen some pretty strange things there, the name Los Angeles Ant would probably work just as well.

Anyway, I had spotted a group of about six large trout holding on top of a big flat rock in about 3 feet of water, and I wanted to show them to Cliff. I was standing about 30 feet below the fish, and it was obvious that they were feeding, moving from side to side taking nymphs and occasionally coming up for an emerger. Cliff pulled up beside me and stood there.

"What do you think of that?" I asked Cliff. I was looking upstream at the rock, thinking that Cliff was looking in the same direction.

"That," said Cliff, "is one hell of a nice fish!"

"Yeah," I replied. "That one on the left will go at least 18 or 19 inches."

"What one on the left?" asked Cliff.

"The one next to that dark crack in the rock," I answered.

"I don't see any dark crack in that rock," said Cliff.

"Jeez, Cliff, the crack in the rock runs for about 4 feet. Look just to the left of it. Man, the thing looks like a submarine."

"I don't see any fish lying along a crack in some imaginary rock of yours, but I sure see one about 20 inches long lying next to that rock about 15 feet to your right," said Cliff.

It was pretty obvious we had been looking in different directions and I had been so zoned in on the fish on the rock that I had missed the hog that was only 15 feet away. On the other hand, not much gets by Cliff. He's not the kind of guy you want to be fishing behind.

"Damn," I said, looking at the fish Cliff had spotted, "you think he's spooked?"

"What have you got on?" Cliff answered.

"A tan LA Ant," I said.

"Give him a drift," said Cliff. So I did.

The hog came up, followed the fly for about 3 feet, almost touching it with his nose, dropped down, and returned to the rock. Cliff and I both simultaneously discovered we had been holding our breath.

"Try him again," said Cliff.

I did, with exactly the same result. I gave it two more casts, and each time the fish came up, followed the fly for about 3 feet, and then returned to his lie.

"He wants it," said Cliff. "Try him again."

"OK," I said, "but this time it's going to be a little bit different."

I cast the LA Ant about 5 feet upstream from the fish and a few feet to the fish's right. As the fly drifted down toward the fish, I started skipping the ant across the current so that by the time the fly was even with the fish, it was dancing right across his nose. He charged, I raised the rod tip, and it was a good solid hookup.

"Have you been skipping that fly like that all day?" asked Cliff.

"Yep," I replied. "Why?"

"Just curious," said Cliff. "So have I; so has Urbie. For that matter, so have Pete and Steve. It's crazy, but we've all just about quit dead drifting the thing. It seems they can't refuse it when it's bouncing along like that."

"Yeah," I said. "I know. What do you think it is?"

"Who cares?" said Cliff. "The technique works like a charm. Let's not get philosophical about it."

Since then, the LA Ant has taken a prominent place in my terrestrial arsenal and in the fly boxes of most of my fishing companions. There have been so many occasions when this has proved to be the "go to" pattern of the day that I often simply start out with one and never bother to change again, unless I break it off or it gets so chewed up that it becomes unrecognizable.

I have had many memorable experiences with this pattern. For example, I took my son with me to Colorado a few years ago, and we fished the Gunnison. On his first cast, a rainbow of about 18 inches came up and took a tan LA Ant. Although he did not land the fish, I had a terrible time trying to convince him that he should try other patterns as well. As far as I know, he never fished another pattern the entire time we were on the Gunnison. Another memorable day was on the Big Thompson River near Loveland, Colorado, where I had hooked and landed three nice browns before the people I was fishing with had even managed to tie a fly to their tippet! Another Colorado River, the Dolores, yielded three nice browns in as many casts, and this happens to be a river noted for its large and selective fish. But this fly, just like all other patterns, is not always the answer, nor do I expect it to be. I have, for example, tried it on the Frying Pan with very little success, but that doesn't mean it might not be a killer there under certain conditions and at certain times of the year.

When I was fishing in the "one-fish contest" during the 2001 Great Outdoor Games, the LA Ant was the first fly I tried, and I immediately raised half a dozen fish with it using the "skip across the current" technique. During the course of the three-hour time period, my partner, Steve Hiner, and I raised quite a few fish with this fly, but never got a solid take. That was too bad, because one of the fish would have won the contest hands down.

On the other hand, one of my acquaintances, Larry Duckwall, has never caught a trout with this particular pattern. I have probably given him two dozen LA Ants, all in different colors and sizes. He is not a particularly good tier, and I feel a little sorry for him, hence I contribute to his rather poorly stocked fly boxes. But for some reason, "Ducky" just can't seem to connect with this fly. I really should not be too surprised at this, however; I've never seen him catch a fish, and it's a well-known fact that Ducky really is not much of a fly fisherman, although he seems to do quite well when he disappears around a bend in the river. What can I say?

I should also mention that I tie this pattern in smaller sizes for fishing mountain and meadow streams for brook trout or small rainbows and browns. These smaller Los Alamos Ants are tied on Tiemco 5212, size 14 or 16 hooks. The triangles used to form the body of these smaller flies are of course cut proportionately smaller to accommodate the smaller hook size.

Others seem to have found this pattern to work as well as I have. Consider the following anecdote from Bob Petti.

This past Saturday evening I was fishing Cairns Pool on the Beaverkill, sort of staying around the edges of the action waiting for the crowd to thin. There were a lot of splashy rises to caddis, so I had tried a slightly weighted hare's ear soft hackle as well as a Snowshoe Caddis, but most of the action was at the head of the pool or along the far side—places I couldn't get to.

Finally, I had a chance to wade into some good water. The sun had already dipped below the hills, and it was cooling down. The splashes were less frequent. The fellow upstream had said size 18 BWO (which was odd considering none of us had seen a BWO all day—lots of Hendricksons, though). So I tied on a size 10 Los Alamos Ant, figuring a buggy, leggy profile at dusk would be too much for the bigger fish to resist.

It's no surprise to you, of course, but the fish *loved* the fly. I missed the best rise, a big buttery slab of fish that rolled over the fly, but I managed to do OK otherwise.

Thanks again. Twice now, on this very pool, your flies have gotten me into fish when otherwise I would have gone fishless. ■

TransparANT

Hook:	Tiemco 101, sizes 14 to 20, or equivalent. Do not use down-eye hooks.
Abdomen:	Formed with tying thread. Piersall silk thread on sizes 14 and 16 hooks is my first choice; use 6/0 or 8/0 tying thread on sizes 18 and 20 hooks. The color of the thread is at the discretion of the tier.
Body coating:	Devcon (or similar brand) five-minute clear epoxy.
Head:	Formed with tying thread. The color can either match or contrast with the color of the thread used to form the abdomen.
Hackle:	Top-quality saddle hackle is ideal if you plan on tying very many of these ants. The color of the hackle should match or contrast with the color of the body.
Wings (if desired):	I use a few strands of nylon organza, a bit of Z-lon, or some other synthetic material for the wings. Tie them in before winding the hackle legs.

A rotary vise should be used when tying this fly.

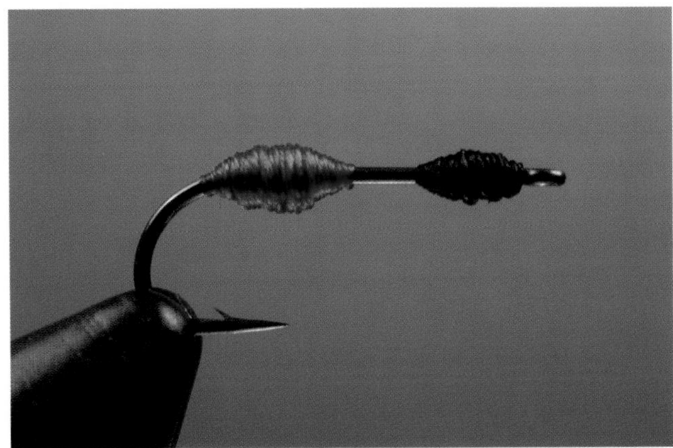

1. Build up the abdomen with thread until it is about three-fourths the final size. Whip-finish, cut and remove the thread, and then reattach the thread behind the eye of the hook. *It is imperative that the portion between the abdomen and head thread wraps be left bare.* If this is not done, the epoxy will flow into the center, and the fly is

ruined. Build up the head directly behind the eye of the hook to about three-fourths the final size. Cut and remove the tying thread. There should be enough bare hook shank between the head and abdomen for adding legs and wings, if they are desired.

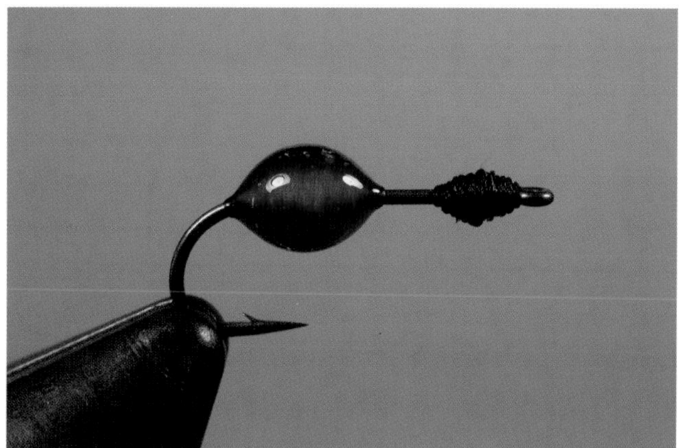

2. Mix up a small amount of five-minute epoxy, and using a needle (bodkin or whatever), pick up enough epoxy to form the abdomen. Experience will show you how much is necessary. While rotating the fly, feed the epoxy from the needle onto the body to cover it and form a nice smooth surface. The epoxy will automatically form the contours of the abdomen; just make sure the thread wraps are evenly covered.

3. To form the head, follow the same procedure as in step 2. Do not allow the epoxy to flow into the eye of the hook. Rotate the fly for about three or four minutes until the epoxy has hardened. Using a pair of fine pointed forceps, with the tips bent to fit through the eye of the hook, grasp the eye of the hook, take the fly out of the rotary vise, and place it on a magnetic strip where it is allowed to cure and harden.

4. When the fly has cured sufficiently (it doesn't take more than thirty minutes), reattach the thread and tie in the hackle for the legs.

5. Wind the hackle once or twice, tie it off, and trim it. If wings are desired, they should be tied in before tying in the hackle used to form the legs. Whip-finish, and remove the thread. ■

Chapter 5

Beetles

Beetles are my favorite of all terrestrial patterns, and I fish them the majority of the time over anything else, even ants. They are a terrific pattern to offer to rising fish when no hatch is evident and are a good "searching" pattern as well. I have without question taken more large trout on beetle imitations than any other fly pattern I carry, and that includes all dry-fly and nymph patterns, as well as other terrestrials. Beetles are incredibly easy to tie, particularly if you are tying with foam. As a matter of fact, I just do not understand why anyone continues to tie beetle patterns with materials like deer or elk hair. The old deer hair Crowe Beetle was, and still is, a great pattern, but it is terribly fragile and seems to explode after only a few fish. On the other hand, foam-bodied beetle patterns will often last for dozens of fish and only seem to get better with a little wear. Besides being easy to tie, foam beetles can be tied in different colors and shapes to mimic many different species of beetles, which can be a primary consideration. If the streamside vegetation is loaded with Japanese beetles, why not use a pattern that effectively mimics them? You certainly do not have to settle for a plain old black deer hair beetle, and if you fish a good foam-bodied Japanese beetle imitation, I'll guarantee your success rate will skyrocket.

Foam-bodied beetle imitations also seem to work no matter where you might be, and they consistently take big fish. A good example of this would be the consistent success of the Firefly pattern on western waters. I don't know how many times someone has said to me, "But fireflies aren't found out west," to which my answer has always been, "Maybe not, but trout don't read entomology books." It has also been pointed out to me on numerous occasions that "Fireflies aren't out yet," to which my answer has always been, "It doesn't matter. I fish the pattern from spring to fall, and I don't see any difference in my success rate." The same holds true for the Japanese beetle. It doesn't matter whether the foliage is covered with them or not, they will consistently take fish.

Although it is nice to tie beetle patterns the same size as the natural insect you are trying to imitate, it is certainly not necessary. I often fish beetle imitations that are considerably larger or smaller than the natural when conditions dictate. If, for example, I am fishing flat-water situations in which one often encounters "spooky" fish, I will use beetles that are considerably smaller than the natural insect, and it does seem to make a difference. But this may not be necessary at all. Sometimes oversize beetle imitations may be just the thing to try. Consider the following communication from my cousin, Conrad Black, who lives in New Zealand. I sent him a care package of some Manuka beetle imitations, and here are the results.

Harrison, those green/Manuka aka Christmas Beetles that you sent me last year just got a third bath two days ago! Fine, fine flies they are indeed! FF@ listers, these are custom Harrison Steeves originals! Hand tied in the US of A! Not mass-produced by a Botswana bushman who has to sit on a Coke bottle to stay awake. They are representative of a beetle specific to Australasia, a shiny metallic green insect that feeds on tea tree or Manuka, and only flies for about a month in early summer. Harrison produced these with his high-density foam, and I looked forward to getting them in the mail like a kid looks forward to Christmas.

Opened the package: beautiful flies, yes indeed, a good twice the size of the natural mind you! But beautiful! Harrison had been tying these for some Aussie, and obviously, the Aussie exaggerated the size. Or so I thought! Turns out the beetles are two times larger in the tropics, and therein starts the tale. This week I had to drive to the far north of New Zealand, and I found a river in the New Zealand "banana belt" that holds trout. I've driven by it a dozen times and never stopped—this is not trout country! Oh, silly me. There is a little river in our "tropics" that is a real winner, half of the water is artesian from a mountain range spine/spline whatever. I hooked a rainbow that was . . .

8 pounds. She did the high hurdle trick and put the trace over a feral banana plant. Ping! Long-distance catch and release.

First fish I've lost to a banana, that's for sure! On the way back from Northland, stopped into the Rangitikei at Springvale, put on a 2X Harry beetle, and put it over two good, good fish. Both refused. Need a 1X in these southern mountains! So I started to fish the run edges, and second cast, you could see a torpedo wake coming for the fly! It amazes me that rainbows can actually see a target from 10 feet or more, but I suppose if the fly's that big, it's hard to miss! My man, Disney could have saved a pile of money spent on *Pearl Harbor* just by shooting over my shoulder! Swissshhhhhhhh. . . . BAM! Man! That wake is a thrill! Another 18 to 19-inch rainbow bites the dust.

Before you get too thrilled, Harry, remember, these are fish that have to make a living somehow, and your double-sized beetles look like a Super Big Mac Combo. Second fish was a real go 'bot, and just before the wake meets the target, I flicked it out of the way. OK, I play with my food, been doing that since Mom put me on solids. Toro! Toro! Eat this if you can [Don Kelly will back me on this, there are times when you *must* prevent fish from eating your fly]. Two days ago, I took the family into the Upper Mohaka and nailed a 5–6 pounder, rainbow, on your terries. You could see the fish coming up, *because* it was a 2X, seeing the fly and saying, "That fly is *not* right!" But like most fat men at a buffet, he said, "If I've walked this far, I might as well have a nibble." (Excuse me for a moment—21$^{3}/_{4}$ inches, 5 pounds, 2 ounces gutted—just getting it ready for Grandma Wendy and the smoker.) Thats it, Harrison, wish I could help, but your flies are too big for my taste, they only hook fish up to 24 inches, 8 pounds. Sorry, Cuzzie.

Cheers . . . CB (Conrad Black)

If that doesn't whet your appetite for beetle patterns, then nothing will.

Bark (Longhorn) Beetle

Hook:	Tiemco 5212, size 10 or 12, or equivalent.
Thread:	Gudebrod 6/0 or equivalent, black.
Body:	Black/white/gray foam cylinders (Livebody brand) from the Dale Clemens Shop, Allentown, Pennsylvania. The foam cylinders are approximately 2 inches long and $^{3}/_{16}$ inch in diameter. Each cylinder is first cut in half and then split with a razor blade along the long axis to give four 1-inch-long, half-round body pieces. Each body piece is then trimmed to a point at one end so it may be easily tied in.
Underbody:	Three or four pieces of peacock herl.
Wings:	Kreinik $^{1}/_{8}$-inch-wide mallard (#850) flat ribbon.
Antennae:	Two bristles (hairs) of javelina (western peccary).
Head underwrap:	Two or three strands of peacock herl.
Head:	$^{1}/_{4}$-inch-diameter disc cut from a $^{1}/_{16}$-inch-thick sheet of black/white/gray Livebody foam.

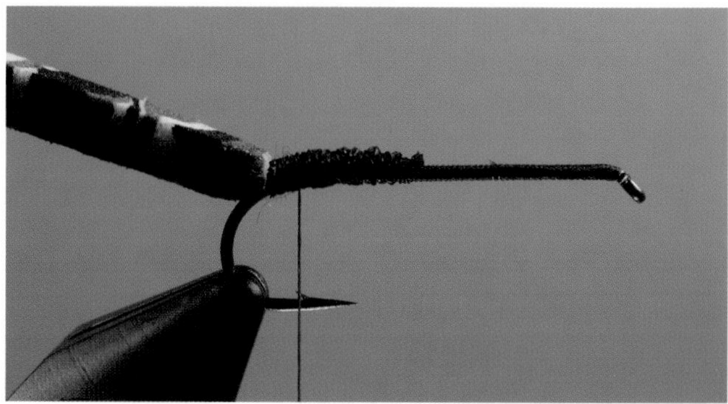

1. Wrap the shank of the hook with thread all the way rearward to the bend of the hook and then forward about one-third the length of the hook shank. Trim one end of the foam body material to a point, and tie it in all the way back to the bend of the hook. Make sure that you tie in the body material with the half round surface down. When it is folded forward to form the body, the half round surface will then be on top, giving the body a classic rounded beetle form.

2. Tie in three or four strands of peacock herl by the tips. Wind the thread forward about three-fourths the length of the hook shank.

3. Wrap the peacock herl forward to this point, tie it off, and trim. The thread is then wound backward to the rear of the fly and then forward again to the point where the peacock herl was tied off. This thread wrap through the peacock herl serves to reinforce the herl. If you follow this procedure, the herl will never break.

4. Fold the body material over the top of the hook shank, and tie it down. Trim away the forward-projecting excess foam. I also trim the remaining foam a bit to eliminate excess bulk and get a neat tapered front to the body, which makes it considerably easier to accomplish the next steps.

5. Tie in the winging material a little distance behind the eye of the hook, and wrap the thread rearward to the point at which the front of the body was tied down. The winging material should extend rearward no farther than the end of the body. Excessively long wings seem to take away from the effectiveness of the fly. Once the winging material is tied in, split it into two equal portions. Separate them using a figure-eight wrap, and tie them down on opposite sides of the body.

6. Tie in two javelina bristles so that the tips extend well past the rear of the body. These bristles do an excellent job of mimicking the excessively long antennae seen on many types of beetles. Separate them with a figure-eight wrap so that they lie well apart from each other and on top of the winging material. Tie them in tightly, and trim the forward-projecting portions.

7. Tie in two or three strands of peacock herl directly in front of the body, and wrap the thread to the eye of the hook.

8. Wrap the peacock herl to the eye of the hook, tie it down, and trim the excess. Wrap the tying thread rearward to a point halfway between the rear of the eye of the hook and the front of the body.

9. Tie in the head disc at this point. The front of the head disc should extend forward to the rear of the hook eye, and the rear of the disc should extend over the base of the wings and antennae. Whip-finish, and remove the tying thread.

This is a slightly modified version of the original pattern, in which the head was formed by twisting two strands of peacock herl and one strand of natural ostrich herl together and then wrapping them forward. I much prefer this modification.

I should offer a little advice at this point on how to split the foam cylinder in order to prepare the bodies. I first tried to do this by holding it with my fingers. That worked just fine for cutting the cylinders in half. But when it came to splitting the inch-long cylinders down the middle, I found out that it was pretty easy to trim off a little of your fingertip in the process. So I took a little block of wood and routed a channel in it slightly larger than the diameter of the foam cylinders and about half as deep. Then I could place the cylinder in the channel, and using a sharp single-edge razor blade, push straight down to divide the cylinder into two equal portions. This works like a charm and saves your fingertips.

This pattern has been a steady producer since its inception and on certain occasions has outfished all other beetle patterns. Although I call it a bark beetle, it probably represents any big long-horned beetle that blunders into the water. Maybe it's the long antennae that contribute to its effectiveness, but I couldn't swear to that because I have never tied any without the antennae to test the hypothesis.

I also tie this pattern with brown and gray foam cylinders, with the heads cut from 1/16-inch-thick sheets of comparably colored foam. These colors have also worked well. Another cylindrical foam you might like to try is that produced by Rainy Riding, which is available in quite a few different colors.

The first time I fished this pattern was on the Dolores River in Colorado. I was standing at the tailout of a pool, watching three nice fish feeding on the other side and figuring how I could make the easiest and most subtle approach to them. In front of me, maybe 15 feet away, was a large boulder, which split the current and formed a nice eddy behind it. While watching the fish on the far side, I idly slapped the Bark Beetle upstream from the boulder. I wasn't really paying attention to anything except those rising fish on the far side. As the fly swept around the boulder, a nice brown came out of nowhere and trashed it. Somehow, probably just a reflex action, I raised the rod tip, managed to get a good hookup, and landed the fish.

It took me a few minutes to calm down, but eventually my pulse rate returned to normal and I picked my way across to a point where I could make a cast to the most downstream of the three feeding trout. But I was in a lousy situation. The current was such that I could only get about 2 feet of good drift before the fly would be snatched away and start to drag. Well, you've got to try, so I made a couple of false casts to get the right distance and let her go. Sure enough, 2 feet of drift and then (no matter how frantically I mended line) the fly started to drag—and I mean it was really dragging—back toward me and away from the fish. That fish never paid any attention to the fact that the fly was dragging. It came after it as though it was starving to death, chased it downstream for a good 3 feet, and slammed it hard enough to jar my wrist. The result was a pretty good rainbow that put on a spectacular aerial show for the next few minutes.

Believe it or not, the second fish (also a rainbow) did the same thing. The minute the fly started to drag, it took off after it and inhaled it. I didn't land that fish, but it was a thrill anyway. I spooked the third fish by nearly hitting it on the head with a sloppy cast, but two out of three is OK by me any day.

Since then, I have fished this fly on many occasions, usually with great success. Like many of the larger terrestrial imitations, the Bark Beetle has proved to be a terrific searching pattern. ■

Disc O'Beetle

Hook: Tiemco 2487, sizes 12 to 18, or equivalent.
Thread: 6/0 or 8/0, depending on the hook size. Color of choice.
Body: 1/16-inch-thick foam disc of the appropriate size to match the hook size. Use the following as a guide:
12 hook—7/16-inch-diameter disc
14 hook—3/8-inch-diameter disc
16 hook—5/16-inch-diameter disc
18 hook—1/4-inch-diameter disc
Underbody: Peacock herl.
Wings: Kreinik flat ribbon, mallard #850. I use the 1/8-inch-wide ribbon for the larger flies (12 and 14) and the 1/16-inch-wide ribbon for the smaller sizes (16 and 18).

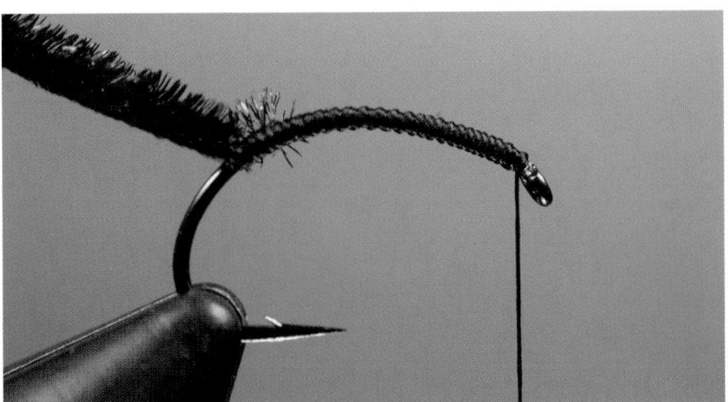

1. Wrap the hook shank with thread back to a point even with or slightly behind the barb. Tie in two to four peacock herl fibers, depending on the size of the fly.

2. Wrap the thread forward to the eye of the hook. Wrap the peacock herl forward to the eye of the hook, tie it off, and trim the excess. Wrap the thread back through the peacock herl and then forward about three-fourths the length of the hook shank.

3. Place the foam disc on top of the hook shank with the front of the disc extending just over the eye of the hook. One-fourth to one-third of the disc should extend forward of the point where the thread is positioned. The forward portion of the foam will form the head, and the remainder, extending toward the rear, will form the body of the beetle. Fold the foam disc evenly over the shank of the hook, and tie it down. At this point a good head and body will be formed. Give it another ten or twelve tight thread wraps so the body will not turn on the shank of the hook.

4. Legs or wings can then be tied in on the sides of the body. For wings, I use either the Kreinik 1/8- or 1/16-inch-wide flat ribbon in mallard color. For legs, I use fine round rubber leg material in colors to either match or contrast with the color of the body. Once the legs or wings are tied in, whip-finish, and remove the tying thread. Trim the wings (or legs) to the appropriate length. I usually tie this beetle with wings no longer (or just slightly longer) than the body of the beetle. A small amount of Zap-A-Gap cement can be applied to the underside of the finished fly. This will prevent the body of the fly from turning on the shank of the hook. ■

Disco Japanese Beetle

Hook:	Tiemco 100, size 14, or equivalent.
Thread:	Gudebrod 6/0 or equivalent, olive or black.
Underbody:	Kreinik Micro Ice Chenille, mallard (#850), or three to four strands of peacock herl. I prefer the Micro Ice Chenille for this pattern, but if you don't have it, then peacock herl is a good substitute.
Body:	3/8-inch-diameter foam disc cut from Metallic Copper Locofoam.
Wing:	Kreinik 1/8-inch flat ribbon, mallard, #850.
Underhead wrap:	Two strands of peacock herl.
Head:	5/16-inch-diameter disc cut from Tiger Beetle Green Locofoam. A 1/4-inch disc can be used for the head if you feel that the 5/16-inch disc is too large.

1. Wrap the shank of the hook with tying thread to the bend of the hook, and tie in a piece of Kreinik Micro Ice Chenille. Wrap the thread forward about two-thirds the length of the hook shank.

2. Wrap the Kreinik material forward to this point, tie it off, and trim the excess.

3. Tie in the foam-body disc. Only a small portion of the front of the disc should be tied down. The rear of the disc should extend to the bend of the hook. Apply a small amount of Zap-A-Gap cement to the top of the underbody wrap, and cement the body disc to the underbody wrap, by pressing it down firmly.

4. Tie in a piece of the Kreinik winging material in front of the body.

5. Separate it into two equal portions. Tie down the separated wings rearward to the front of the body.

6. Tie in two strands of peacock herl, and wrap the thread forward to the eye of the hook. Wrap the peacock herl to the eye of the hook, tie it off, and trim away the excess.

7. Wrap the thread rearward to a point about halfway between the front of the body and the eye of the hook.

8. Tie in the head disc at this point with about a dozen firm thread wraps. The front third of the head disc should extend just over the eye of the hook, and the rear of the disc should extend well over the body of the fly. Then turn the fly upside down in the vise, and apply either head cement or Zap-A-Gap to the thread wraps under the head. Fold the rear of the head disc forward, apply a small bit of Zap-A-Gap to the body beneath the head disc, and then cement the head disc to the body disc with a little pressure. The bond should be almost immediate. ■

Double Disc O'Beetle

Hook:	Tiemco 100, size 12, or equivalent.
Thread:	Gudebrod 6/0 or equivalent, color of choice.
Underbody wrap:	Kreinik Micro Ice Chenille, color of choice, or peacock herl.
Body:	3/8-inch-diameter disc cut from 1/16-inch-thick Locofoam. The color of the Locofoam is the choice of the tier, and it can be tied in with the metallic surface of the foam either up or down. If Locofoam is not available, the body disc can be cut from any 1/16-inch-thick sheet foam.
Underhead wrap:	Peacock herl.
Wings:	Kreinik flat ribbon, 1/8 inch wide, mallard, #850.
Head:	5/16-inch-diameter disc cut from Locofoam. The color of the head can either match that of the body or contrast with the body. Tie the head disc in with the metallic surface up. If Locofoam is not available, any 1/16-inch-thick sheet foam may be used.

1. Wrap the shank of the hook with thread to the rear of the hook, and tie in a single strand of Micro Ice Chenille or two or three strands of peacock herl. I much prefer the Micro Ice Chenille for this pattern.

2. Wrap the thread forward about two-thirds the length of the hook shank. Wrap the underbody material forward to this point, tie it off, and trim the excess. If peacock herl is used, then wrap the tying thread back to the

point where the peacock herl is tied in and then forward again. This will reinforce the herl and prevent it from breaking.

3. Tie in the body disc at the point where the underbody material was tied down. You only need to tie in a small portion of the body disc at the front. The rear of the disc should extend rearward to the bend of the hook.

4. Place a small amount of Zap-A-Gap cement on the top of the underbody material, and press the body disc down.

5. Tie in a piece of the Kreinik ribbon in front of the body, and trim it so that it extends no further rearward than the end of the body.

6. Separate the Kreinik ribbon into two equal portions, and tie the wings down to the front of the body and on opposite sides of the body.

7. Tie in a couple of strands of peacock herl, and wrap the thread forward to the eye of the hook.

8. Wrap the peacock herl forward to the eye of the hook, tie it off, and trim the excess. Wrap the thread rearward to a point about halfway between the front of the body and the eye of the hook.

9. Tie in the head disc at this point so that about one-third of the disc projects forward to the eye of the hook and two-thirds extends rearward over the body and the wings. Whip-finish, and remove the thread.

10. Fold the head disc into an upright position, and place a small drop of Zap-A-Gap on the top of the body disc. Then press the head disc down, and cement it firmly to the body disc. This will insure that the wings of the fly remain separated. Turn the fly upside down, and place a small drop of head cement or Zap-A-Gap cement on the thread wraps under the head. This insures that the wraps will never come loose and firmly cements the head to the front of the fly. ■

Firefly

Hook:	Tiemco 5212, size 14, or equivalent.
Thread:	Gudebrod 6/0 or equivalent, black.
Body:	A 1/8- to 3/16-inch-wide strip cut from 1/8-inch-thick, black, closed-cell foam (Evasote or Fly Foam).
Underbody:	Two to four strands of peacock herl.
Butt:	Kreinik medium round braid, fluorescent yellow, #054.
Wings:	Kreinik 1/8-inch-wide flat ribbon, mallard, #850.
Wing case:	Kreinik 1/8-inch-wide flat ribbon, beetle black, #005HL.

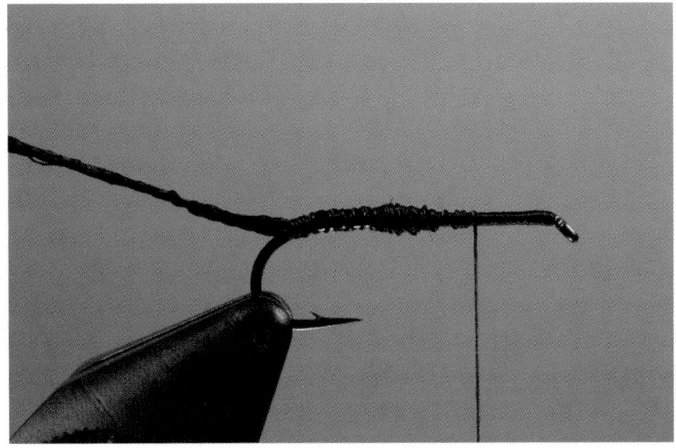

1. Wrap the shank of the hook with tying thread. Starting at a point in the middle of the hook shank, tie in the wing-case material to the bend of the hook. Wrap the thread forward two-thirds the length of the hook shank.

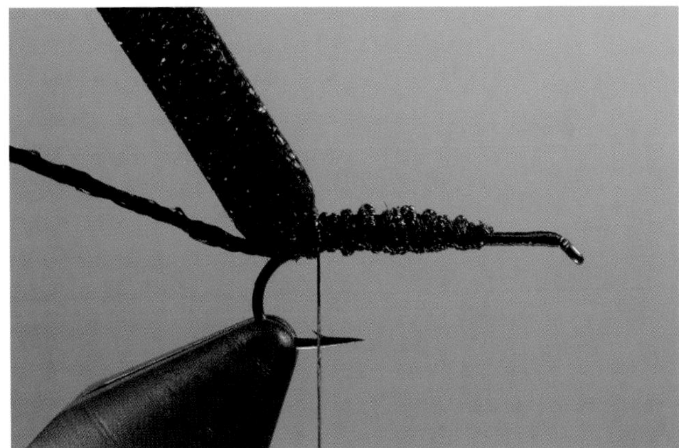

2. Tie in body foam, and continue to tie it in back to the bend of the hook. This will prevent the body from turning on the hook shank.

3. Tie in three or four strands of peacock herl, and wrap the tying thread forward to the eye of the hook.

4. Wrap the peacock herl forward to the eye of the hook, tie it off, and trim the excess. Wrap the thread back to the rear and then forward about 1/8 inch.

5. Tie in a piece of the butt material rearward; then wrap the tying thread forward about 1/8 inch.

6. Form the butt by wrapping the butt material forward three turns. Tie it off, and trim the excess. Wrap the thread forward through the peacock herl to a point about 1/8 to 1/16 inch behind the eye of the hook.

7. Fold the body foam forward, and tie it down. Cut the forward-projecting portion of the foam even with the front of the eye of the hook to form the head.

8. Tie in a piece of winging material projecting backward to the fluorescent butt. Trim the forward-projecting portion flush with the front of the head. Separate the winging material into two equal portions on either side of the body. Fold the wing-case material forward

between the wings, and tie it down. Trim the excess wing-case material flush with the front of the head. Whip-finish, and remove the thread.

I tie this particular pattern in many sizes besides 14. Two of my favorite sizes are 16 and 19. However, tying these smaller sizes necessitates a few changes in materials. For a size 16 Firefly, I use the standard Tiemco 5212 dry-fly hook, cut the 1/8-inch foam in thinner strips, and use the Kreinik fine braid for the fluorescent butt and the Kreinik 1/16-inch-wide ribbon in beetle black and mallard for the back and wings, respectively. Because a size 16 is the smallest size available in the Tiemco 5212 hook, I tie the size 19 on the Tiemco 102Y (regular-size shank, black). You could, of course, tie the fly in a size 18 instead of 19 on any standard dry-fly hook. Why did I choose 19? Good question, for which I have no answer other than I like the size 19 because it's just a bit smaller. I also believe that the black finish on the hook helps when you are casting to really picky fish. On the size 19 (or 18), I use 1/16-inch-thick foam cut into strips of the appropriate width. Use Kreinik 1/16-inch-wide beetle black ribbon for the wing case, or you can omit the wing case on a fly this small. The wings are tied with 1/16-inch-wide Kreinik mallard ribbon. If the wing case is omitted, the wings may be easily separated by using a single figure-eight wrap. For the butt on a size 19 Firefly, I use a single strand of the Kreinik Flash in a Tube, fluorescent yellow, and make enough wraps to give a nice little fluorescent yellow butt. If you desire, you can pick apart a piece of either the medium or fine fluorescent yellow braid to get a single strand of material for these little guys.

I have used all colors of the Kreinik fluorescent materials for forming the butt on these Fireflies. They all work, but because I started out with fluorescent yellow, I tend to stay with this color.

I should also point out that the smaller sizes of this pattern are absolutely deadly on picky fish in flat-water situations. The size 19 Firefly, for example, has on many occasions been the pattern of the day on both Armstrong's and DuPuy's Spring Creeks.

One day on DuPuy's Spring Creek when I was fishing with Dave Braine and Miller Williams the size 19 Firefly was worth its weight in gold. They were working a group of fish above the upper culvert, toward the end of the property, with very little success. There were enough PMDs hatching to get the fish up and moving, and I think they had thrown every variation of artificials at these fish. I was sort of standing back from the bank watching the whole thing and got this crazy notion to try one of these little-bitty size 19 Fireflies. So I knotted one on to the 6X tippet and casually flipped it out, maybe 20 feet, to a fish holding tight to the bank in still water. He came right over and took it!

Dave yells up to me, "What the hell are you doing?"

"Catching a fish. What does it look like?" I yelled back. "I don't see you guys doing anything outstanding."

Four fish later, Dave and Miller gave up and came up to where I was sitting on the bank. Not a word was spoken. They both held out their hands, and I forked over a couple of these little Fireflies to each of them. For the next few hours, it was nonstop action for all of us.

OK, that's a good example of how effective these little Fireflies can be, and I've had the same experience on many different rivers (the Watauga in Tennessee, the Smith in Virginia, and the San Juan in New Mexico are three that immediately come to mind). But what about the old standard size 14 Firefly? Listen, I'll be perfectly frank with you (I hate to use the word "honest," because you're then immediately suspect). I have fished this particular fly from Tennessee and Virginia through Pennsylvania and New York, as well as in Montana, Idaho, Wyoming, and Colorado, and day in and day out, it has proved to be an outstanding pattern. Of all my terrestrial patterns, this is the number one "go to" pattern, and I'll usually try it before anything else. The nice thing about it is that I know it's not just me who has had incredible success with this fly. Many of the guys I fish with use this pattern as much as I do and with the same degree of success. I'll be glad to give out names and phone numbers to anyone who wants to give them a call. Just as an example, a few months ago I sent a wellknown Canadian fly fisherman a shipment of Fireflies. He had been in touch with me about this Firefly pattern and was dying to give it a try. Because he was going to fish the English chalk streams, I was of course more than happy to send him a good handful of Fireflies (14) to try on these hallowed waters. I figured the chalk streams would be the ultimate test. Not long ago I received an e-mail from him in which he told me that he cast to twelve fish with the Firefly and had eleven takes. I'll take that success ratio any day.

There are other instances in which this pattern has proved unbelievably effective. The first time I ever fished this pattern I took more than 100 (that's not a misprint) trout on Virginia's Jackson River. My fishing partner that day took more than forty, but he didn't start using it until about 1:00 P.M.! Want another example?

The phone at home rang one evening, and when I answered it, I thought Donald Duck was on the line. It turned out to be a guy named Dave Norwood who lives in Allentown, Pennsylvania, and fishes extensively on the Little Lehigh. Well, Dave's excitement level was off the scale, but he finally calmed down enough so that I could make sense out of what he was trying to tell me. It seems as though Ed Koch had given Dave some of the Firefly patterns a few days before, and Dave had gone over to the Little Lehigh to give them a shot. Let me tell you something about this stream. It gets pounded! Plain and simple, it's a stream that is fished very heavily. The rule there is usually tiny flies; long, fine tippets; careful wading; and a handful of fish at day's end.

It seems that Dave had gone over to the stream that morning, tied on one of the Fireflies that Ed had given him, and started fishing. At the end of the day, he had taken 126 fish! Now, I've fished with Dave since then, as a matter of fact on the Little Lehigh, and I trust him. Normally he would never—and I mean never—take that many fish on purpose. Like most of us, Dave quits fishing after a point—a dozen or maybe two dozen is a very, very satisfying day on any stream. But Dave told me, "Harrison, I just couldn't stop." I guess he felt pretty much the same way I did that day on the Jackson when I took more than 100 on this pattern. I think everyone has probably had this sort of experience. You're in the zone, your casts are straight and accurate, the fish are coming out of nowhere to take the fly, you can't do anything wrong, the hours scoot by like clouds in the wind, and you come out of it at the end of the day dazed and confused. It's hard to describe the feeling. I imagine it's like being addicted to something: You just want more and more, and you simply can't stop.

After Dave had finished telling me all this, I said, "Dave, I have no idea what you were doing wrong. I guess I'll have to come up there and show you how to fish that pattern." Sometimes you get lucky and come up with the right answer at the right time.

It's one thing to take a whole bunch of fish on a particular pattern, and sure, that can be an incredible experience. But sometimes—and I think actually the great majority of the time—most of us remember those days when you really have to work hard at it. Things aren't always easy, and that's good for the character. And really, I believe that those who have been fly-fishing for some time reach a point when numbers of fish don't mean nearly as much as they did when they first started. I find more and more that it's not numbers but specific fish I remember and specific patterns I took those fish with. The Firefly has certainly accounted for the great majority of the "specific" fish I have taken with it since its birth more than a decade ago. Has it really been that long ago? Strange, it seems like only yesterday.

I think everyone in the angling world has heard of Henry's Fork, which just happens to be one of my five favorite rivers. If I had to pick one river out west to fish for the rest of my life, I'm pretty sure it would be Henry's Fork. Why? Well, it just "gets ahold on you" and won't let go. The fish are broad shouldered, strong, and selective, and you're going to work your butt off for every one of them. If you take a handful in a long day, you're going to be a mighty happy angler. Besides that, there's the mystique of the river. It's difficult to describe. There's just no other place like it, at least in my mind.

Sometimes when I fish Henry's Fork, I'll just park right across from Mike Lawson's place, sit on the bank, and wait for something to happen. Other times I'll gear up and start wandering downstream into the Railroad Ranch section. Sometimes I opt to go upstream a ways, or even down below Osborn's Bridge. It really doesn't matter.

I remember one day in particular when I decided to just take an easy hike way downstream to a certain stretch I especially enjoy. This place is no secret. It's been written about many times, so I'm not giving anything away here, but I like to fish it because most folks just don't want to walk down to it. That's fine with me. So I just ambled on down the bank, looking for rising fish, poking along and taking my own sweet time. Talk about a dead day—this day wasn't just dead, it was in the process of being autopsied. There was absolutely nothing going on at all. Henry's Fork can be like that, as anyone who fishes it can tell you. One day it rolls over and rewards you, the next day it's just likely to give you a boot to the family jewels. I was beginning to consider turning around and heading on back to the van. But I'm a stubborn sort of guy, I was past the halfway point, and figured "Might as well go ahead and do it."

When I reached the area I had set out for, I headed across to the far bank. I really like this place! There's a deep channel over there, the high grass hangs way over the water, and there's usually—but not always—a few fish feeding on whatever might fall into the water. It's an absolutely prime place for a terrestrial pattern. Sure enough, there were three fish, spaced about 30 feet apart, sipping "stuff" out of the surface film. Yeah, "stuff" is the best way to describe what they were feeding on, because there's no way you're going to know exactly what they are taking. As far as I could see, there was really nothing on the water, and yes, I looked hard.

I even took out the little net I carried and spent ten minutes trying to collect something, anything, that might give me a clue. No luck.

So, without thinking too much about it, I tied on one of the size 14 Fireflies and headed for the fish farthest downstream. OK, let's not go into the details of the next forty-five minutes. What happened was simply this: The fish farthest downstream took the Firefly on the third drift, when I finally managed to get the cast where I wanted it. I was lucky on the next fish, managed to make a pretty decent cast, and he took it on the first drift. The third fish took the Firefly on the second drift. I landed two of these fish (the first and the third), which is a little better than average for me considering all the weed beds and the tendency of fish in this water to do the old submarine dive into them—usually after a blistering initial run. How big were they? Who cares? I quit carrying a tape measure years ago. All I can say is that the frame of the net I carry measures a tad more than 20 inches long. The first fish went more than halfway up the handle, and the other was probably well into the handle too.

When something like this happens, I used to continue fishing, but not any more. After landing the third fish, I hooked the fly in the keeper, waded back over to the bank, and began the trek back to the car. On the way I ran into another fish, maybe a foot from the bank, that was rising every now and then. Sure, I cast to this fish—what did you expect? The Firefly landed dead even with the fish and about 6 inches to the right, between the fish and the bank. He exploded on it, and I missed him. I reeled in, cut the Firefly off the tippet, and headed on back to the van. Time for a cold beer and a replay of the morning. I was more than satisfied.

I could go on and on with stories and anecdotes about the Firefly. It's probably my all-around favorite terrestrial pattern, and I am pretty sure that it has become the same for a lot of my fishing buddies too. One thing, though, is that you have to get used to fishing it. It rides low in the water and can be difficult to see under certain conditions, even though it's a size 14. Let me give you an example. One day in August, I was guiding a fellow on Virginia's Smith River, and we were fishing the Firefly. This fellow missed twenty-seven fish in a row! That's right, twenty-seven! I know because I started counting after he missed the first four. It turned out that he never saw the fish take the fly, even in calm water. The fact of the matter is that in many cases the take is so subtle and gentle that unless you're used to fishing this pattern, you might be unaware that a fish has taken it. The problem is exacerbated when you happen to be fishing into the shade of overhanging vegetation along the bank. In many instances, the take is nothing more than a gentle sip, and yes, it is difficult to see. I've frequently had people that I'm fishing with look on in amazement when I raise the rod tip and have a fish on because they've never seen the take. I guess I've fished this pattern for so many years that I have developed a sixth sense as to where it is, even in broken water or in the shade. If you have trouble seeing this fly, simply tie in a little bit of fluorescent Antron yarn as the last step in the tying procedure (after you've tied in and trimmed the wing-case material), and trim it so that it isn't too long. This will help you to keep track of the fly, and it apparently does not detract from the effectiveness of the pattern. ■

Japanese Beetle (Original)

Hook:	Tiemco 100, size 10 and 12, or equivalent.
Thread:	Gudebrod 6/0 or equivalent, olive.
Body:	A strip of foam about 1/4 inch wide cut from either black or olive 3/16-inch-thick closed-cell foam (Evasote or Fly Foam).
Wing case:	Copper-colored Swiss straw.
Underbody:	Three or four strands of peacock herl.
Wings:	Kreinik 1/8-inch-wide, flat ribbon, mallard, #850.
Thorax:	Two or three strands of peacock herl twisted together.

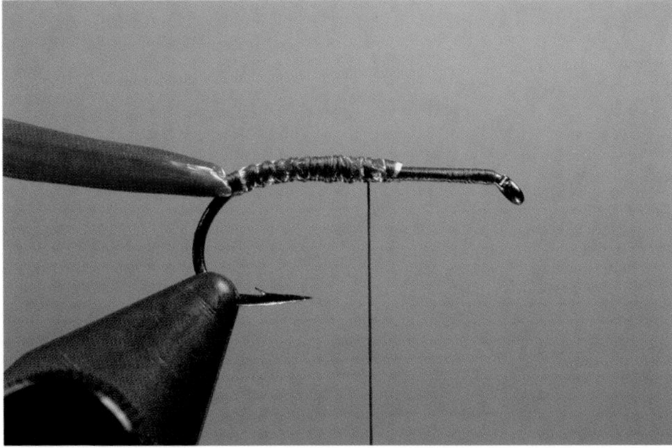

1. Wrap the thread on the hook shank to the rear of the hook, and then wrap it forward to a point just slightly forward of the middle of the shank. Tie in about a 3-inch piece of copper-colored Swiss straw on the hook shank. Tie the Swiss straw in by wrapping the thread rearward to the bend of hook. Once this is done, wrap the thread forward to a point slightly past the middle of the hook shank.

2. Tie in the piece of body foam. Tie the foam down by wrapping the thread rearward to the bend of the hook.

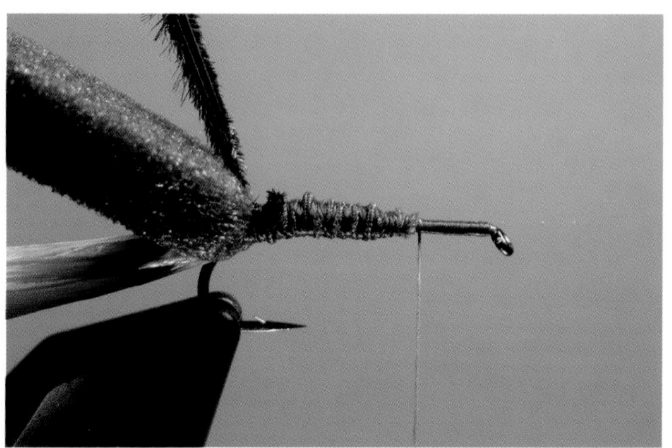

3. Tie in the tips of the peacock herl fibers. Wrap the thread forward about two-thirds the length of the hook shank.

4. Wrap the peacock herl underbody material forward, and tie it down. Trim away the excess. Wrap the thread back and then forward through the peacock herl to strengthen it. This procedure is much more satisfactory than simply twisting the herl strands together for added strength.

5. Fold the body foam over the underbody and forward, but do not stretch the foam during this procedure. You want the body to be robust and "fat" rather than thin. When doing this procedure, I put almost no tension on the foam. Tie the foam down with about six firm thread wraps, but be careful with the amount of tension you use. Foam, although it is pretty tough material, can be cut with too much thread tension, but a little practice is all that's necessary. Once the foam is securely tied down, pull it toward the eye of the hook (stretch it), and trim away the forward-projecting excess. By using this "stretch and cut" procedure, a minimum of foam is left ahead of the point where it is tied down. Wrap the thread over the remaining forward-projecting foam and then forward about $^{1}/_{16}$ inch.

6. Tie in a piece of Kreinik winging material, extending backward no farther than two-thirds the length of the body. The wings on this fly should be relatively short, so pay attention to your proportions. Trim away any excess material. Separate the winging material into two equal portions on either side of the foam body, and tie them in rearward to the front of the body.

7. Fold the Swiss straw forward over the body to form the wing case and to separate the wings. Tie it down, and trim the excess.

8. Tie in two or three strands of peacock herl by the tips. Grasp all of the herl butts together with a pair of hackle pliers or a circuit tester, and twist them together.

9. Wrap the twisted herl forward, two to four wraps, to form the thorax. Tie the herl down, and trim away the excess material. Form a small thread wrap "head" in front of the peacock herl thorax. Whip-finish, and remove the thread.

Harrison:

Your first book turned me on to terrestrial patterns. I had none in my fly boxes before your book—now I have a fly box devoted only to them. Although even more of a neophyte then than I am now, and initially taught to fish by someone who almost only used an Adams, your book really enlightened me to the role of terrestrials in fishing!

Several years ago on Second Creek (West Virginia), I caught seven big browns in a row on your beetle pattern, which was more fish than I had ever caught in a day there before that. Accompanying me on this trip was a person who considered me his fly-fishing protégé, and he was fishing a Griffith's Gnat—catching none. After my third brown, he asked what I was fishing. I showed him. He laughed at it, thinking it was too "sparkly" with the Kreinik wings. He asked for one after the fifth brown and promptly caught two in the pool in which he was fishing the "midge cluster." I now tie a variation of them, using copper-colored nail polish for the backs on the foam rather than Swiss straw. Caught my largest trout ever—a 22-inch brown in Second Creek—this summer on a size 18 black foam ant with black Krystal Flash legs, a pattern I tied from your book. From hoppers on Mossy Creek to ants on a creek in Pennsylvania, where I have seen numerous trout and couldn't get them to hit anything else, I have learned to go to terrestrials, and almost all patterns come from your book or are my own variation of those patterns.

—Steve Ferris

I've always had a fascination with Japanese Beetles, probably because they were in such abundance when I was a kid growing up in Alabama. I remember that they used to decimate my grandparents' roses every year and that I used to earn a little pocket money wandering around the garden, picking these pests off the roses (along with some other beetle that infested the candytuft), and dropping them into a jar of kerosene. My cousin and I were paid "by the beetle," so believe me, we kept careful count. Anyway, Japanese Beetles, regardless of their pesky nature, are really quite striking little critters when viewed up close. The iridescent greens, metallic browns, and white spots along the side of the abdomen give them a certain charm, and I can't help but think that this lovely coloration makes them doubly attractive to trout.

I was never able to fish Pennsylvania's Letort Spring Creek in its heyday, but I would have loved to watch the regulars on the stream chumming up browns by throwing Japanese Beetles into the Letort's tricky little currents. That would have been a tremendous experience for anyone, and I'm sorry I missed it. This was where Vince Marinaro perfected his Japanese beetle imitation, which was nothing more than a larger and slightly modified version of his famous Jassid. He also came up with his "coffee bean" beetle, which was another (and apparently impractical) solution for a successful imitation of the Japanese beetle. It was on this same stream that Don Dubois first presented Marinaro and the other Letort regulars with his foam rubber beetle imitations, for which Marinaro relegated him to hell for using synthetics to tie flies. If Marinaro had lived long enough, I think that he would have eventually embraced all the new and wonderful synthetic materials available to us now. But perhaps not: I understand he was pretty stubborn and contrary, quite opinionated, and was not in the habit of backing off a single inch.

There is no question about the attractiveness of the Japanese beetle as a food item for trout. When it is abundant, they will absolutely gorge themselves on it, and the imitations of this beetle have provided my fishing partners and me with some memorable experiences. Some years are better than others for Japanese beetles (and worse for gardeners I suppose), but on many streams in my area, I always look forward to the blooming of the grapevines and multiflora rose along certain trout streams. The growth and flowering of these plants herald the return of the Japanese beetle, along with some great surface activity, and believe me, we take full advantage of it. But long after the beetles are gone, the trout will continue to readily take imitations of this insect, so don't make the mistake of relegating this pattern to your dustbin once the naturals have departed. I continue to fish this pattern well into the summer and fall simply because it is still a top producer. ■

Locoskin Japanese Beetle

Hook:	Tiemco 100, size 12, or equivalent.
Thread:	Gudebrod 6/0 or equivalent, black or olive.
Wing case:	3/16-inch-wide strip cut from Copper/Green Swirl Locoskin.
Underbody:	3/8-inch-long piece cut from a 3/16-inch-wide strip of 1/16-inch-thick closed-cell foam, any color.
Body:	1/2-inch-by-1-inch strip cut from single-sided Green Swirl Locoskin.
Underhead wrap:	Peacock herl.
Head:	Formed by folding the wing-case material rearward over the underhead wrap.
Legs:	Fine round rubber legs, black.

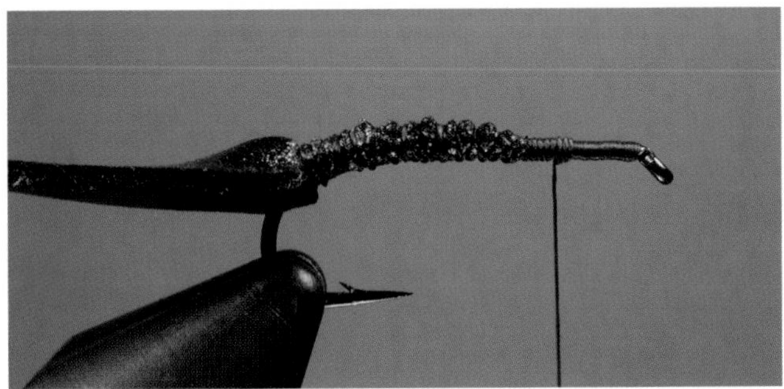

1. Wrap the shank of the hook with tying thread to the rear of the hook, well behind the barb. Wrap the thread forward about half the length of the hook shank. Trim the wing-case material to a point, and tie it in with the copper side down. Tie it in rearward to a point behind the barb of the hook. Wrap the thread forward about two-thirds the length of the hook shank.

2. Tie in the front of the piece of underbody foam at this point with a few tight thread wraps, and then wrap the thread rearward, loosely, over the foam underbody. Tie in the rear of the underbody foam tightly, and wrap the thread forward loosely to the front of the underbody and then to a point just behind the eye of the hook. Trim a piece of the Locoskin body material so that it is approximately 1 inch long by 1/2 inch wide (wide enough to extend a little past the underbody foam). Leave the protective backing on the Locoskin until you are ready to apply it to the underbody foam.

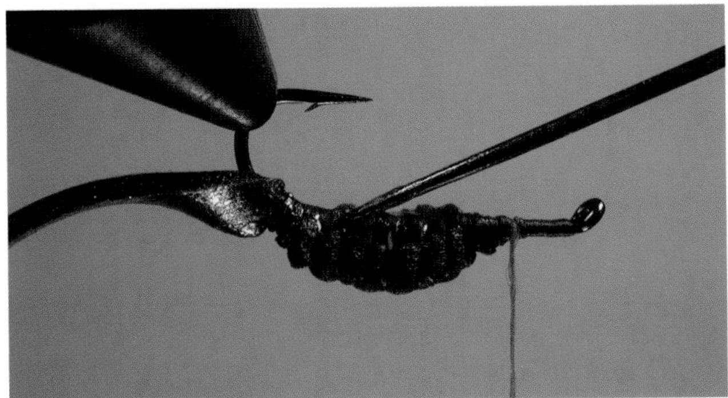

3. Rotate the fly upside down in the vise, and apply Zap-A-Gap cement to the thread wraps. Using a needle, spread the cement over the thread wraps and onto the underside of the underbody foam.

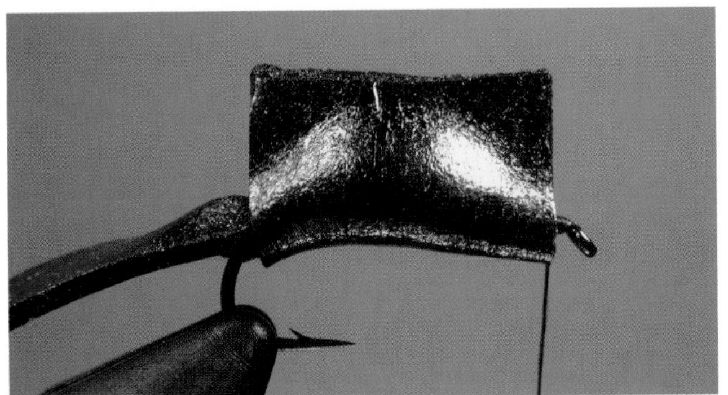

4. Turn the fly right side up in the vise. Peel the protective backing from the Locoskin, put it under the fly, and fold it up and over the underbody foam. Pinch it together at the top so that the adhesive backing adheres.

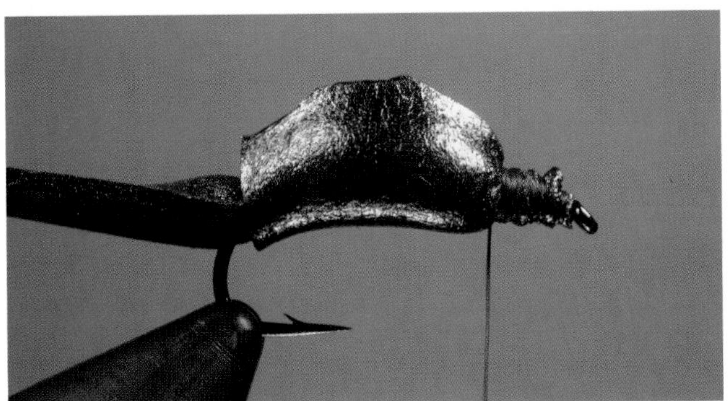

5. Trim the top of the Locoskin to the contours of the underbody foam, but do not trim away so much that the Locoskin separates. A little practice is all that is necessary. Wrap the thread rearward, and tie down the front of the Locoskin body material. When done correctly, a space equal to about one-fourth the length of the hook shank or a little less should be left between the front of the body and the eye of the hook. Put a small amount of Zap-A-Gap cement on the top surface of the Locoskin wing-case material, and spread it evenly with a needle. When spread, the cement should cover an area just a little longer than the length of the body.

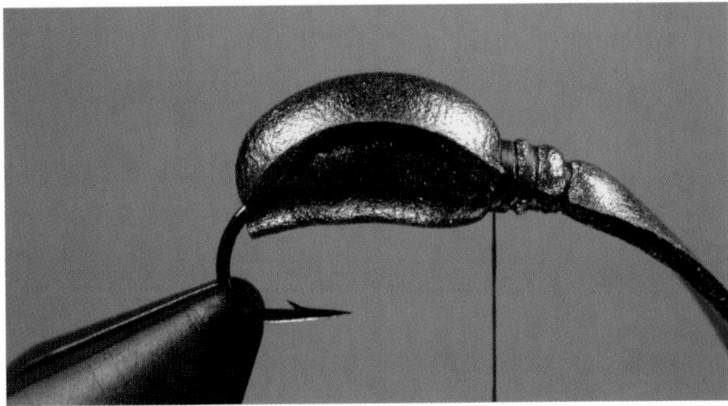

6. Fold the wing-case material forward, tie it down at the front of the body, and then tie it down all the way to the eye of the hook.

7. Wrap the thread rearward to the front of the body, and tie in two or three ostrich herl fibers. Wrap the ostrich herl forward to the eye of the hook and then rearward to the front of the body. Tie off the ostrich herl, and trim the excess.

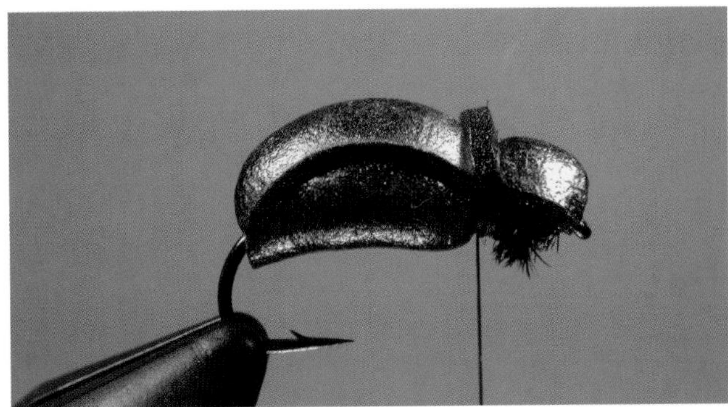

8. Fold the wing-case material back over the ostrich herl underwrap, tie it down, and trim the excess.

9. Add rubber legs on both sides of the fly, and trim them to the desired length. Rotate the fly upside down, and apply a small amount of Zap-A-Gap to the thread wraps under the body. ■

Kiwi Fleetle

Hook:	Tiemco 5212, size 12, or equivalent.
Thread:	Gudebrod 6/0 or equivalent, black.
Body:	A $^{3}/_{16}$-inch-wide strip cut from $^{1}/_{8}$-inch-thick black closed-cell foam (Evasote or Fly Foam).
Underbody:	Three of four strands of peacock herl.
Wing case:	Metallic green Swiss straw.
Wings:	Kreinik $^{1}/_{8}$-inch-wide flat ribbon, mallard, #850.
Thorax:	Two or three strands of peacock herl and one strand of black or natural (gray) ostrich herl twisted together.

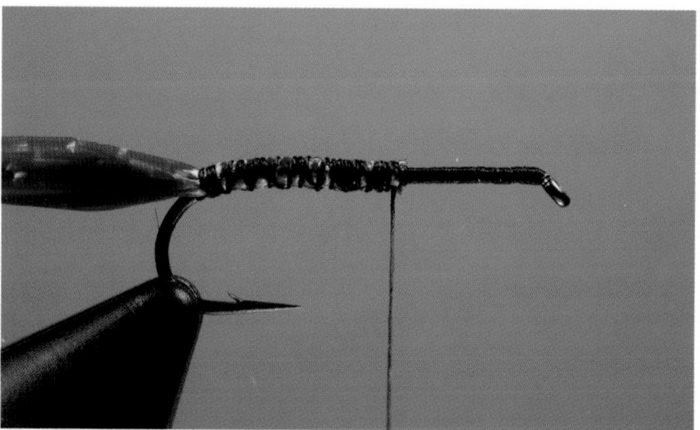

1. Wrap the thread on the hook shank to the rear of the hook, and then wrap it forward to the middle of the hook shank. Tie in the Swiss straw wing-case material at this point, and tie it down rearward to the bend of the hook. Wrap the thread forward to the middle of the hook shank.

2. Tie in the foam body material, and continue to tie it down rearward to the hook bend.

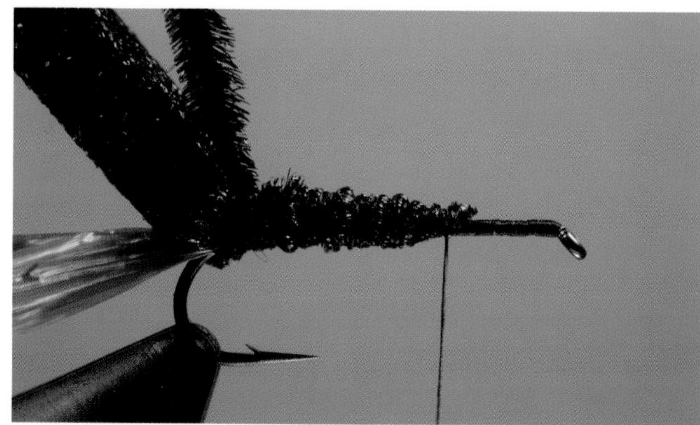

3. Tie in the peacock herl underbody material. Then wrap the thread forward to slightly ahead of the middle of the hook shank.

4. Wrap the peacock herl forward, tie it off, and trim the excess. Wrap the tying thread rearward through the herl and then forward. This is done to reinforce the herl underbody.

5. Fold the foam body material forward over the underbody, and tie it down tightly just forward of the herl underbody. Do not stretch the foam. Once the foam is tied down, pull the foam forward, stretching it slightly, and cut away the excess. Stretching the excess foam forward allows a minimum to be left ahead of the body when it is cut. Wrap the thread over any excess foam that is projecting forward.

6. Tie in a piece of the Kreinik winging material so that it projects backward over the body. The wings on this fly should be no longer than about three-fourths of the body length. Trim away the forward-projecting portion of the winging material. Separate the winging material into two equal portions on opposite sides of the hook shank.

7. Fold the Swiss straw over the foam body and forward. Tie it down just in front of the body, and trim the forward-projecting excess. This will keep the wings separated and on opposite sides of the hook shank.

8. Tie in the tips of two or three peacock herl fibers and one ostrich herl fiber. Trim them to equal length (about 2 inches). Grasp the butts of all the herl fibers, and twist them together. The most useful item I have found for this procedure is a circuit tester from the local electronics shop, but a pair of hackle pliers does a reasonable job.

9. Form the thorax by wrapping the twisted herl forward. Two to four wraps will usually do it. Tie the herl down, and trim away the excess. Wrap the head, whip-finish, and remove the thread.

I first tied this pattern at a fly-fishing show in Denver for a gentleman from New Zealand. He came by my table, started up a conversation, and we of course got on the subject of terrestrial patterns for Australia and New Zealand. He gave me the specs on the beetle pattern he wanted—size, color, etc. I got busy, and when he returned a few hours later, I had a handful of these ready for him. This pattern apparently worked well for him, because I started getting requests a few months later from some of the Down Under crowd for pattern directions. Well, when it came to naming this fly, the Kiwi designation immediately came to mind, but here in the states we don't have this beetle. We do, however, have the greenbottle flies, so taking a little from each group of insects, I came up with the "Fleetle" designation.

So, when I fish this pattern, what am I trying to imitate? A land fly or a beetle? Does it really matter? I don't think so, and neither do the trout. I have yet to see one thumbing through a field guide to the insects of North America before deciding to eat an imitation.

This is one of those patterns that I always carry but somehow tend to overlook, and I shouldn't, because on those occasions when I have fished it, the results have been most rewarding.

I vividly recall one brown trout on a certain Virginia river that refused everything I threw at it. It would come up and take a look at everything, but was just not going to take anything. After casting to this fish for about forty-five minutes, I gave up, went over to a rock, and sat down. I started going through the terrestrial collection and pulled out one of the Kiwi Fleetles. "Well," I thought, "why not?"

So I tied on the Kiwi Fleetle, waded back out, made one cast, and this trout took it like it was going to be his last meal.

Now we have to ask a few questions. Was it the rest that I gave the fish that prompted it to take the next pattern I presented? If this were the case, would the fish have taken a Jassid, an orange flying ant, or some other pattern just as readily as it took the Kiwi Fleetle? Listen, you can't answer these questions, so don't bother to ask them unless you just want to get involved in the metaphysical aspect of the sport. This is a one-shot deal. You can't repeat the experiment, *ever.* But speculation like this can be a lot of fun, even though you can't come to any conclusions. ■

Tiger Beetle

Hook:	Tiemco 5212, size 14, or equivalent.
Thread:	Gudebrod 6/0 or equivalent, black.
Body:	A 3/16-inch-wide strip of 1/16-inch-thick Tiger Beetle Green Locofoam.
Underbody:	Three or four strands of peacock herl.
Wings:	Kreinik 1/16-inch-wide flat ribbon, mallard, #850.
Underhead wrap:	Two strands of peacock herl.
Head:	7/32-inch-diameter disc cut from 1/16-inch-thick Tiger Beetle Green Locofoam.

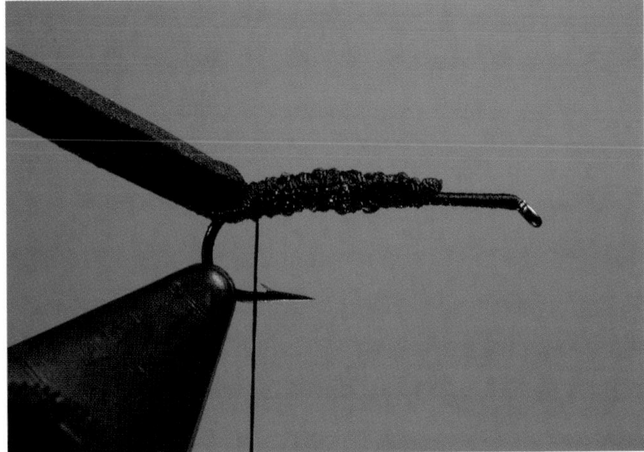

1. Attach the thread to the hook shank, wrap it rearward to the bend of the hook and then forward about two-thirds the length of the hook shank. Tie in the foam body piece at this point, and continue tying it in to the rear of the hook. Remember to tie in the body foam with the metallic side down.

2. Tie in the tips of three to four strands of peacock herl, and wrap the thread forward two-thirds the length of the hook shank. Wrap the peacock herl forward to this point, tie it off, and trim the excess. Wrap the tying thread rearward through the peacock herl and then back forward.

3. Fold the foam body material forward, and tie it off. Trim the excess, and wrap the thread forward to the eye of the hook.

4. Tie in a piece of the winging material, separate it into two equal portions, and tie down the wings on opposite sides of the hook shank back to the front of the body.

5. Tie in two or three strands of peacock herl, and wrap the tying thread forward to the eye of the hook.

6. Wrap the peacock herl forward to the eye of the hook, tie it down, and trim the excess. Wrap the tying thread rearward to a point halfway between the eye of the hook and the front of the body.

7. Tie in the head disc with the front one-third extending forward slightly over the eye of the hook and the rear two-thirds extending backward over the wings and front of the body. Whip-finish, and remove the tying thread. ■

Basic Black Beetle

Hook:	Tiemco 5212, sizes 14 and 16, or equivalent.
Thread:	Gudebrod 6/0 or equivalent, black.
Body:	A strip cut from 1/8-inch-thick black closed-cell foam (Evasote or Fly Foam) for hook sizes 14 and 16. The width of the strip will vary depending on hook size. In general, a 3/16-inch-wide foam strip works well for a size 14 hook, and a 1/8-inch-wide strip works well for a size 16 hook.
Underbody wrap:	Three strands of peacock herl.
Wing case:	Kreinik 1/8-inch-wide flat ribbon, beetle black, #005HL for a size 14 hook. For a size 16 hook, use the Kreinik 1/16-inch-wide flat ribbon.
Wing:	On size 14 beetles, use Kreinik 1/8-inch-wide flat ribbon, beetle black, #005HL. On size 16 beetles, use Kreinik 1/16-inch-wide ribbon, beetle black, #005HL.

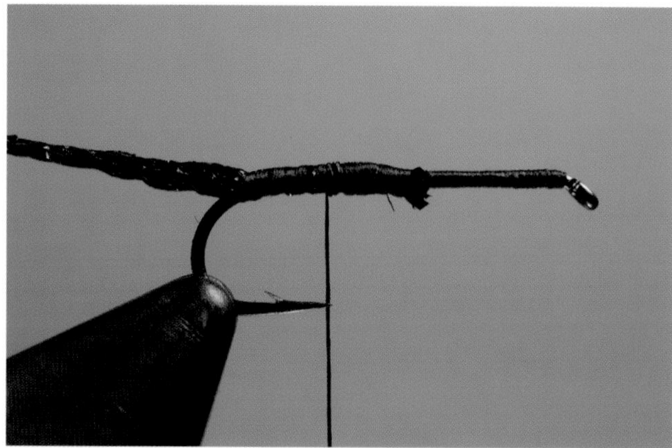

1. Wrap the shank of the hook with tying thread rearward to the bend of the hook. Then wrap the thread forward about one-half the length of the hook shank, and tie in a piece of the Kreinik wing-case material. Tie down the wing-case material rearward to the bend of the hook.

2. Wrap the tying thread forward to a point about two-thirds the length of the hook shank, and tie in the foam-body piece rearward to the bend of the hook.

3. Tie in the peacock herl underbody material, and wrap the tying thread forward to the eye of the hook.

4. Wrap the peacock herl forward to the eye of the hook, tie it down, and trim the excess. Wrap the tying thread rearward to the bend of the hook and then forward to a point slightly behind the eye of the hook. This reinforces the herl and will prevent it from breaking.

5. Fold the foam-body strip forward (do not stretch the foam), and tie it down about 1/16 inch behind the eye of the hook. Trim away the forward-projecting excess.

6. Tie in the winging material on top of the foam body at the point where the body was tied down. The rear-projecting portion of the wing material should be shorter than the body. Trim away the forward-projecting excess. Separate the wing material into two equal portions on either side of the body.

7. Fold the wing-case material forward between the wings, and tie it down. Trim away the forward-projecting excess material. Whip-finish, and remove the thread. Turn the fly upside down in the vise, and apply a small amount of head cement or Zap-A-Gap to the thread wraps under the body of the fly. ■

Sinking Japanese Beetle

Hook:	Tiemco 3769, size 10, or equivalent.
Thread:	Gudebrod 6/0 or equivalent, olive or green.
Body:	Kreinik heavy braid, mallard (#850) and emerald (#009HL). One 9-inch strand of each is enough for the bodies on three beetles.
Wing:	Kreinik 1/8-inch-wide flat ribbon, mallard, #850.
Wing case:	A 6-inch piece of copper-colored Swiss straw.
Thorax:	Kreinik fine round braid, caddis larva green, #015.

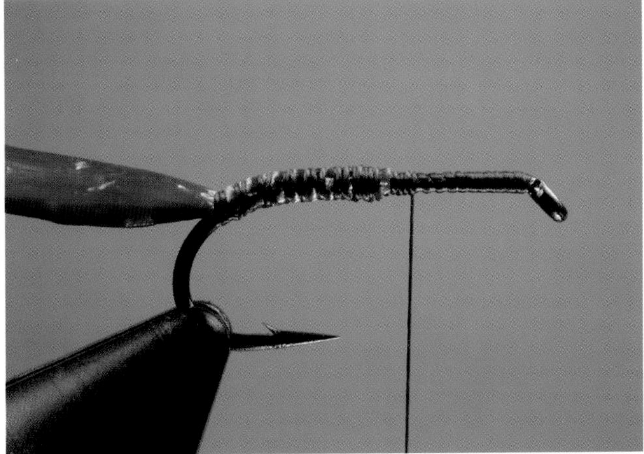

1. Wrap the shank of the hook with tying thread to a point well behind the barb of the hook and then forward about one half the length of the hook shank. Tie in the Swiss straw at this point and tie it in rearward to the bend of the hook. Wrap the thread forward to about the middle of the hook shank.

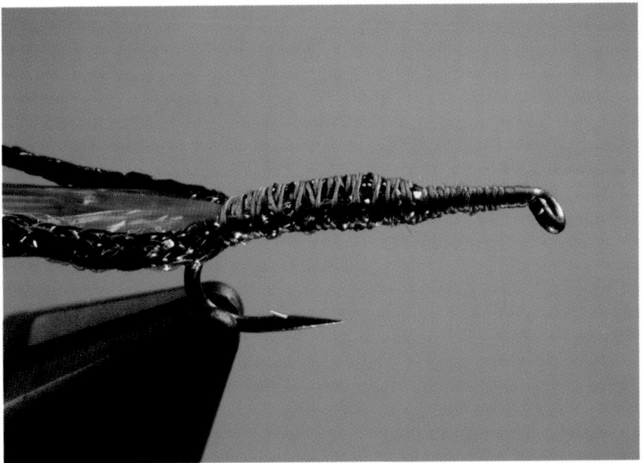

2. Tie in the two strands of body material on opposite sides of the hook shank, with one tied in slightly behind the other to produce a forward taper. Tie both strands down rearward to the same point as the Swiss straw. Wrap the thread forward slightly, whip finish, and cut and remove the thread.

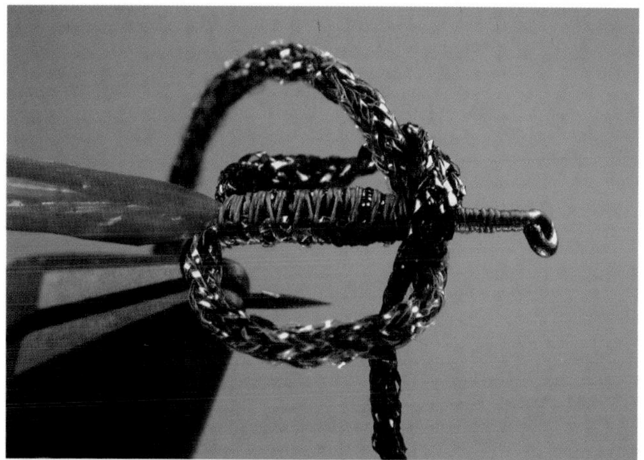

3. The body of the Sinking Japanese Beetle is then formed using the overhand knot procedure. A simple overhand knot (the same knot used to tie your shoelaces) is tied with the two strands of body material. The first knot can be tied either above or below the hook shank, but you must then follow the same procedure for each successive knot. The color of the top and bottom of the body is determined by the placement of the strands of the body material when tying the knot. The strand of body material that is behind the other strand when the knot is tied will determine the color of the back. The other strand of body material will then determine the color of the abdomen. Be consistent when tying the knot, or it will not work out correctly. Once the knot is *loosely* tied, bring it forward and slip the eye of the hook through the middle of the knot.

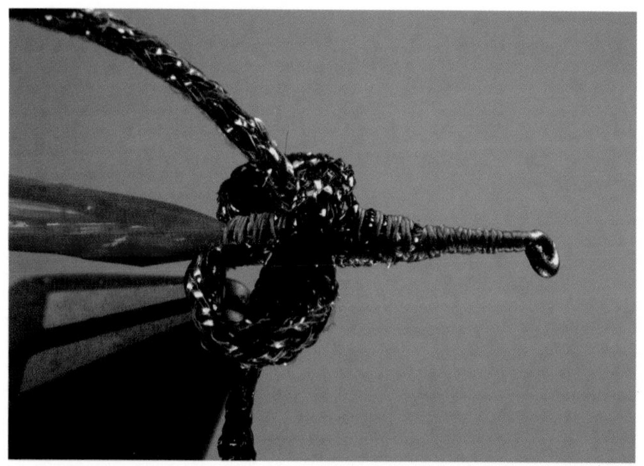

4. Move the knot toward the rear of the hook. When it is at the point where the Swiss straw was tied down, tighten the knot by pulling on the two strands of body material.

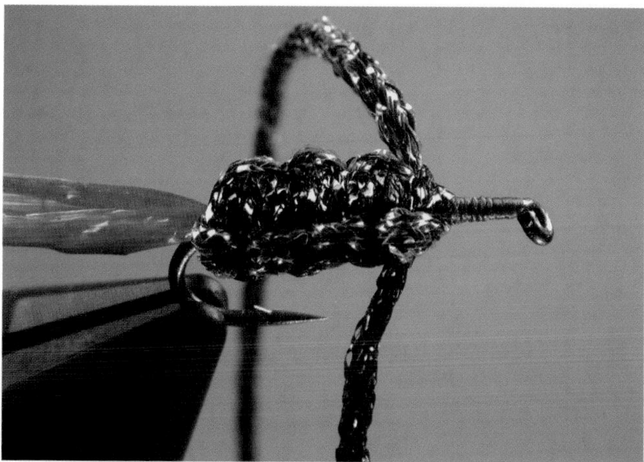

5. Form the body of the Sinking Japanese Beetle by tying a series of seven overhand knots, tightening each as you work forward.

6. Once the body is formed, tie off the two strands of body material, and trim the excess.

7. Tie in the winging material at the front of the formed body, and separate it into two equal portions. The wings should be no longer than the body.

8. Fold the Swiss straw forward between the wings, tie it down, and trim the forward-projecting excess material.

9. Tie in the material used to form the thorax.

10. Wrap the thread to the eye of the hook, and then wrap the thorax material forward three or four times. Tie off the thorax material and trim the excess. Form a thread head behind the eye of the hook. Whip-finish and remove the thread. Coat the head with either head cement or Zap-A-Gap.

My first Japanese beetle pattern was not a floating pattern but this sinking imitation, and I tied it because I was convinced that many of these beetles were sucked under in the riffles. These sunken beetles then floated for quite a way downstream, and only then did some float slowly back to the surface. I surmised that many of them never made it back to the surface but were taken by trout. I was intrigued by this idea. Sure, others had thought about this, and the old Lacquered Ant pattern was devised for just this sort of situation, but it was the only pattern that had been specifically devised to imitate a sunken terrestrial. Others fished sunken terrestrials, but these were nothing more than dry patterns with a split shot added.

Both the floating and the sinking Japanese beetle patterns have been top producers for me and occupy a prominent position in my terrestrial arsenal. I fish both of them pretty much in the same manner—that is, casting to the bank and under the overhanging vegetation. If the vegetation along the bank just happens to have a lush growth of multiflora rose or wild grapevines, then so much the better. It doesn't take long for lunker fish to position themselves in those areas where Japanese beetles are prevalent.

When fishing any beetle pattern to the bank, and the Japanese Beetle is one of my favorites, I do a great deal of blind casting. These "bank" fish are not constantly feeding and rise only intermittently, so in many instances you may not even be aware of their presence. My usual technique is to start up a bank, casting upstream at about a 45-degree angle to the bank and putting the fly as close to the bank as possible. Usually, if a fish is holding along the bank, you'll have a take within a few seconds, but I always allow the fly to drift as far as possible before making the next cast. Why? Well, if you've seen as many fish as I have come 4, 5, or more feet to take a beetle, the reason soon becomes obvious.

I'll usually make one or two casts and then move upstream 4 or 5 feet and repeat the procedure. You cover a lot of territory using this technique, you will spook a few fish that you don't see, but you'll catch a lot more fish than you spook. One thing I have learned with this technique is that landing the beetle imitation either behind or to the side of a fish is often the best thing you could do. The fish "feels" (or "hears" if you prefer, but that's not quite right) the fly land on the water, turns, and takes it with little or no hesitation. In many instances, you'll actually see the fish or its wake as it heads for the fly. If you're like me, it takes a great deal of willpower to wait for that fish to inhale the fly, rather than jerking it out of its mouth at the last second. Something else I have discovered is that there is no such thing as a bad cast when fishing beetles (or any other terrestrial) to the bank. No matter where the fly lands, *let it drift!* It's amazing how far a fish will come to take a beetle pattern, so don't jerk the fly off the water after a few seconds. Play out the drift, wait, and see what happens. I can almost guarantee you'll get a few major surprises.

I fished a sinking beetle for the first time on Virginia's Smith River. The multiflora roses were in full bloom, the Japanese beetles were everywhere, and I had just finished designing and tying my first handful of sinking Japanese Beetles. I was excited, to say the least. After hiking along the railroad tracks for a while, I cut through the finger of woods that led to one of my favorite pools, stopped on the bank, and strung up the rod. The mist was still on the river, but the sun was beginning to slant into the water, and I just knew this was going to be a great day. After knotting one of the new Japanese Beetle patterns to the 5X tippet and applying just a touch of strike putty about 18 inches above the fly, I slipped into the water and headed for the far bank.

I love this pool. Most guys head for the deep chute in the middle and just flog it to death with nymphs; still others head down to the tailout where there are always a bunch of dinks rising. Me, I head for the far bank. Years of fishing this river have taught me where the bigger fish lie, and it isn't in the middle or the tailout—it's the far bank under the heavy crown of vegetation. Large maples, beech, "musclewood" (American horn beam), and other trees, along with rhodedendron and assorted bushes, extend well out over the water. Besides, the water is a good 12 to 18 inches deep along that bank, but not one angler in a hundred has ever bothered to wade over and take a look. I guess it's because the water looks about 6 inches deep from where they stand in the middle of the run. What more could a good fish ask for? Great cover, a constant supply of assorted terrestrials dropping into the water, super oxygenation from the upstream riffle, and all the anglers concentrated in the wrong places. Well, almost all, because my partners and I head for the banks. We've learned what might be there.

At any rate, that morning I was fat with anticipation. But after about thirty minutes, my high level of excitement had turned into the beginnings of disappointment. Nothing! Not a single good take on that sinking Japanese Beetle that looked so like the real thing. After another thirty minutes with no action, the small seed of disappointment had grown into a mature bush and started to set flowers. Frustrating to say the least. So, I waded back to the far bank, took a seat, and let the old feeble mind wander around a bit trying to think of what I might be doing wrong. I couldn't figure it out. Everything seemed to be set up correctly, there wasn't enough strike putty on the tippet to spook fish, and the fly was sinking nicely and was the right distance from the indicator. I knew it was, because I had seen it barely hesitate quite a few times as it ticked over the rocks on the streambed. So I sat there in frustration, wondering what was wrong. Then slowly, like the sun coming up on your deer stand when it's 15 degrees, something began to dawn on me. What if those little "ticks" of the indicator had not been the fly bouncing over the rocks? What if they were due to fish gently taking the fly and letting go of it? Well, I wasn't used to this sort of take. I was used to the dead stop or the violent movement of the indicator when fishing nymphs. If these little ticks were indeed takes, then it was something new to me.

There had been plenty of time for the fish to quiet down, so I headed back over toward the far bank and started to work my way back upstream. After a few casts, the indicator ticked. I raised the rod tip and was into a pretty good fish. A short while later, it happened again. About that time, I figured I had probably had more than a dozen fish take that sinking Japanese Beetle on my first trip up the bank, and I never even knew it! I took another half dozen fish as I worked my way back up the bank, the best being a lovely 14-incher. Each time the indicator even looked as though it hesitated, I raised the rod tip. OK, some of the ticks were rocks, but most of them were fish gently mouthing the fly. The only thing I could figure was that a drowned beetle was just such easy pickings that there was no rush. A fish would simply ease over, open its mouth, and gently close down on the beetle. No hurry, no panic, just a slow deliberate take. It was fantastic.

I have no idea how many fish I took that day on the Sinking Japanese Beetle, but it was quite a few. Since then I've learned that there are certain days when the sinking beetle will outfish the dry imitation, and vice versa. I don't know why, but if the fish aren't coming to the dry, you can bet your rear end I'll go to the wet in short order. Sinking Japanese Beetles, sinking Fireflies, sinking Epoxy Beetles, sinking Black Beetles—they all have a time and place when nothing, and I mean nothing, in your fly boxes will outfish these deadly little terrestrial imitations. ■

Epoxy Beetle

Hook:	Tiemco 2302 or equivalent. The size of the hook for this pattern is dependent on how large a beetle you wish to tie. I've used everything from 8 to 16 for this pattern.
Thread:	6/0, color depending on the body color of the fly.
Body:	Kreinik round braid, large or medium, depending on the size of the fly. Color of the braid is at the option of the tier.
Wing:	Opalescent Pearl, Peacock, or Root Beer Krystal Flash. I've used all of these and can't see that the color makes that much difference. If I had to pick one color for the wings, I would probably select Opalescent Pearl.
Wing case:	Dyed black turkey quill, sprayed with artist's fixative.
Thorax/head:	Kreinik round braid, medium or small, depending on the size of the fly. The colors used can either match or contrast with the colors used for the body.

These instructions are given for an Epoxy Beetle tied on a Tiemco 2302 hook, size 10.

1. Attach the thread to the hook shank. Wind it all the way to the bend of the hook, then forward approximately two-thirds the length of the shank. Select the two colors and the correct diameter of the Kreinik material you wish to use to form the body. For this size beetle, use the heavy Kreinik braid. Some of the color combinations I have used are emerald/mallard, black/purple, emerald/black, black/black, and bronze/black. Let your imagination run wild with this pattern when selecting the body colors. No matter what you choose, there is probably a beetle somewhere that comes in those colors. Tie in the two selected strands of body material on opposite sides of the hook shank, and tie them down all the way rearward to the bend of the hook. Wrap the thread forward to the point where the body material was tied in. Whip-finish, and remove the tying thread. You can't do the overhand knot technique used to form the body with the thread attached to the hook shank. (Well, you can, but it's a much more complicated procedure and requires the use of crochet needles. Forget it! It's much easier to do it the old-fashioned way.)

2. Form the body of the beetle using the overhand knot procedure as described for the Sinking Japanese Beetle (see page 54) until you have reached a point two-thirds of the way up the hook shank. For this size beetle, nine overhand knots are required to form the body. Reattach the thread to the hook shank, tie down the two strands of body material, and trim the excess. Whip-finish, and remove the thread. The body is now ready to be coated with epoxy.

3. Mix enough five-minute epoxy to coat the body of the beetle. It takes less than you think. A little practice will give you a good idea of how much is needed. A true rotary vise is almost mandatory for this step. Once the epoxy is well mixed, coat the body of the fly evenly while rotating the fly. A needle chucked into a pin vise is ideal for performing this procedure. Continue rotating the fly until the epoxy hardens, then allow it to cure for about one hour before performing the next step.

4. Reattach the thread to the hook shank, and wind it back to the front of the body. Tie in about twelve strands of Krystal Flash, and trim them to the desired length (extending rearward to the bend of the hook). Tie in two strands of Kreinik fine braid on opposite sides of the hook shank. Wrap the thread forward, whip-finish, and remove the thread.

5. Form the head of the beetle using the overhand knot technique. For this size beetle, it takes four knots to form the head. Reattach the thread, tie down the Kreinik material used to form the head, and trim the excess.

6. Coat the finished head, including the thread wraps behind the eye of the hook, with five-minute epoxy while rotating the fly in the vise. Once the epoxy has hardened, allow it to cure for about an hour. Reattach the thread between the body and head of the fly.

7. Tie in the wing-case material. Trim the wing-case material to the same length as the Krystal Flash wings, split it down the middle with a fine needle, and trim away any forward-projecting excess wing-case material. If desired, rubber legs can be added at the same point at which the wing case was tied in. Coat the thread wraps with Zap-A-Gap cement. ■

Chapter 6

Grasshoppers, Crickets, and Their Relatives

Synthetic materials are ideal for tying all of the insects that fall into this category. In the past, there have been many patterns designed for this group of insects that are tied only with natural materials, but the judicious use of synthetics as well as natural materials only enhances imitations of these insects. My favorite patterns use both synthetic and natural materials and are attempts to create imitations that are more durable, less bulky, and lighter; float more naturally; and are easier for the average person to tie. Foam is an ideal medium for tying imitations of this group of insects. The varying thickness of different types of foam, the colors that are available, the flotation properties, the durability, the ability to cut different shapes from foam, and the light weight of the material all contribute to its desirability. Other synthetic materials used in conjunction with foam allow the tier to create impressionistic patterns that are extremely effective. I still use certain natural materials for many of my patterns simply because I have yet to find an acceptable substitute. So far nothing has appeared on the market that, to my way of thinking, is an acceptable substitute for turkey quills, peacock herl, ostrich herl, and elk hair, all of which I use on a regular basis.

Colorado Hopper

Hook:	Tiemco 5212, size 8, or equivalent.
Thread:	Gudebrod 6/0 or equivalent, brown.
Tag:	Red Kinky Fiber.
Body:	A 1/4- to 3/8-inch-wide strip cut from 1/16-inch-thick brown foam.
Underbody:	1/8-inch-thick closed-cell foam (Evasote or Fly Foam), tan, olive, or gray, depending on the color of the abdomen of the natural hopper. Cut a strip about 1/8 inch wide from the foam sheet, and stretch it by pulling it between your fingers so that it becomes shiny. This takes a little practice. Too much force and the foam will break, but this procedure preps the foam so that it ties in and wraps much more easily.
Ribbing thread:	Gudebrod, size G, brown.
Wings:	Bright red Kinky Fiber.
Wing case:	Turkey quill sprayed with artist's fixative.
Underhead wrap:	Dubbing, color to match that of the underbody foam.
Legs:	Brown, medium-size, round rubber legs. The legs can also be formed by knotting two strands of round rubber leg material and trimming them as is done for the Crystal Butt Cricket.
Head:	A 3/8-inch-diameter disc cut from brown or tan 1/16-inch-thick foam.

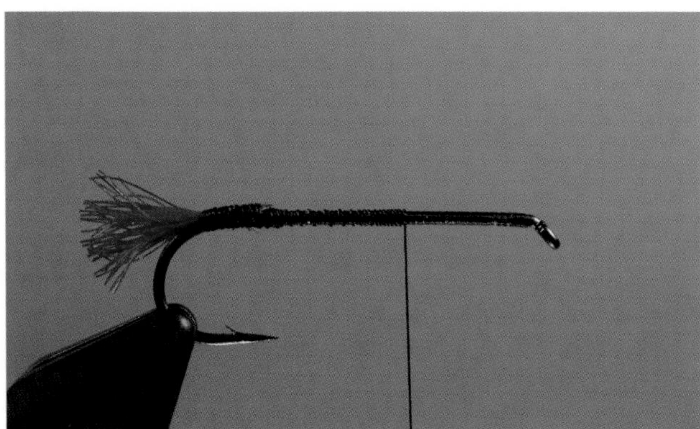

1. Attach the tying thread to the hook shank, and wrap it rearward to the bend of the hook. Tie in the Kinky Fiber tag, and trim it to length.

2. Wrap the thread forward about two-thirds the length of the hook shank. Begin tying in the strip of body foam at this point, and continue tying it down to the rear of the hook.

3. Tie in an 8- to 10-inch piece of the ribbing thread.

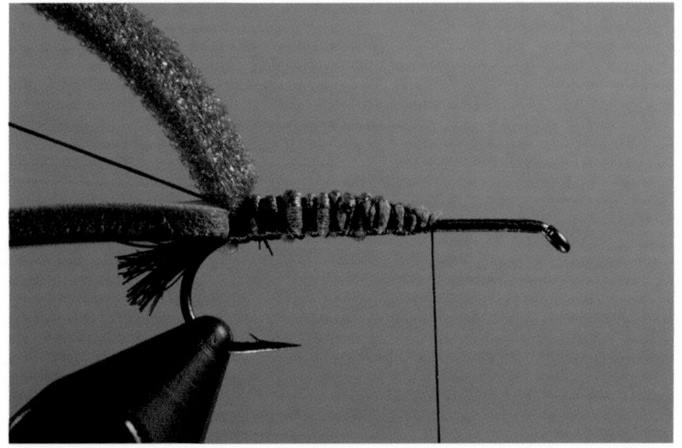

4. Trim the stretched underbody foam to a point, and tie it in. Wrap the tying thread forward about two-thirds the length of the hook shank.

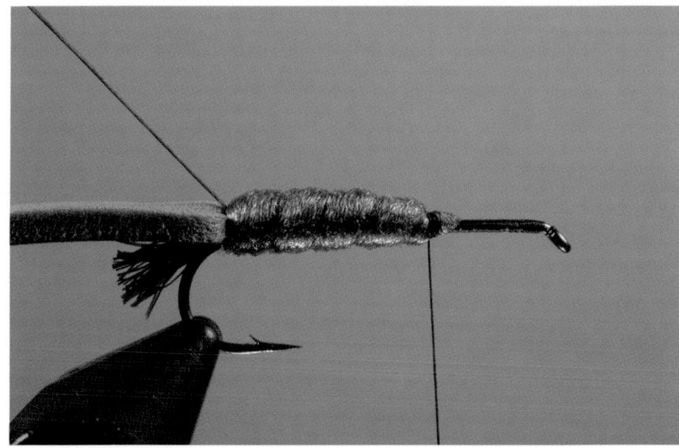

5. Wrap the underbody foam forward, tie it off, and trim the excess.

6. Fold the strip of body foam forward, tie it off, and trim the excess. Tie the trimmed end of the foam down firmly with thread wraps.

7. Wind the ribbing thread forward about five turns to form a segmented body, tie it down, and trim it.

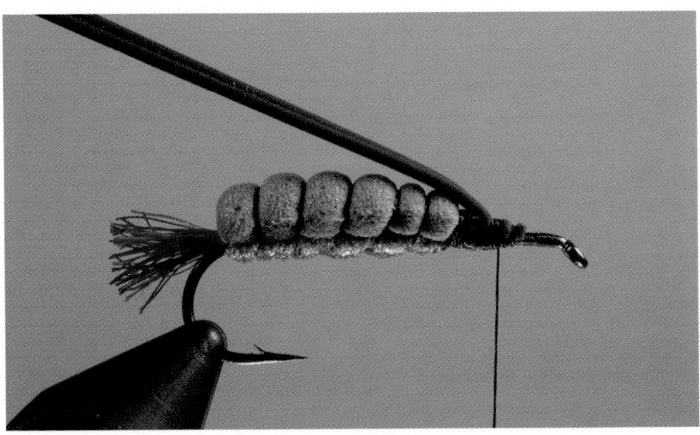

8. Tie in two unseparated rubber legs, and trim them to the desired length.

9. Separate the legs and tie them in on opposite sides of the body.

10. Tie in a clump of red Kinky Fiber, separate it into two equal portions, and tie the wings down on opposite sides of the body. A few initial figure-eight thread wraps will help to keep the wings separated. Trim the wings so that they extend over the rear of the hook bend.

11. Tie in the turkey quill wing case by the thin end. The thick portion of the quill should extend rearward and be trimmed to the same length as the wings.

12. Wrap the tying thread to the eye of the hook. Wax the thread, and apply enough dubbing to form a good ball of dubbing behind the eye of the hook. The dubbed area should extend rearward almost to the point at which the legs were tied down. Leave about $^{1}/_{16}$ inch of bare thread wrap between the dubbed area and the front of the body.

13. Tie down the head disc on the bare thread-wrapped portion of the fly between the dubbed region and the front of the body. Approximately one-third of the disc should extend forward to or just over the eye of the hook. The rear portion of the head disc should extend

well over the legs, wing case, and wings of the fly. Rotate the fly in the vise, and apply a small amount of Zap-A-Gap cement to the thread wraps under the head.

14. If desired, add eyes by applying a small drop of black E-Z Shape Sparkle Body on the sides of the front of the head. Eyes can also be added by using a permanent black marker.

I first tied and fished this hopper on a river in Colorado, which of course accounts for the name. I remember that I got up fairly early that morning and headed for the river full of enthusiasm and hope, tied on a Crystal Butt Hopper, and proceeded to start flailing away. Because nothing was rising, I figured my best bet was to see if I couldn't pound a few fish up by slapping this hopper along the bank and through the runs coming into the head of pools. OK, I did manage to hang into a few, and one was a pretty good brown (which I broke off), but it was tough going. You know how it gets after a couple of hours of abusing your rotator cuff—I headed over to the bank to take a break. When I reached the bank, I just about lost it when I heard what I thought was a rattlesnake cut loose. I was really tuned into rattlesnakes on this river because the summer before a friend of mine, Todd Fields, had a pretty bad experience with one. He had driven to the river, forgotten to pack his wading shoes, and headed for the stream wearing a pair of Teva sandals.

Well, wet wading this river is no real problem, but wet wading in rattlesnake country during a particularly dry summer is not advisable. As it turned out, Todd was sneaking up on some nice risers, concentrating on them instead of where he was going. You guessed it! He stepped on one of these low-shouldered devils, which promptly responded by sinking its two front teeth into Todd's foot. Todd made it back to his truck OK, but he had a thirty- or forty-minute drive to the nearest town with a hospital. When he got there, it turned out they had no antivenin. It seems that all of the antivenin in the United States had gone to the southern states because of an overabundance of snakebite incidences. What followed was not pleasant, to say the least, and resulted in Todd being out of action for the next three or four months.

Back to the rattle on the bank. Because of Todd's experience, my first stop on the way to Colorado was the Cabela's store in Sidney, Nebraska, where I purchased a pair of snakeproof leg guards. So what if I had them on? That buzz still scared the hell out of me, and I jumped about 3 feet backward, stepped on a slick rock, and planted my butt firmly in the water. Actually, it didn't feel too bad on a hot day. Besides, I figured my pants could probably use a little washing.

I made my way back over to the bank and started poking around in the high grass with the rod tip (I'll sacrifice a rod tip any day rather than get nailed by a rattler). After a few tentative pokes in the grass I was rewarded with the sight and sound of a big hopper heading for the hills. What really struck me about this critter was the fact that it had bright—and I mean really bright—red wings. I had to have one and get a closer look.

How many of you have tried to catch these big western flying hoppers? Let me tell you, it isn't easy, but I finally managed to snag one in the net and get a good close look. Sure enough: bright red wings!

I always carry a tying kit when I go out west, so I headed back to the van, broke it out, and luck was with me. Stuck in the bottom of the box was some red Kinky Fiber that looked like it would do the trick. One hour and half a dozen flies later, I headed back to the river with high hopes. To make a long story short, the hopper lived up to my expectations, and I was rewarded with about a dozen nice trout, the largest of which pushed the 21-inch mark. I figured this was pretty good for what looked like a slow day on the river.

Strangely enough, this was the only river on which I encountered this particular red-winged hopper, but I fished it on other rivers anyway. On some water, it worked beautifully, even though there appeared to be none of these hoppers around. Maybe it had something to do with the well-known attractive qualities of the color red, maybe not, but it seemed to work better than other hoppers on certain rivers. On other rivers, let's be frank about it, I couldn't *buy* a fish with it, but they would readily take either the Crystal Butt Hopper, an LA Ant, or a Schroeder's Parachute Hopper (which, by the way is a terrific terrestrial pattern). Some things just can't be explained, but that's what makes this sport so interesting. ■

Crystal Butt Cricket

Hook:	Tiemco 5212, size 8, or equivalent.
Thread:	Gudebrod, 6/0 or equivalent, black.
Tail:	Peacock Krystal Flash.
Body:	A 1/4- to 3/16-inch-wide strip cut from 1/16-inch-thick black foam or from Northern Lights Locofoam.
Underbody:	Kreinik Micro Ice Chenille, mallard or peacock.
Ribbing:	Gudebrod size G thread, black.
Legs:	Black, round rubber leg material, medium size. Two strands are knotted and trimmed to form the legs.
Wing:	Black elk hair.
Underhead wrap:	Fine black dubbing.
Head:	A 3/8-inch-diameter disc cut from 1/16-inch-thick black foam or Northern Lights Locofoam.
Eyes:	E-Z Shape Sparkle Body, yellow.

1. Attach the thread to the hook shank, and wrap the thread to the rear of the hook. Tie in a small bunch of Krystal Flash, and trim the Krystal Flash to form a butt about 3/8 inch long.

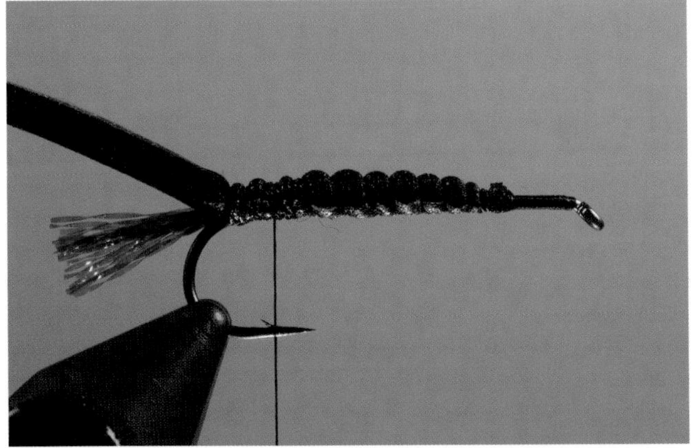

2. Wrap the thread forward about two-thirds the length of the hook shank. Tie in the body foam at this point, and continue to tie it down to the bend of the hook.

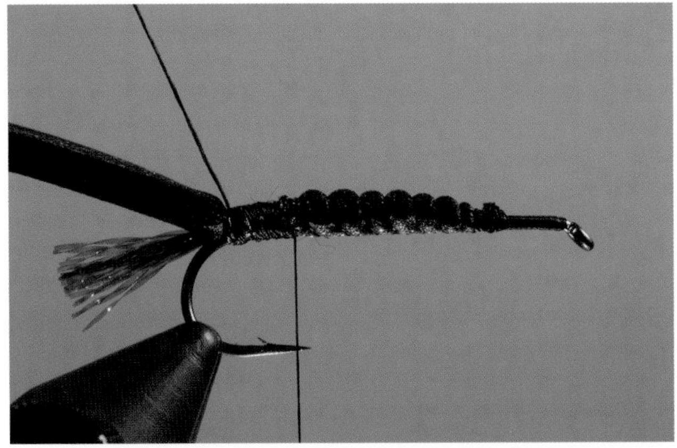

3. Tie in about a 10-inch piece of ribbing thread.

4. Tie in a piece of the Micro Ice Chenille. Wrap the thread forward about two-thirds the length of the hook shank.

5. Wrap the Micro Ice Chenille forward to this point, and tie it down. Trim the excess.

6. Fold the foam forward and over the Micro Ice Chenille. Tie it down, and trim away the forward-projecting excess.

7. Rib the body by making five or six turns of the ribbing thread. Tie off the ribbing thread, and trim the excess.

8. Tie in the legs on opposite sides of the hook shank, directly in front of the formed body.

9. Tie in a clump of black elk hair at the front of the body (even the tips of the hair in a hair stacker before tying it in). The wing should project rearward slightly over the bend of the hook. Trim away the forward-projecting elk hair, and tie down the butts.

10. Wrap the thread forward to the eye of the hook, apply a small amount of dubbing to the thread, and wrap the dubbing rearward, leaving a small area of undubbed thread between the front of the body and the rear of the dubbed forward portion.

11. Tie in the foam head disc on top of the bare thread wraps. The front third of the head should extend forward at least to the eye of the hook, and the rear two-thirds should extend back over the wing and the legs. Whip-finish, and remove the tying thread. Apply a small amount of Zap-A-Gap to the thread wraps under the head.

12. Add eyes by applying a small dot of E-Z Shape Sparkle Body material on opposite sides of the head. Allow the eyes to dry overnight.

One of my favorite patterns of Harry's is the Crystal Butt Cricket. This last December was a particularly warm one. On the off chance that I might find some trout, I headed up to Big Hunting Creek in Maryland. In the five hours that I fished, I caught and released twenty-two fish, all taken on the Crystal Butt Cricket. The fish were all between 9 and 14 inches, and most of them were stream-bred browns. Not a bad way to spend a midwinter day. Fishing terrestrials during the darkest part of winter is something that a person wouldn't normally do; however, day in and day out, terrestrials do make an appealing meal for most fish. Who am I to argue?

—Pat Devney ■

Crystal Butt Hopper

Hook:	Tiemco 5212, size 8, or equivalent.
Thread:	Gudebrod 6/0 or equivalent, brown or tan.
Crystal butt:	Pearl Root Beer Krystal Flash.
Body:	A $^{3}/_{16}$-inch- to $^{1}/_{4}$-inch-wide strip cut from Tan Opal Locofoam or plain $^{1}/_{16}$-inch-thick tan foam. I prefer to use the Tan Opal Locofoam for the body. In some locations, the predominant body color of the hoppers is dark brown, in which case I would use plain brown $^{1}/_{16}$-inch-thick foam for the body.
Ribbing:	Gudebrod thread, size G, tan or brown.
Underbody:	A $^{1}/_{8}$-inch-wide strip cut from $^{1}/_{8}$-inch-thick gray closed-cell foam (Evasote or Fly Foam), stretched to achieve a shiny effect. You can also use white, gray, or olive foam for the underbody, depending on the predominant color of the hopper in the area.
Legs:	Brown, medium-size, round rubber legs. The legs for this pattern can be tied in the same manner as those for either the Colorado Hopper or the Crystal Butt Cricket.
Wing:	Natural elk hair.
Wing case:	Section of turkey quill, sprayed with artist's fixative.
Dubbing:	Any fine dubbing will do. The color should match or contrast with the color of the body.
Head:	A $^{3}/_{8}$-inch-diameter foam disc, cut from either Tan Opal Locofoam or $^{1}/_{16}$-inch-thick regular tan foam.
Eyes:	E-Z Shape Sparkle Body, black, or black permanent marker.

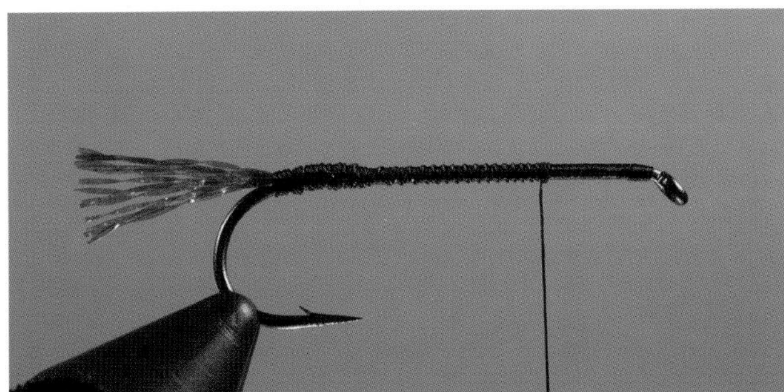

1. Wrap the hook shank with thread to the bend of the hook, and then wrap the thread forward about $^{1}/_{8}$ inch. Tie in about twelve strands of the Krystal Flash butt material, and wrap the thread back to the bend of the hook. Trim the butt to about $^{3}/_{8}$ inch in length.

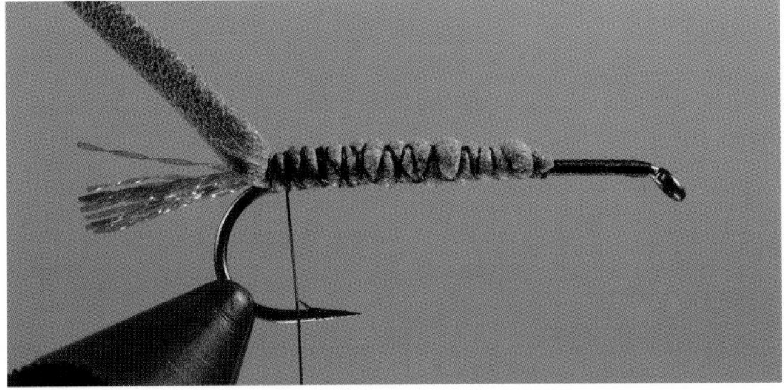

2. Wrap the thread forward about two-thirds the length of the hook shank. Tie in the body foam at this point, and tie it in rearward to the bend of the hook.

3. Tie in about a 10-inch strand of the ribbing material.

4. Trim the stretched underbody foam to a point, and tie it in. Wrap the tying thread forward about two-thirds the length of the hook shank.

5. Wrap the underbody foam forward, and tie it off at this point.

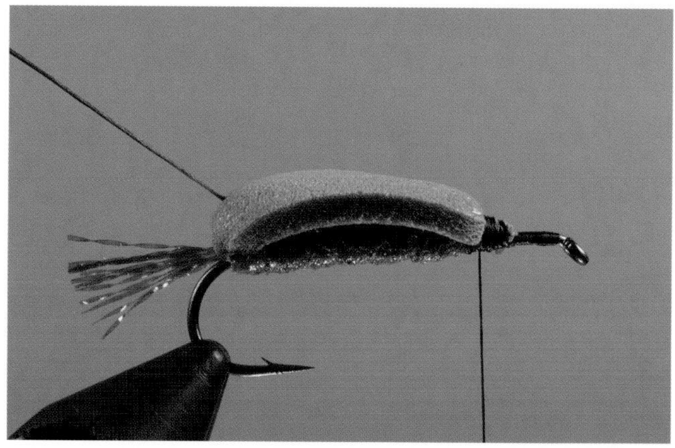

6. Fold the body foam forward, and tie it down at the same point at which the underbody wrap was tied down. Trim the forward-projecting excess body foam.

7. Rib the body with five or six turns of the ribbing thread, tie it off, and trim the excess.

8. Tie in two unseparated rubber legs, and trim them to the desired length.

9. Separate the legs and tie them down on opposite sides of the hook shank, even with the front of the completed body.

10. Cut a small clump of elk hair, even the tips in a hair stacker, and tie it in by the butts. The tips should extend past the bend of the hook. Trim the butts, and tie the elk hair down tightly.

11. Tie in the turkey quill wing case, and trim it so that it is no longer than the tips of the elk hair wings. Trim the forward-projecting excess, and tie it down. Wrap the tying thread to the eye of the hook.

12. Wax the tying thread, and apply the dubbing. Build up a good clump of dubbed thread behind the eye of the hook by wrapping the dubbed thread rearward. Leave about a $^{1}/_{16}$-inch-wide bare thread wrap behind the dubbing. The dubbing forms a reinforced area so the head will not slide forward.

13. Tie in the foam head disc behind the dubbed portion and over the bare thread wrap. The front third of the head disc should extend to the eye of the hook, and the rear two-thirds should extend well over the wing case, wings, and body of the fly. If desired, tie in a piece of fluorescent Antron yarn on top of the foam disc, and trim it to form a "quick sight" spot. Whip-finish, and remove the thread. Apply a small amount of Zap-A-Gap cement to the bare thread wraps under the head.

14. Add black E-Z Shape Sparkle Body eyes, and allow them to dry for about twelve hours before fishing the fly. Eyes can also be added using a black permanent marker, in which case the fly can be fished immediately.

I've had many successful days with the Crystal Butt Hopper, and I am not the only one for whom this pattern has worked well. Consider the following from Dave Lewis, a well-known rod builder from Harrisonburg, Virginia. Dave spends the summer out west and often has occasion to fish hopper patterns.

It was late July or early August on one of the upper meadows of the Gallatin that I seemed to see that Harrison Steeves's foam hopper for the first time. Harry and I had been fishing Mossy Creek together the previous spring, and as we watched a brown rise to some sulfurs, he dropped two of his big ruddy brown foam hoppers into the big compartment of my fly box. Over time they had shifted about and sunk beneath the Madam Xs and the Sofa Pillows and disappeared.

A very picky cutbow was working a sparse emergence of mahogany duns along a deep-cut bank. I floated several sizes of Sparkle Duns over him and never got a nod. Most of the late morning I had been using the Madam X and had taken several wonderful strong fish. It looked like I needed to return to the big fly. I tied on the traditional one with white legs in a size 10 long shank hook. A nice hooking cast put the fly a couple feet above the big boy at just about the right time for him to come up for another mahogany dun. He slowly rose under the big fly and drifted back beneath it for about 3 feet before drifting away and back to his hold deep along the bank. Twice more he followed but never took, finally giving up on my offerings altogether.

Knowing trout will often come to a different pattern after a good long look at an unacceptable one, I reached for a smaller Madam X with brown legs. As I rummaged through the big end compartment for the smaller fly, one of the two foam hoppers Harry had given me way back in the spring crept in amongst the bunch. It was as if I saw it for the first time. Something sort of lit up in my mind's eye, and I went for it.

The same cast got the fly in a perfect position, and the trout came to it as if the world had just come crashing down. The take was an explosion. None of that careful scrutiny the other flies had been subjected to. I thought at the time that the trout's reaction at that moment was much the same as mine just moments before. We both seemed to see the fly for the first time, and it was right.

I continued to use the same fly several more times that summer for those picky, difficult trout. Many times I found fish that would ignore careful, precise offerings of hatch-matching accuracy and throw all caution to the gravels for the big foam hopper. I can tell you, like the trout, it made me a believer.

—Dave Lewis ■

Flying Hopper

Hook:	Tiemco 410T, size 8, or equivalent.
Thread:	Gudebrod 6/0 or equivalent, yellow.
Underbody wrap:	Three or four yellow ostrich herl fibers.
Body:	A 1/4-inch-wide strip of 1/8-inch-thick, yellow closed-cell foam (Evasote or Fly Foam).
Legs:	Round rubber legs, medium size, brown.
Wings:	Golden pheasant crest feathers.
Wing case:	Turkey quill, treated with artist's spray fixative.
Underhead wrap:	Yellow ostrich herl.
Head:	A 3/8-inch-diameter disc cut from 1/16-inch-thick brown foam. A larger-diameter disc may be used for the head if desired.
Eyes:	Black E-Z Shape Sparkle Body or black magic marker.

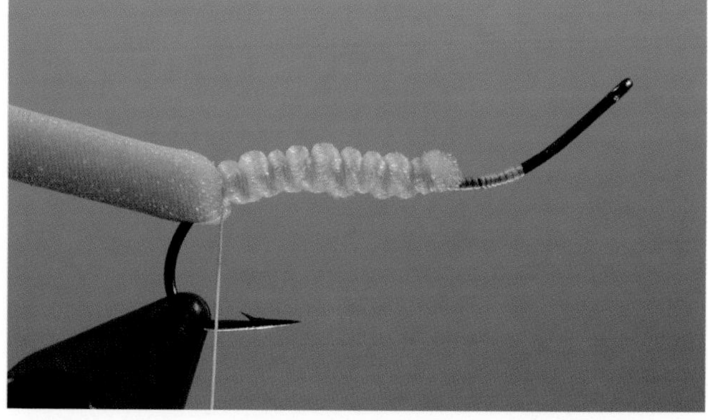

1. Wrap the shank of the hook with tying thread to a point behind the barb of the hook. Then wrap the thread forward about two-thirds the length of the hook shank. Trim the body foam to a point, and tie it in. Continue tying in the body foam to the rear of the hook.

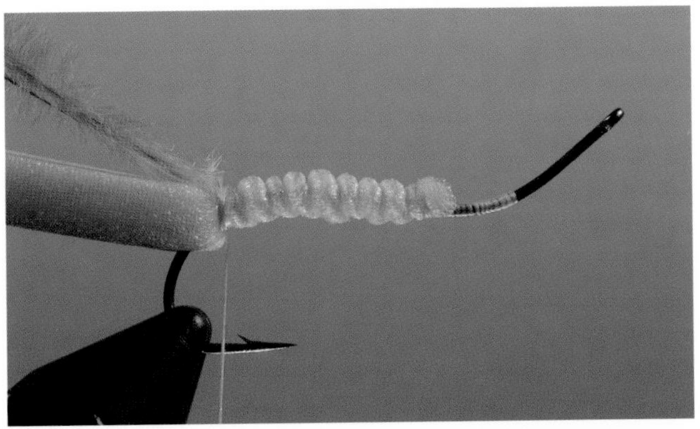

2. Tie in three or four yellow ostrich herl fibers. An alternative body wrap is a strip of yellow closed-cell foam. If foam is used, stretch it gently before tying it in and wrapping it forward. This gives it a nice sheen, thins it down, and makes it easy to wrap.

3. Wind the tying thread forward about two-thirds the length of the hook shank, just to the point where the shank of the hook begins to bend upward. Wrap the ostrich herl forward to this point, tie it off, and trim the excess.

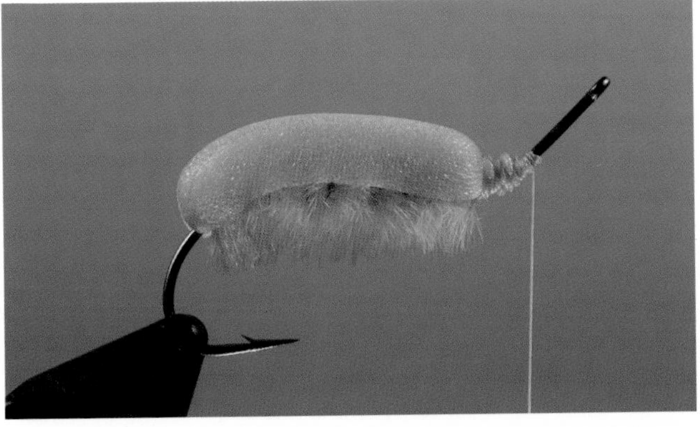

4. Fold the foam body over the hook shank, and tie it off. Do not stretch the foam. You want the body of this hopper to be full and bulky. Trim the front of the body foam, and tie down the excess.

5. Tie in two unseparated round rubber legs in front of the body, and trim them to the desired length.

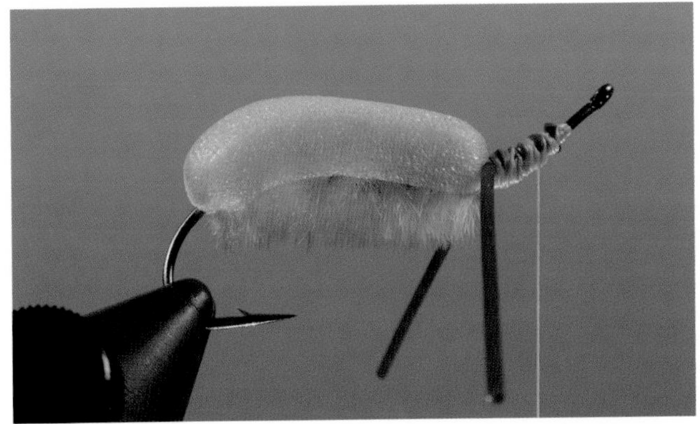

6. Separate the legs, and tie down the separated legs on opposite sides of the hook shank. The legs should be tied down rearward to the front of the body.

7. Tie in a good clump of golden pheasant crest fibers. Separate them into two equal portions with a couple of figure-eight wraps so that they lie on opposite sides of the body. Tie them down rearward to the front of the body. The wings should extend over the rear of the fly.

8. Tie in a quill section taken from a turkey wing or tail feather. The thin end of the quill should be tied in with the heavier butt portion of the wing pointing rearward. Trim the turkey quill to the same length as the wing fibers, and split it in the middle with a needle.

9. Tie in a couple of yellow ostrich herl fibers, and wrap the thread forward to the eye of the hook.

10. Wrap the ostrich herl to the eye of the hook, tie it down, and trim the excess. Wrap the thread rearward to a point halfway between the eye of the hook and the front of the body.

11. Tie in the head disc so that the front third extends to, or slightly over, the eye of the hook. The rear of the head disc should extend over the front of the body, the base of the wings, and wing case. Rotate the fly in the vise, and apply a small amount of Zap-A-Gap cement to the thread wraps beneath the head. Add the eyes on the sides of the head if desired. Only a small drop of E-Z Shape Sparkle Body material is necessary.

I had one of the strangest experiences of my fly-fishing career one day with this pattern. Cliff Rexrode, Pete Bromley, and I were fishing a lake that held some very nice rainbows. I tied this big hopper on just to see how it floated and what it looked like in the water. After a few short casts, I began to lay out a little more line and was casting about 40 feet out from the bank. At one point, I gave the fly a quick 3-foot strip, and the hopper dove under. When it floated to the surface, the fly did the strangest thing I have ever seen. It started to rotate in the water. As I stood there watching this big hopper turning over and over, a pretty good rainbow came out of nowhere and nailed it. Well, that called for a little more experimentation. Sure enough, if you stripped this fly in about 3 feet, it would twist the tippet enough to cause the fly to rotate three or four times, and it drove the rainbows crazy. I have no idea how many fish hammered that fly when it was rotating, but the movement of the fly seemed to be irresistible to them.

Since that day, I have tried this hopper pattern on quite a few rivers, and in slow-moving sections, the "strip and rotate" technique can be deadly. Not all of these hoppers will do this, though, and I have yet to dissect one of those that rotates to find out just what is different about it. I can say that when I get one that rotates, I put it in a separate compartment and fish it very, very carefully. I certainly do not want to sacrifice it to a tree! ■

Katydid

Hook:	Tiemco 5212, size 8, or equivalent.
Thread:	Gudebrod 6/0 or equivalent, fluorescent yellow or yellow.
Underbody and tag:	A 1/16-inch-wide strip cut from 1/8-inch-thick yellow Evasote or Fly Foam.
Body:	A triangle cut from Pearl Chartreuse Locofoam or plain 1/16-inch-thick bright green foam. The triangle is slightly more than an inch in length and is 3/8 inch wide at the base. Trim away the points at the base of the triangle so that it will tie in easily.
Wings:	Twelve to sixteen strands of Pearl Krystal Flash.
Legs:	Medium-size round rubber legs, chartreuse.
Head underwrap:	Fine yellow dubbing.
Head:	A 7/16-inch-diameter disc cut from Pearl Chartreuse Locofoam or bright green 1/16-inch-thick foam.
Eyes:	Black E-Z Shape Sparkle Body or permanent black marker.

1. Attach the thread to the hook shank, and wrap the thread rearward to a point just behind the barb of the hook. Tie in the underbody foam with a short tag extending rearward over the bend of the hook. Wrap the thread forward about two-thirds the length of the hook shank.

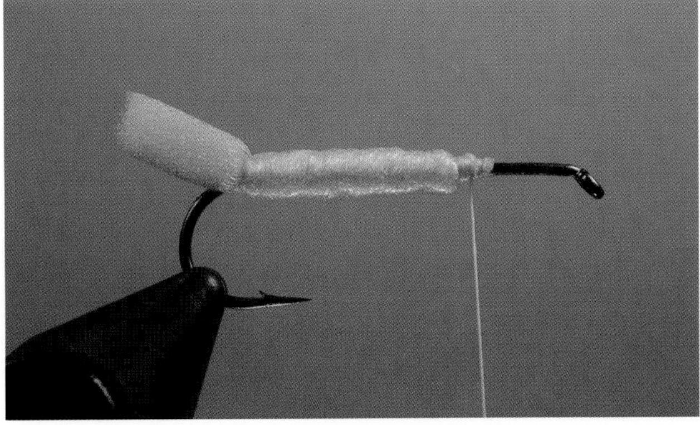

2. Wrap the underbody foam forward, tie it off, and trim the excess. If you stretch the foam slightly as you are wrapping it, the underbody will be smooth and shiny. Trim the rear tag to a point.

3. Tie in twelve to sixteen Krystal Flash strands. Trim the ends so that the wings extend well over the tag at the rear of the fly.

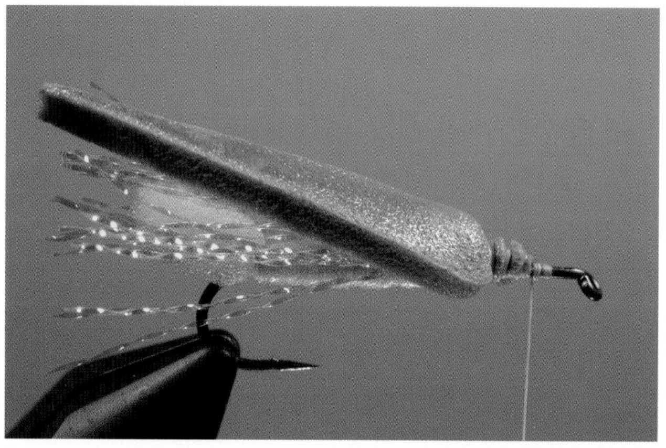

4. Tie in the body foam at the same point. The base of the triangle used for the body is tied in with the tip of the triangle pointing rearward and extending slightly past the tips of the wings.

5. Tie in two unseparated rubber legs in front of the point where the body was tied down, and trim them to the desired length.

6. After the legs are tied in, separate them, and tie them down so that they lie on opposite sides of the hook shank. Tie them down rearward to the front of the body.

7. Wrap the tying thread forward to the eye of the hook. Wax the thread, and apply the yellow dubbing. Wrap the dubbed thread rearward, leaving an undubbed area of thread about 1/16 inch wide in front of the body.

8. Tie in the foam head disc on top of the bare thread wraps. The disc should be tied in so that the forward third extends just to the eye of the hook and the rear two-thirds projects rearward over the front portion of the body.

9. Tie in a single strand of rubber leg material on either side of the head so that a portion of the legging material will extend both forward and backward. Trim the forward- and backward-projecting portions of the rubber legs to the desired length. Whip-finish, and remove the thread. Treat the thread wraps under the head with a small amount of Zap-A-Gap cement.

10. Add the eyes on the sides of the head using either a spot of the E-Z Shape Sparkle Body material or permanent black marker.

I should fish this pattern more frequently than I do. For some reason, I seem to overlook it most of the time, but on those occasions when I have used it, it has been deadly. One incident really stands out:

I was hiking up the bank of a western river, making my way to an area where I knew big fish would be taking advantage of the late afternoon and evening caddis hatch. After about 50 yards or so, I noticed that the tall grass was crawling with big green hoppers that were frantically trying to get out of my way. It also occurred to me that trolls throwing rocks in the water did not cause the sucking sounds I heard!

Sure enough, quite a few of these big green hoppers were landing in the water and were being inhaled by some very respectable browns. I cut back the tippet to 4X, tied on one of the big green Katydid patterns, and eased into the water. What followed was one of those unforgettable times when you seem to enter fly-fishing nirvana. One good brown after another fell to that Katydid, and at the end of a couple of hours and three flies, I had to go sit on the bank and recover.

Strangely enough, I have never encountered these big green hoppers on any other river, eastern or western. I can assure you, though, that when I fish this particular river, I will never be without a couple of dozen of these big green Katydids. ■

Chapter 7

Miscellaneous Insects

Black Widow (Trout)

Hook:	Tiemco 100, size 12, or equivalent.
Thread:	Gudebrod 6/0 or equivalent, black.
Tag (butt):	A 5/32-inch-diameter disc cut from Metallic Red Locofoam.
Underbody:	Kreinik Micro Ice Chenille, peacock or black.
Body:	A 3/8-inch-diameter disc cut from Northern Lights Locofoam.
Underhead wrap:	Two or three strands of peacock herl.
Head:	A 1/4-inch-diameter disc cut from Northern Lights Locofoam.
Legs:	Fine round rubber legs, black.

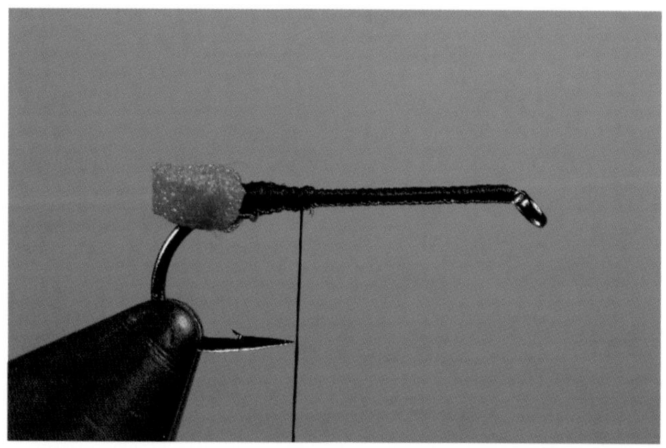

1. Attach the thread to the hook shank, and wrap it rearward to the bend of the hook. Wrap the thread forward, and tie in the front of the tag (butt) disc so that the disc extends rearward to a point even with the bend of the hook. The tag disc should be tied in with the metallic side down.

2. Tie in the Micro Ice Chenille just in front of the tag, and wrap the thread forward about two-thirds the length of the hook shank.

3. Wrap the Micro Ice Chenille forward to this point, tie it off, and trim the excess.

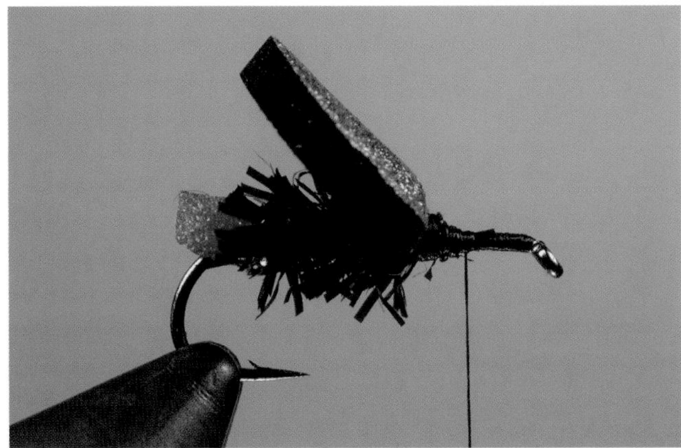

4. Tie in the front of the body disc so that the disc extends rearward over the tag.

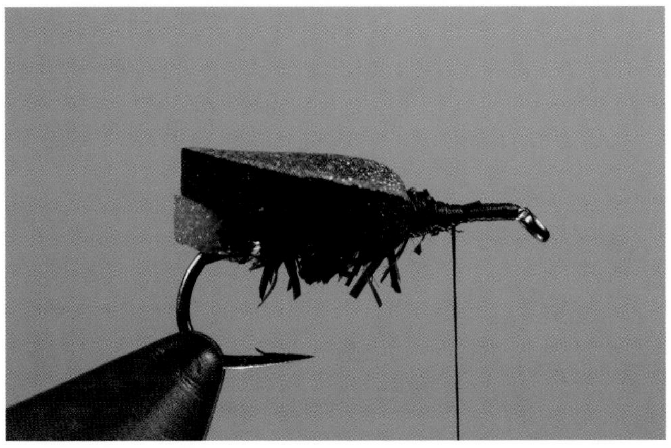

5. Apply Zap-A-Gap to the top of the underbody wrap and the top of the tag (butt) disc. Press the body disc down so that it bonds to the top of the underbody wrap and the top of the tag.

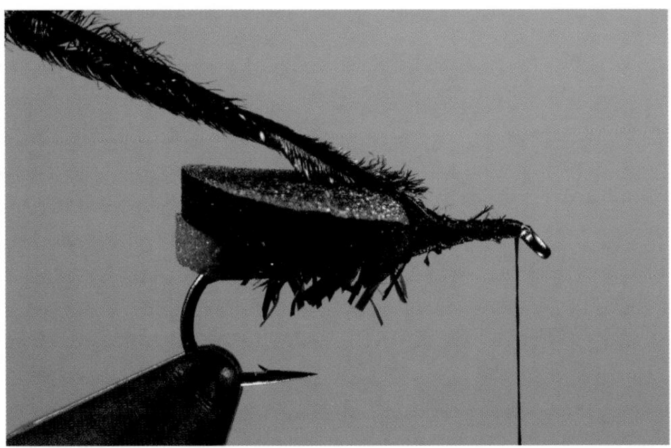

6. Tie in two to three strands of peacock herl, and wrap the thread forward to the eye of the hook.

7. Wrap the peacock herl forward to the eye of the hook, tie it down, and trim the excess. Wrap the thread rearward to a point about halfway between the front of the body and the eye of the hook.

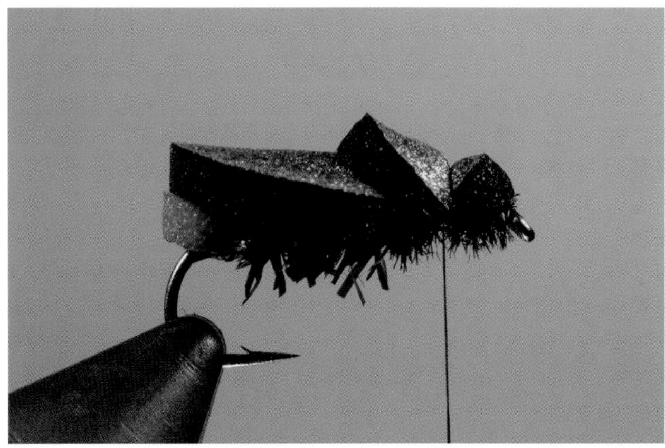

8. Tie in the head disc so that two-thirds of the disc projects rearward over the body disc and one-third projects forward to a point just behind the eye of the hook. Apply a small amount of Zap-A-Gap to the underside of the head disc, and press it down on top of the body disc so that the two bond together.

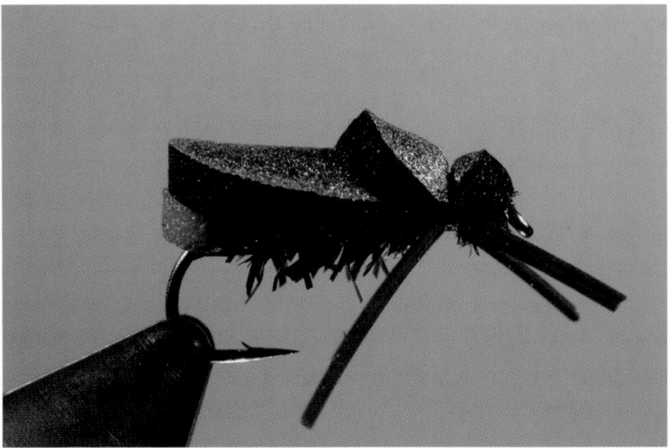

9. Tie in two unseparated strands of round rubber leg material on either side of the head disc.

10. Once the legs are tied in, they are then separated to give four legs on either side of the fly. Apply a small amount of Zap-A-Gap to the thread wraps under the head. ■

Disc Head Cicada

Hook:	Tiemco 7989, size 6, or equivalent (light wire salmon dry-fly hook).
Thread:	Gudebrod 6/0 or equivalent, black.
Underbody wrap:	Three or four strands of orange or white ostrich herl.
Body:	A 3/8-inch-wide strip of 1/8-inch-thick Evasote or Fly Foam.
Legs:	Round rubber legs, medium size, black.
Wings:	Pearlescent Root Beer Krystal Flash, about twenty-four strands.
Underhead wrap:	Peacock herl.
Head:	A 1/2-inch-diameter foam disc cut from 1/8-inch-thick black Evasote or Fly Foam.
Eyes:	Red E-Z Shape Sparkle Body.

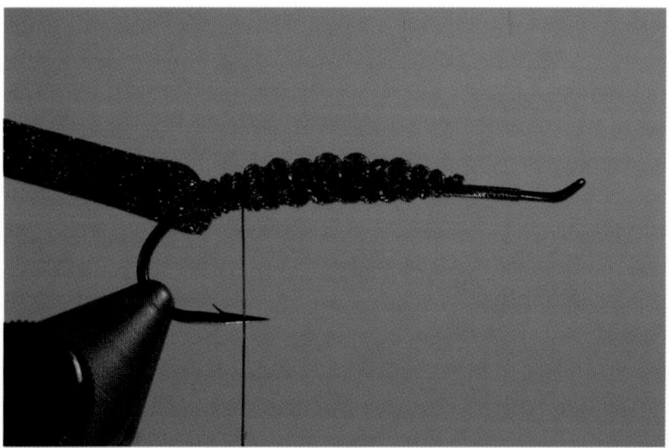

1. Attach the thread to the hook shank, and wind it rearward to a point behind the barb of the hook. Wrap the thread forward to a point about 3/8 inch back from the base of the hook eye (at the end of the open eye). Tie in the body foam at this point, and continue tying the foam in rearward to a point behind the hook barb. Wrap the thread forward and then rearward again to firmly attach the body foam to the hook shank.

2. Tie in three or four ostrich herl fibers at the rear. Wind the thread forward to the rear of the open eye of the hook.

3. Wrap the ostrich herl forward about two-thirds the length of the hook shank, tie it down, and trim. If the ostrich herl is not long enough to wrap the entire underbody, simply tie in three or four more herl fibers and continue.

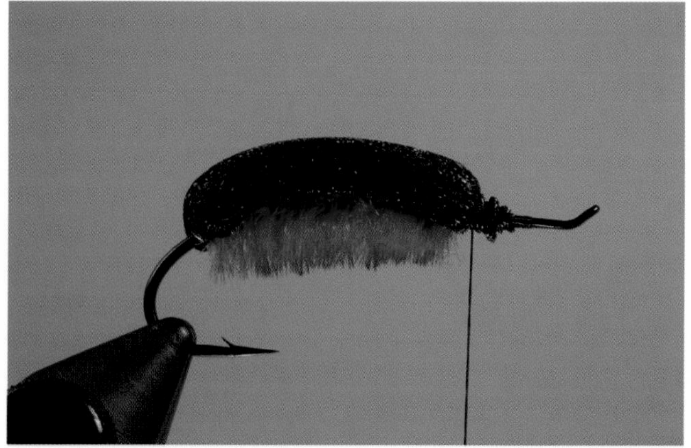

4. Fold the body foam forward, and tie it down with about a dozen good thread wraps. Trim the excess, and tie down any forward-projecting foam.

5. Tie in four unseparated round rubber legs in front of the body, and trim them to the desired length.

6. Split them down the middle, and tie in two unseparated legs on either side of the hook shank (a single figure-eight wrap helps to do this once they are separated). Tie them down firmly rearward to the front of the body.

7. Tie in a clump (about twenty-four strands) of Krystal Flash in front of the body. Separate it into equal portions, and tie down the wings on opposite sides of the body. They should project upward and above the legs. Trim the wings so that they extend at least to the bend of the hook.

8. Tie in three or four strands of peacock herl at the front of the body, and wrap the thread to the eye of the hook.

9. Wrap the peacock herl to the eye of the hook, tie it off, and trim the excess. Wrap the tying thread rearward to a point halfway between the front of the body and the eye of the hook.

10. Tie in the foam head disc firmly on top of the peacock herl. The front third of the foam disc should extend over the eye of the hook, and the rear two-thirds should extend over the base of the wings and the front of

the body. Whip-finish, and remove the thread. Separate the rubber legs, and apply either head cement or Zap-A-Gap to the thread wraps under the head.

11. Add the eyes by placing a drop of red E-Z Shape Sparkle Body on either side of the head. Allow the eyes to dry overnight before fishing the fly.

This pattern originated as a very slight modification of the UFO and for a very specific purpose: fishing a hatch of seventeen-year locusts. This doesn't happen frequently, but it does occur much more often than most people realize. As I understand it, there are actually three or four broods of these insects, and in an area where they are abundant, you might get a fairly constant hatch of these things every year. Utah's Green River is a pretty good example of this sort of phenomenon, and I was lucky enough to hit it once during this time. What can I say? I've never seen so many big fish so eager to take any fly that was big and black. I have been lucky enough to encounter more than one of these hatches.

Shortly after I returned from a fishing trip to Pennsylvania, I got a phone call from a friend, Clay Mook, who lives in Roanoke, Virginia, with the news that there was a major hatch of cicadas on Smith Mountain Lake.

"So what?" I thought to myself, but his next bit of information really caught my attention. Huge carp were apparently cruising the banks, sucking down cicadas as fast as they hit the water. Now my adrenaline level hit an all-time high. Big carp on a fly rod is about as close to fishing for redfish as you can get, and catching them on the surface will really increase your heart rate. That night I tied up a dozen cicadas and, the next day, along with a neighbor of mine, Hans Rott, loaded up the canoe and gear and headed for the lake to meet Clay.

Clay was right. Big carp were everywhere, cruising, slurping down cicadas, and acting stupid for a change. Now, you talk about exciting fishing—this was about as exciting as it gets. We eased the canoes along the bank looking for schools of cruising carp and cast the cicada patterns a good 10 feet or so in front of the lead fish. One of the carp would usually break away from the group, cruise over to the fly, ease up underneath the thing, and gently suck it in. Then all hell would break loose. We experienced broken tippets (even though we were using 2X tippet material) and straightened hooks. I began to wish I had tied these cicadas on saltwater hooks instead of the light wire salmon hooks. Some of the carp took off on blistering runs; others went for the bottom and slugged it out. At one point we heard Clay yell, and we looked up to see that he was into a carp so big it was towing his canoe around. None of them came easily, and we had a great afternoon.

We had only been into a few fish when Hans reached down in his bag and pulled out a stringer. "Uh-oh," I thought, "what now?"

"Keep six of the little ones," he said.

"What for?" I asked. "You going to fertilize your garden?"

He gave me a withering look. "Have you ever eaten carp?"

"No," I said, "and I don't plan on starting to either."

He gave me a grin. "You will when I fix it," he said. "In Austria carp is a delicacy. It's the standard dinner every Christmas. You have any idea what a fillet from one of these is worth in Austria?"

Dumb question. How would I know something like that?

"Each fillet would cost about $20 American. If we keep six of fish, we'll have more than $200 worth of fillets."

Who was I to argue with this mad Austrian gourmet cook? So we wound up stringing six of the smaller ones to take back with us.

At the end of the afternoon, we pulled up to the dock, and as Hans hauled about 30 pounds of fish out of the water, this young Asian woman came streaking down the dock. She was obviously very excited about these fish, and it was even more obvious that she would love to have one of them. So Hans took one off the stringer and handed it over. Talk about a happy lady! She said she was going to cook it for dinner that evening. Now my curiosity was really aroused.

"Let's see," I thought to myself. "Austrians eat them, Asians eat them. Isn't gefilte fish made from carp? Maybe I've been missing out on something."

We took my dry bag, emptied it out, bought some ice, and dumped in the five remaining fish.

To make a long story short, the next day my wife and I went over to Hans's house for dinner. The first bite convinced me that Americans had indeed been missing out on something. It was absolutely delicious, and Hans convinced me that he had done nothing special to make it so. I was an instant convert, and for those of you who would like to try carp as table fare, I am including Hans Rott's procedure and recipes for cooking this much-maligned delicacy:

The carp has a very fine skin, which should be used after scaling, with almost all preparations. The carp also has a good number of bones. Raking is a Midwestern method of preparation, which sadly destroys the fish. If you fillet the fish carefully, you will reduce all the structural bones. Then, while eating, methodic paring apart of the fillets, first along the nerve line and then halfway up from there, will remove all the bones as you go along. It is really very easy and can be done in a civil manner.

Traditional Christmas Carp (Viennese)

$2^1/_2$ pounds carp
1 stick light salted butter (You can always use pork lard or render fatback yourself. This will add a different flavor after frying.
Bread crumbs (I always add a little crushed pepper to them.)
Flour
2 eggs
A spritz of milk

Gut the carp; keep the roe or the milt in a bowl. The liver is very good in pond fish, but usability might vary with the water the fish came from.

Fillet the carp and cut into six pieces.

Take three bowls: put a handful of flour into one; break the eggs into the next, add a little salt and milk, and whip with a fork until well blended; and put bread crumbs generously into the third bowl. In the same sequence, dip the salted fish pieces into the flour, pat the flour onto the fish, dip thoroughly into the egg mix, and then immediately into the bread crumbs, making certain the fish is covered all around and the crumbs are well patted on. Gently place into the heated butter in a flat skillet over low heat, and fry until golden brown. Turn the fillet, and brown the other side.

Small roasted potatoes rolled in chopped parsley make a wonderful accompaniment.

As a salad, a very lightly marinated iceberg lettuce is mild enough to support the fine flavor of the fish without competing with the wine.

The marinade is very simple: one part white wine vinegar mixed with four parts water, a dash of salt, and sugar to make the vinegar just lightly piquant. Place the lettuce in the marinade no sooner than one hour before serving.

A dry Gewürztraminer (Oregon or Washington State if you can't get anything from Styria or lower Austria) is the preferred wine. A dry Washington Riesling will do well also, as would a Pinot Gris (except the Veneto varieties, which are too light).

Serve very soon after cooking.

Boiled Carp

2 to 3 pounds carp
$^1/_2$ cup white apple cider vinegar
1 sliced or coarsely chopped carrot
1 small parsnip
$^1/_2$ cup parsley
1 small white onion
About 20 to 30 peppercorns (red peppercorns if available)
Pinch of thyme and 2 bay leaves
2 teaspoons of caraway seed
3 large shallots
4 to 6 sticks of clarified butter

Scale, gut, and wash the fish. In order to be able to remove it from the pot or fish steamer without breaking, wrap it in cheesecloth, twisting both ends and knotting them. This makes good handles.

Place the other ingredients into a fish pan (poacher) or large pot, and boil for twenty minutes. Add the fish, making certain that the liquid always covers the fish. Simmer for thirty minutes.

Clarify the butter, or just melt it, and sauté three large, finely chopped shallots until they turn glassy.

Place the fish carefully on a large platter, remove the cheesecloth, and pour the butter over it.

Serve with napkin dumplings.

Napkin Dumplings

6 stale kaiser rolls, diced and browned in butter
2 eggs
1/2 cup flour
1/4 cup chopped parsley
2 teaspoons of salt

Mix ingredients in a large bowl, and if needed, add a little milk. Cover with saran wrap and let sit for about an hour.

Place a shallow rack in a large pot, and add salted water to just touch the rack. Roll the mixture into a thick roll, 4 to 5 inches in diameter, and wrap the roll in a white cooking towel or napkin. Fold the ends up; you'll need them to carry the dumplings.

Bring water to a boil, and place the dumplings, towel and all, on the rack. Cover and steam for twenty minutes. Remove and slice.

Meanwhile, you can reduce the stock you boiled the fish in to make about one cup. Flavor with a little white wine to taste, and thicken with arrowroot.

Serve the fish whole, and place the dumplings on a platter with the sauce for them.

Here are two wonderful ways to use the milt and the roe.

Take a good fish stock (Knorr makes cubes that are locally available and really good). In a pot, simmer one quart of water and dissolve the stock. Add lemon juice for slight acidity; two young carrots, sliced; one parsnip, sliced; three sprigs of parsley; a small yellow onion; and five cloves. Boil for thirty minutes over low heat, and then add the roe and the diagonally sliced milt. Simmer for twenty minutes, and salt to taste. Serve in flat soup bowls.

You can, of course, make your own stock with another carp and the head and bones of the one you filleted.

The trickiest way, but I also believe one of the best, is to sauté the roe in butter. Heat is critical so the roe cooks through without becoming hard on the outside.

Dip the roe in flour after lightly salting it. In a large skillet, heat butter just hot enough to sear the roe. The best way I found to do this is to place the roe into the butter and keep sliding it around by moving the pan. Reduce the heat, and slowly fry on both sides, making certain that the roe does not get too brown. Remove to a hot platter.

Blanch a couple of sprigs of parsley, chop, and squeeze dry. Squeeze a little lemon juice over the roe, and sprinkle it with the parsley. If you like spice, use a little Tabasco. Brown the remaining butter and pour over the parsley and the fish. Serve immediately. A dry California sparkling wine will make this an elegant and delicious appetizer.

Guten appetit.

—Hans Rott

The Disk Head Cicada is also being used to imitate large South American beetles. Not too long ago, I picked up a fly-fishing magazine, and lo and behold, there was my Cicada pattern pictured in an article on fishing for big browns in Chile! There are apparently some monster beetles there, and the guys were using the cicada pattern to imitate these whopper terrestrials.

Jim (Coz) Costelnick, a guide from New York, who stopped by my tying table at the 1999 Charlotte show, confirmed this. He grabbed a handful of the cicadas to take to Chile with him and made the comment that they should really be bigger. "Bigger!" I thought. "How big does this blasted beetle get?"

A few weeks later, Coz called me up and asked how big I could tie this pattern, and if I could make them really big, could I possibly get them to him right away? Again, it was off to the tying bench, where I hauled out some 2X long streamer hooks. The end result was a dozen of the biggest terrestrial patterns I have ever tied, which were sent overnight to Coz. A month later he called me with a one-word comment: "Fantastic." Then he told me that they could have been even bigger! What do you do? ■

Disco Damselfly

Hook:	Tiemco 100, size 12, or equivalent.
Thread:	Gudebrod 6/0 or equivalent, blue.
Tail:	A 3-inch piece of Kreinik medium round braid, kingfisher blue, #006, and a 3-inch piece of Kreinik fine round braid, high luster black, #005HL.
Body:	Blue dubbing.
Wing support:	A 1/4-inch-diameter disc cut from 1/16-inch-thick Damsel Blue Locofoam. If Locofoam is not available, use standard bright blue 1/16-inch-thick sheet foam.
Wings:	Approximately twelve to sixteen strands of Pearl Krystal Flash.
Head underwrap:	Fine blue dubbing.
Head:	A 5/16-inch-diameter foam disc cut from 1/16-inch-thick Damsel Blue Locofoam or 1/16-inch-thick bright blue sheet foam.
Legs:	Silli-Legs, black or black with any color of metallic flakes.
Eyes (if desired):	Black E-Z Shape Sparkle Body or permanent black marker.

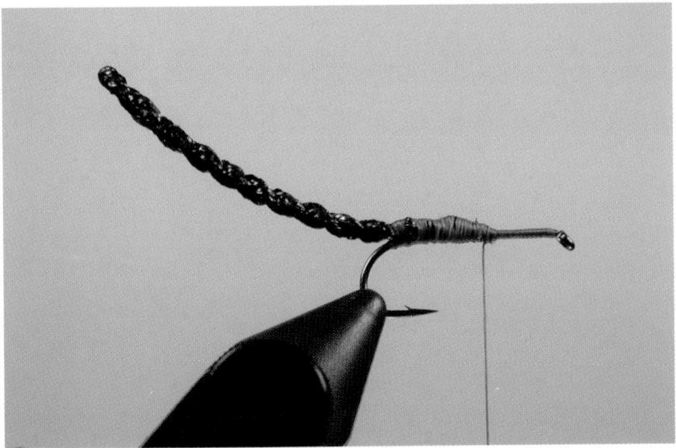

1. Wind the thread to the rear of the hook shank and then forward about half the length of the shank. Twist the two pieces of Kreinik tailing material together to form a tight spiral. When done properly, this gives a neat "barber pole" effect. Once the pieces of tail material are tightly twisted together, bend them over the shank of the hook, and then pull them forward over the eye of the hook. They will immediately twist up on themselves to form a neat tail for the fly. This technique is referred to as *furling* and has been around for years. Tie in the furled tail material in the middle of the hook shank. Continue to tie it down to the rear of the hook shank. If the furled tail starts to loosen up a little, it can be twisted in the appropriate direction as the tail is tied down rearward. Treat the tail with a few drops of Zap-A-Gap cement, and allow it to dry for a few minutes.

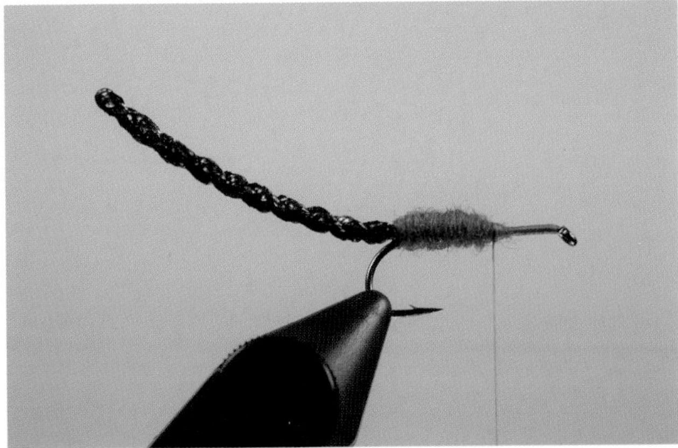

2. Wax the tying thread, and apply a little blue dubbing. It won't take much dubbing to form the body. Wrap a dubbed body forward to the point where the tail was tied in.

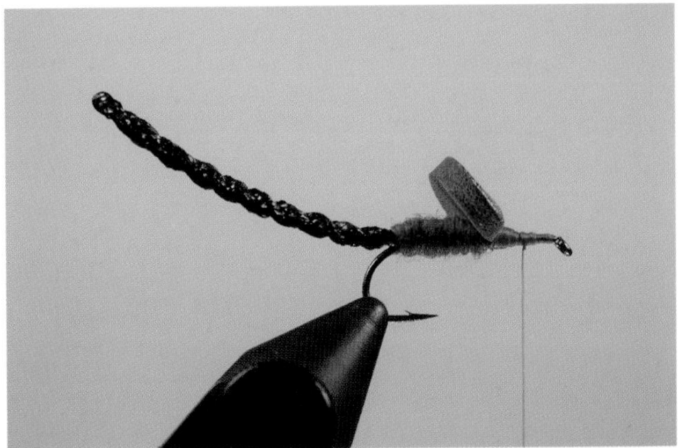

3. Tie in the front of the wing-support disc so that it extends rearward over approximately half of the dubbed body.

4. Tie in the Krystal Flash winging material just in front of the wing-support disc, and wrap the thread rearward.

5. Separate the winging material into two equal portions, divide them, and tie them down on opposite sides of the wing-support disc.

6. Wrap the thread to the eye of the hook. Wax the thread, and apply a small amount of blue dubbing. Wrap the dubbed thread rearward until it is almost even with the point at which the wings were tied in. Leave a small portion of thread between the dubbed underbody and the point at which the wings were tied in. This is where the head disc will be tied down.

7. Tie in the head disc between the dubbed front of the fly and the wing-support disc. About one-third of the disc should project forward to the eye of the hook, and the rear two-thirds of the disc should extend rearward over the wing-support disc. Apply a very small amount of Zap-A-Gap between the head and wing-support disc. This is easy to do if one first folds the head disc forward and applies a small drop of the adhesive with a sewing needle. Press the two discs together, and the bond is almost instantaneous.

8. Legs are added by tying the Silli-Leg's material on opposite sides of the head. Trim the legs to the desired length. Whip-finish, and remove the thread. Apply a little Zap-A-Gap to the thread wraps under the head.

I have had a lot of fun with this particular pattern on everything from smallmouth bass and bluegills to trout in some of the most unlikely places. One of the places where you would not normally think about fishing this pattern is on the fabled Henry's Fork of the Snake River. I know this sounds like heresy on this hallowed water, home of some of the great hatches, but if you have ever wandered the banks, you'll see tons of blue damsels flitting about in the tall grass. If you can ever take your eyes off the middle of the river and learn to tell the difference between rising whitefish and rising trout, you might see that there are a lot of big rainbows lying smack up against the bank just waiting for something to fall in. It could be a beetle, an ant, or a hopper. It could be, and frequently is, one of these blue damselflies, and if you have a pattern that mimics these, you're in luck.

I dearly love to fish the hatches on Henry's Fork, but I get just as much fun out of wading close to the bank and "head hunting" for bank feeders. The blue damselfly pattern has often produced more fish than any other pattern under these circumstances. "More" on Henry's Fork usually means the difference between two or three fish and a dozen. I think most people would agree with me that a dozen fish on this water is a memorable day, and the blue damsel has done it on more than one occasion for me. ■

Egg-Laying Caddis

Hook: Tiemco 100, sizes 10 to 16, or equivalent.
Thread: Gudebrod 6/0 or equivalent, color to match or contrast with the body color.
Egg sac: Small foam discs, 1/8 to 3/16 inch in diameter (or even smaller depending on the size of the fly) cut from sheets of 1/16-inch-thick bright green, dark green, or chartreuse foam.
Body: Any fine dubbing can be used to form the body. The color should match or contrast with the color of the foam used to form the wing.
Body hackle: Color to match the body dubbing.
Wing: A Locofoam triangle or a triangle cut from regular 1/16-inch-thick sheet foam, color to match or complement the body color. The triangle should be about an inch long and 3/8 inch wide at the base. This size can be used on all of the different hook sizes because it is trimmed to the correct length after it is tied in and cemented in place.
Front hackle: Color to match that of the body hackle.

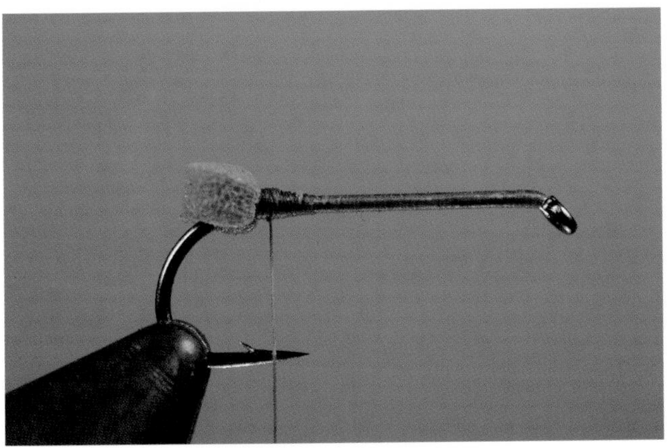

1. Wrap the shank of the hook with tying thread to the bend of the hook. Wrap the thread forward a short distance, and tie in the front of the disc used to form the egg sac.

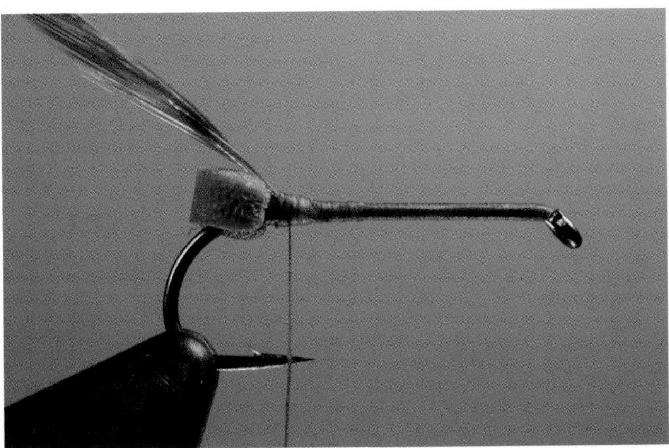

2. Tie in the body hackle just in front of the egg sac.

3. Wrap the thread forward about three-fourths the length of the hook shank, wax the thread, and apply the dubbing. Dub the body rearward to the point at which the body hackle was tied in and then forward again.

4. Wrap the hackle forward to the end of the dubbed body, tie it off, and trim the excess.

5. Trim the top of the wrapped hackle flush with the top of the dubbed body.

6. Tie in the foam body triangle by the tip at the front of the dubbed body. The base of the triangle should extend well over the rear of the hook.

7. Apply Zap-A-Gap to the top of the dubbed body and the top of the foam egg sac. Use only enough to dampen the dubbing and the top of the egg sac. Rotate the fly upside down in the vise, and press the foam wing triangle down onto the treated body and egg sac. Turning the fly upside down allows you to make sure the wing triangle is cemented evenly to the body and egg sac. In other words, you can see what you are doing! The foam wing should bond almost immediately to the body and egg sac. Trim the body hackle so that it is no longer than the gape of the hook.

8. Tie in the front hackle.

9. Wrap it forward about four turns, and tie it off. Wrap the head, whip-finish, and remove the thread.

10. Remove the fly from the vise, trim the rear of the foam wing to the desired length, and cut a V-shaped notch in the rear of the wing.

11. The tip of the V-shaped notch should be even with the rear of the egg sac. ■

Fliedermouse

Hook:	Tiemco 5212, size 10, or equivalent. This pattern can be tied on larger- or smaller-size hooks by varying the size of the discs used to form the body and the head.
Thread:	Gudebrod 6/0 or equivalent, color to match that of the body.
Tail:	Elk hair, color to match or contrast with the body color.
Body:	A 7/16-inch-diameter disc cut from Locofoam or standard 1/16-inch-thick sheet foam. The color of the disc is at the discretion of the tier. On other hook sizes, adjust the size of the disc accordingly.
Wings:	Elk hair, color to match or contrast with the color of the body.
Head:	Two 3/8-inch-diameter discs cut from Locofoam or standard 1/16-inch-thick sheet foam, color to either match or contrast with the body color. On other hook sizes, adjust the size of the discs accordingly.

1. Attach the thread to the hook shank, and wrap the thread rearward to the hook bend. Tie in a clump of elk hair to form the tail, and wrap the thread forward about two-thirds the length of the hook shank.

2. Rotate the fly upside down in the vise, and tie in the front of the body disc *under* the hook shank.

3. Turn the fly upright in the vise, and apply a small amount of Zap-A-Gap cement evenly to one-half of the body disc and the thread wraps on the hook shank. Fold the body disc upward, and pinch it together. The bond should be almost immediate. Turn the fly upside down again, and trim a little away from the rear of the foam disc under the hook shank. This will effectively increase the hook gape.

4. Tie in the first head disc immediately in front of the body disc. Place a small amount of Zap-A-Gap on the front portion of the body disc, and cement the first head disc in place.

5. Tie in a clump of elk hair directly in front of the first body disc.

6. Separate the elk hair into two equal portions on either side of the first head disc (a figure-eight thread wrap can be used to keep the wings separated), and tie them down to the front of the first head disc.

7. Tie in two or three strands of peacock herl in front of the elk hair wings, and wrap the thread to the eye of the hook.

8. Wrap the peacock herl to the eye of the hook, tie it off, and trim the excess. Wrap the tying thread rearward to a point about halfway between the eye of the hook and the front of the first head disc.

9. Tie in the second head disc. Approximately one-third of the second head disc should extend forward to the eye of the hook, and two-thirds should extend rearward over the wings and the first head disc. Wrap the second head disc firmly in place, whip-finish, and remove the tying thread.

10. Fold the second head disc forward, and apply a small amount of Zap-A-Gap cement to the top of the first head disc. Press the two discs together. They should bond almost immediately. This step will insure that the wings will remain separated. ■

Motivator

Hook:	Tiemco 5212, size 8 or 10, or equivalent.
Thread:	Gudebrod 6/0 or equivalent, black.
Body:	Black closed-cell foam, 1/16 inch thick, cut in the shape of a triangle. The triangle should be approximately 1 inch long with a 3/8-inch-wide base. The corners at the base of the triangle are trimmed slightly to make it easier to tie in the body. The triangle can be cut from either Northern Lights or Green Swirl Locofoam or standard black 1/16-inch-thick sheet foam.
Thread for spinning loop:	Gudebrod size G, red or yellow, depending on the color of the deer hair used for the underbody.
Underbody:	Red or yellow deer hair, spun in a dubbing loop.
Hind legs:	Round rubber legs, black, small size.
Hackle:	Furnace or brown.
Underhead wrap:	Two or three strands of peacock herl.
Head:	A disc cut from either Locofoam (Northern Lights or Green Swirl) or from standard black 1/16-inch-thick sheet foam. Use a 1/4-inch-diameter disc for a size 10 fly and a 3/8-inch-diameter disc for a size 8 fly.
Front legs:	Round rubber leg material, black, small size. One piece is tied in on either side of the head to form two legs on each side at the front of the fly.

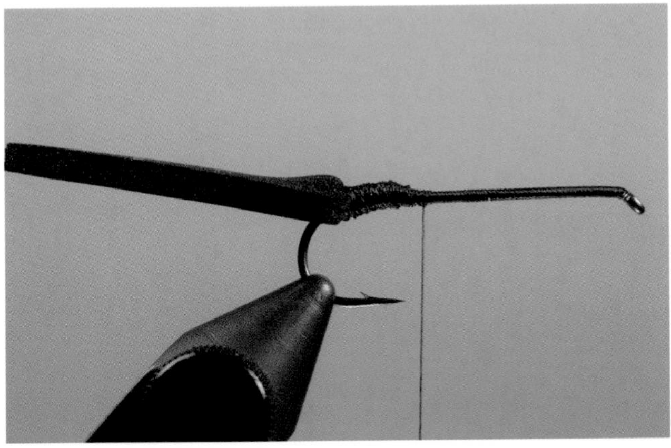

1. Attach the thread to the hook shank, and wrap it rearward to the bend of the hook. Tie in the body triangle, with the tip of the triangle pointing to the rear. Trim the corners off the base of the triangle before tying it down.

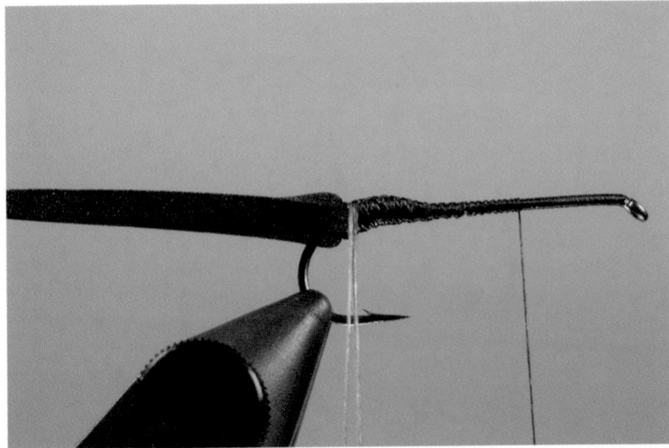

2. Wrap the tying thread forward slightly. Form a dubbing loop with the Gudebrod G thread, and tie it down all the way to the rear of the hook shank. Wrap the tying thread forward about two-thirds the length of the hook shank.

3. Cut a bunch of deer hair (quantity is determined by the size of the hook), trim the tips, and spread the hair evenly in the dubbing loop. Spin the dubbing loop so that the deer hair now forms a deer hair "hackle."

4. Wrap the spun deer hair forward about half the length of the hook shank. Tie it down, and trim the excess.

5. Trim the deer hair underbody to the shape illustrated.

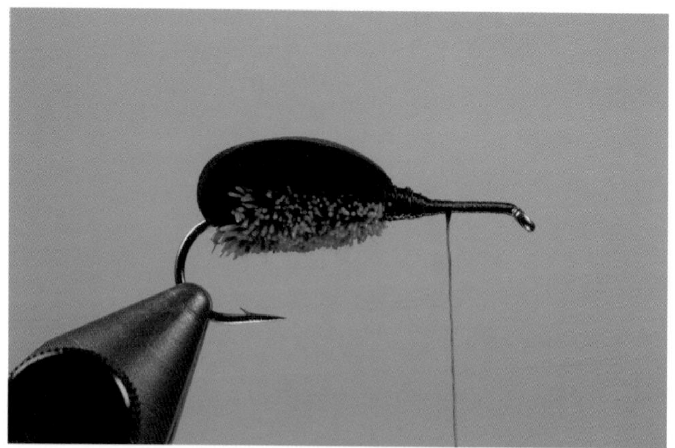

6. Fold the foam triangle forward over the trimmed deer hair underbody, tie it down, and trim away any excess foam.

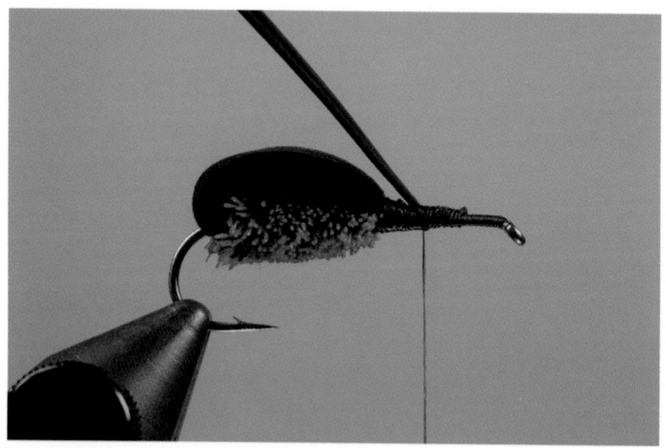

7. Tie in two unseparated rubber legs in front of the completed body. Trim them to the desired length.

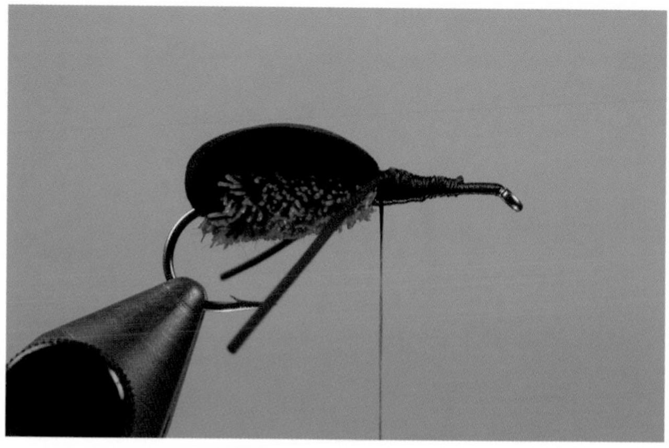

8. Separate the legs, and tie them down so that they lie on opposite sides of the trimmed underbody.

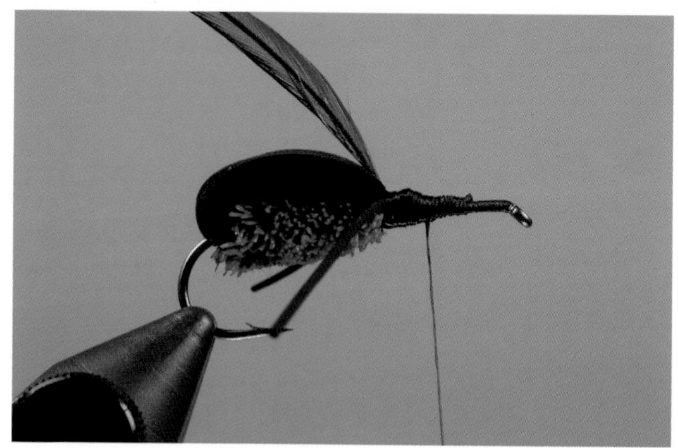

9. Tie in a single hackle fiber.

10. Wrap the hackle forward three or four turns, tie it down, and trim away the excess. Wrap the tying thread forward a short distance.

11. Tie in three or four strands of peacock herl in front of the hackle, and wrap the tying thread to the eye of the hook.

12. Wrap the peacock herl forward to eye of hook. Tie it down, trim away any excess, and wrap the thread backward about half the distance between the eye of the hook and the front of the hackle.

13. Tie down the foam head disc with the front of the disc extending to the rear, or just slightly over, the eye of the hook.

14. Tie in a single piece of round rubber leg material on either side of the head to form two legs on each side. Trim the legs to the desired length. Whip-finish, and remove the thread. Apply head cement or Zap-A-Gap to the thread wraps under the head of the fly. ■

Plumpy

Hook:	Tiemco 5212, sizes 10 to 16, or equivalent.
Thread:	Gudebrod 6/0 or equivalent, color to match or contrast with the body.
Tail:	Elk body hair, color of choice. The color can either match or contrast with the color of the body.
Body:	Disc cut from Locofoam or standard 1/16-inch-thick sheet foam. Use the following to match the disc size to the hook size: 10 hook—7/16-inch-diameter disc 12 hook—3/8-inch-diameter disc 14 hook—5/16-inch-diameter disc 16 hook—1/4-inch-diameter disc As far as the body color is concerned, I tie these with different colors of Locofoam. I particularly like the Tan Opal, Gray Opal, Northern Lights, Pearl Yellow, Metallic Red, and Pearl Orange.
Wing:	Elk body hair, color of choice.
Hackle:	Color of choice.

1. Wrap the tying thread rearward to the hook bend, then forward about 1/8 inch, and tie in a small clump of elk hair for the tail. Wrap the thread forward about three-fourths the length of the hook shank.

2. Turn the fly upside down in the vise, and tie in the body disc under the hook shank. Just a small portion of the front of the disc should be tied down. The rear of the disc should be even with the front of the tail. No thread wraps should be visible at the rear of the fly when the body has been completed.

3. Turn the fly right side up in the vise, and using a fine needle, apply a small amount of Zap-A-Gap cement evenly to half of the foam body disc and the thread wraps on the hook shank. Fold the disc up and over the hook shank, and squeeze the halves together. They should bond almost instantaneously if the correct amount of cement has been used. Turn the fly upside down again, and trim a small amount of foam from the underside at the rear of the fly. This will effectively increase the hook gape.

4. Wrap the tying thread forward to a point about halfway between the front of the body and the eye of the hook. Cut a clump of elk hair, even the tips in a hair stacker, and tie the elk hair with the tips extending forward over the eye of the hook. Trim away the rear-projecting elk hair butts and wrap them down tightly. Wrap the thread forward, pull the elk hair wing into an upright position, and wrap the thread in front of the now upright wing. Wind the thread around the base of the wing to form a typical parachute-style wing.

5. Wrap the thread rearward to the front of the body, tie in the hackle, and wrap the thread to the eye of the hook.

6. Wrap the hackle forward about three to four turns behind the parachute wing and then three or four turns in front of the parachute wing. Form the head, and whip-finish.

I really like this pattern. I know that other foam-bodied Humpies have been designed, but this is the only one I know of with the entire body formed from a single piece of foam. It is so easy to tie and so effective that it now occupies a prominent spot in my fly box. I love the original Humpy pattern, but I absolutely refuse to tie them. Tying a couple dozen Humpies would, for me, be the equivalent of being relegated to hell. For some reason, I can never get the proportions right. They all look different to me, and I just cannot seem to get the technique down. I suppose if I did sit down and tie a few hundred of them, it would become a lot easier, but I am not going to do that. I'll go along with most other folks and continue to buy the old-style Humpy if I feel that I need any.

On the other hand, the Plumpy is a piece of cake to tie, and I can turn out a couple dozen in no time at all—for me, that's the bottom line. Not only is this fly simple to tie, it also seems to be just as effective as the original Humpy pattern and can be tied in many different colors. In other words, the sky is the limit for this particular foam-bodied fly. I have tied them in all the standard Humpy colors plus just about everything else imaginable, from purple to all black.

The first time I tested this fly was on the West Branch of the Delaware River in New York. I actually can't say that I *tested* it there, because I only made two casts with it, but the experience is worth recounting.

Pete Bromley and I arrived at the second angler's parking area below Deposit, New York, within seconds of each other. Considering that Pete had driven up from Raleigh, North Carolina, and I had driven from Blacksburg, Viriginia, that was pretty remarkable, but things like this seem to happen to us with frightening regularity. After exchanging the usual insults, we geared up and headed for the river.

When we arrived at the high bank, we stopped to check the situation out. Right in front of us, about 30 feet from shore, a nice trout was rising.

I looked at Pete and said, "I've got to try something."

"What?" said Pete.

"Just a new pattern I've been messing around with," I replied. "It's called a Plumpy. I haven't even cast the thing yet."

"Go for it," said Pete. "You going to come in from behind him?"

"Naw," I answered. "I think I'll just cast off the bank and see what happens."

I knotted a tan-bodied Plumpy to the tippet, worked out what I figured was enough line to reach the fish, and made the cast. A gust of wind picked up the line and killed the cast. I stripped the line in and started all over again. This time the cast landed even with the fish but about 3 feet to the right. The fish shot over and slammed the fly, missed it, and as the fly floated downstream, the fish raced back about 10 feet and slammed it again. This time there was a solid hookup.

It was hard to tell who was the most surprised: Pete, the trout, or me. There I stood, 10 feet above the water on a steep bank, playing a nice 14-inch brown.

I turned to Pete and in my best English accent said, "I say, old chap, would you mind sliding down the bank and netting that fish for me?"

"You can be such a jerk sometimes," Pete replied. "Yeah, I'll do it, but you owe me."

Pete beat his way down through the brush, netted the fish, slipped the Plumpy from its jaw, and returned the fish to the river.

He looked back up toward me, grinned, and said, "Looks like you might have something hot here."

"Who knows?" I said. "That didn't prove anything other than a blind hog will find an acorn every now and then. I'll have to fish the thing a whole lot before we'll know anything."

But deep down I had the feeling that he was right. After all, the original Humpy had to be one of the best all-purpose patterns ever designed, and this wasn't that much different.

My feelings about this pattern were confirmed later that summer on numerous occasions, on both western and eastern streams. It proved to be an incredibly good searching pattern for riffle water, and when tied in the larger sizes, it worked equally as well in heavy water. I tried it in all different colors and sizes, and the ones I found to be most effective were those tied with tan, yellow, orange, and red bodies, the standard colors for the original Humpy.

Not long ago, I had the occasion to fish an outstanding eastern brook trout stream. Before hiking in to the stream, I tied on a size 16 orange-bodied Plumpy, figuring that with the high-water conditions at the time, it would probably work fairly well. The brookies trashed the fly for the rest of the afternoon, and because I wanted to see how the foam body would hold up, it was the only fly I used that day. At the end of the afternoon, the body was a little chewed up, but the fly was still very fishable, and I was quite pleased with the results. ■

UFO

Hook:	Tiemco 400T, size 10, or equivalent.
Thread:	Gudebrod 6/0 or equivalent, black.
Underbody wrap:	Three or four strands of peacock herl.
Body:	A 3/16- to 1/4-inch-wide strip cut from 1/8-inch-thick black sheet foam (Evasote or Fly Foam).
Legs:	Round rubber legs, black, medium size.
Wings:	About fourteen to sixteen strands of Pearlescent Olive Krystal Flash.
Eyes:	Red E-Z Shape Sparkle Body.
Head:	A 3/8-inch-diameter disc cut from 1/8-inch-thick black sheet foam (Evasote of Fly Foam).

Any 2X long light wire hook can be used to tie this pattern, but I much prefer the Tiemco 400T (swimming nymph hook). The wide gape of this hook has excellent hooking properties, its light weight is definitely a plus, and the upward bend of the hook at the forward portion provides a good reference point for maintaining the correct proportions of the fly.

1. Attach the thread to the hook shank, and wind it rearward to a point well behind the hook barb. Wrap the thread forward to the beginning of the upward bend of the hook shank. Tie in the body foam at this point, and continue tying in the body foam rearward to a point well behind the hook barb. Wrap the thread forward and then rearward again to firmly attach the foam to the hook shank.

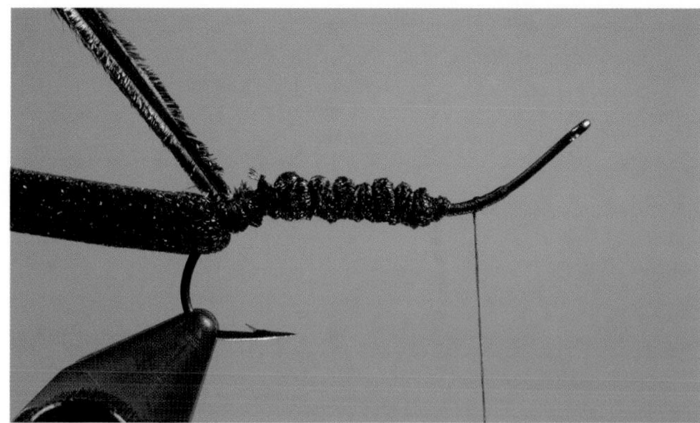

2. Tie in three or four peacock herl fibers, and wrap the thread forward to the upward bend of the hook shank.

3. Wrap the peacock herl forward to cover the entire underbody, tie it down, and trim the excess. Wrap the thread rearward and then forward through the herl. This step insures that the herl will not break after hooking a few fish.

4. Fold the body foam forward, and tie it down in front of the underbody wrap. When folding the foam forward, it is important that you do not stretch the foam. Tie down the foam with about twelve tight thread wraps. Now stretch the forward-projecting foam, and trim away the excess. When you stretch the foam before trimming it, there will be less bulk left to tie down. Then tightly tie down the remaining forward-projecting foam.

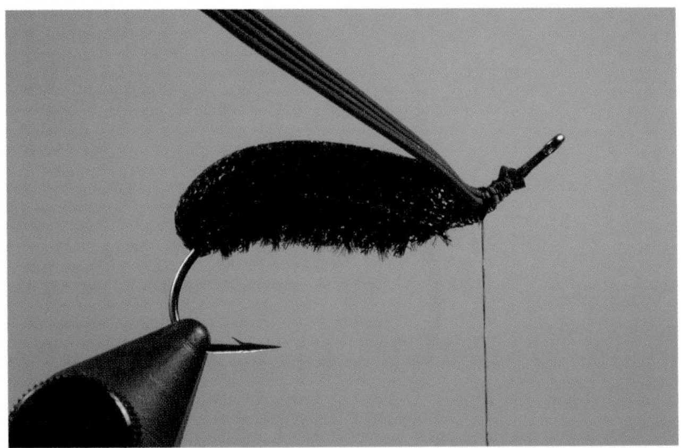

5. Tie in four unseparated round rubber legs a little in front of the body, and trim them to the desired length.

6. Separate them in half (split them in the middle), and tie down two unseparated legs on either side of the hook shank back to the front of the body.

7. Tie in the Krystal Flash winging material in front of the body. Trim the rear-projecting portion of the winging material so that the wings extend slightly over the rear of the body.

8. Separate the winging material into two equal portions, and tie the wings down on opposite sides of the body. When done correctly, the wings should project slightly upward and remain above the legs.

9. Wrap the thread forward slightly, and tie in three or four strands of peacock herl. Wrap the thread to the eye of the hook.

10. Wrap the peacock herl forward to the eye of the hook, tie it down, and trim the excess. Wrap the thread

rearward to a point halfway between the front of the body and the eye of the hook.

11. Tie in the foam head disc firmly on top of the ostrich herl. The front of the disc should extend forward to a point just behind the eye of the hook. Tie in the disc so that the front third forms the head and the rear two-thirds extends over the base of the wings and the front of the body. Whip-finish, and remove the tying thread. Separate the legs, and apply a small amount of Zap-A-Gap to the thread wraps under the head.

12. Add E-Z Shape Sparkle Body eyes on opposite sides of the head. Allow the eyes to dry for a few hours before fishing the fly.

When I first tied this pattern, I had no particular terrestrial insect in mind. It was one of those things that just looked good, and it was a simple tying procedure that didn't take much time. I tied about six of the things, stuck them in one of the terrestrial boxes, and figured I'd use them when the need arose. That didn't take very long, but what was strange was that I wasn't the first one to test it out. The first cast with one of the UFOs was made by a friend named Doug Hudgins, whom I fish with on occasion. He made the cast to a little brown trout of about 10 inches on Virginia's Smith River.

I had seen Doug anchored in one spot for about half an hour and had gradually worked up to him. It turned out he had been casting to this particular fish for the entire time with no success. We went through the usual fisherman's litany.

"What have you tried?"

"Everything."

"Don't believe I know that pattern."

"Right. Let's see: Orange Ant, Firefly, Sulfur, Blue Wing Olive, little PT Nymph, and a couple of other things. He takes a look at everything one time and that's it."

So I pulled out the experimental box, and we took a look. I fished out one of the UFOs and handed it to Doug. "Give this a shot."

"What is it?" asked Doug.

"Beats me," I said. "It doesn't have a name yet."

"Well," said Doug, "I'll have to switch back to 5X tippet. I've got 7X on right now."

"Naw, just tie it on and give it a couple of casts. All I really want to see is how it looks on the water. Besides, you're only casting about 20 feet."

So Doug tied this unnamed fly on and flipped it out. This little brown streaked over and took it as though he was starving. I'll have to admit I was just as surprised as Doug was. I figured right then that there might just be something special about this pattern.

Since then, my fishing buddies and I have had some remarkable times with this pattern, but none of us can remember who first called it the UFO or when the name was coined. It really doesn't matter because it's not the name but the effectiveness of this thing that impressed us the most. Three occasions immediately come to mind.

It was shortly after the experience that Doug and I had with this fly on the Smith River that I took off for Colorado. Now, although I would like to name the river I fished, I've been warned not to by those with whom I fish it. They're bigger, younger, and meaner than I am, so I think you'll forgive me. Anyway, a guy named Eric Kraimer, who was working for the Scott Rod Company at the time, met me on the river. We set up camp, got everything in order, and headed down to the water.

Eric and I stood there looking at this gorgeous run coming into the head of a pool and gradually tailing out into a long flat. Nothing was rising, and no bugs were coming off.

"Hmmm, don't know what to try," said Eric. "Looks like maybe it's nymph time."

"I don't know," I replied. "Just for the hell of it, try this thing," and I handed him one of the UFOs.

You know, it's easy to see skepticism, and it was written all over Eric's face when he took a look at this fly. He squinted his eyes, looked at me kind of funny, and said, "You're joking."

"Aw, come on, Eric, just give it a couple of casts."

So Eric tied on the UFO, made a couple of false casts, and dropped it in the middle of the run. The fly made about a 2-foot float, and there was one incredible explosion. Of course Eric missed the fish. He wasn't ready for that, and frankly, neither was I.

Eric stood there with the rod tip down in the water, the UFO trailing at the end of the line, and this goofy look on his face.

He turned and looked at me. "How big do you think that brown was?" he asked.

"Don't know," I replied. "How big do they get here?"

"Big," said Eric.

"Well, then," I grinned, "he was big. Will that do?"

"Yeah, it'll do," said Eric. "He was big."

Eric tried for that fish a couple more times over the next few days. He never took it, but each time he tried, that monster brown would come out of nowhere and slam the UFO. Each time, he wasn't ready for it. I think his nerves were shot.

I don't mind telling you about this next stream. The Little Lehigh is pretty well known, and that's where it happened. Anybody who has ever fished the Little Lehigh knows what it's like. Lots of flat water, picky fish, and heavy angling pressure all combine to make it pretty tough. I was fishing it during late summer, and Tricos were everywhere. My partners on this occasion were three of the regulars on the stream (Dave Norwood, Lincoln Palmer, Bob Miller) and Ed Koch. Bob had been kind enough to fork over half a dozen of his exquisite Trico patterns for the occasion, and I was looking forward to trying them out. I did, but for some reason, I simply could not get a fish to even look at them. So, being an ornery cuss, I put on a Firefly and had a great morning, but that wasn't the high point of the day. That came right at the end.

I was walking back to the car and spotted everybody sitting on a bench under a big willow tree. About that time, Ed came walking up the bank to join us.

"What's going on?" said Ed.

"Well," said Lincoln, "there's a couple of nice fish rising under this willow tree. We've all tried for 'em, so you guys might as well give it a shot too."

Ed tied on a little orange ant, floated it down to the fish, and they turned up their noses. He tried a couple of other patterns. Nothing.

"OK," said Ed. "Your turn."

Well what do you do in a situation like this? There I am with three guys who fish this water all the time and Ed Koch. You've got four super fly fishermen sitting there, and it's your turn to screw up.

"Oh, what the hell," I thought to myself. "Might as well screw it up good."

So I opened up the box, took out a size 8 UFO, and tied it on.

"What is that thing?" one of them asked.

Of course, everyone had to take a look, and I took some heat for even thinking this thing would work on that water. Ed, however, looked at it, got a funny little grin on his face, and said, "I don't know guys, wait and see."

I dropped down below the fish, crossed over to the other side of the stream, and laid out enough line to cover the lower fish. With my usual beautifully accurate technique, I made the first cast to the lower of the two fish. Do you ever make those casts when you know immediately that it's going to be terrible and there's nothing you can do about it? I mean, you know it the second you release the line? The fly is in the air, on the way, and there's no calling it back? Worst of all, it's in front of four guys sitting there watching you? It was one of those casts. The fly landed at least 2 feet behind the fish and a foot off to one side. I expected the fish to hit the afterburners and evaporate. It didn't. It charged the fly, slammed it, and of course, I missed the fish. There was a chorus of comments from the bank, most being unprintable.

My cast to the second fish was better. The UFO landed well above the fish, and the fish rose to meet it as it came over him. It was a good solid hookup and a short fight. I left the stream and returned to the bench under the willow tree.

I'll never forget Bob Miller's comment: "Where do you get the stuff to tie those things?"

Another experience with the UFO happened on DuPuy's Spring Creek. I'll make it short. Steve Hiner and I were fishing a major PMD hatch with very little success, so I decided to try the UFO. You know what it's like. It's one of those "oh, why not" thoughts. So I tied on a UFO, and a good fish hit it on the first cast. On about the third cast, I took another fish. Steve came over, took a UFO, tied it on, and the same thing happened to him. So there we were, on one of the fabled western spring creeks, fishing for "picky, spooky, and highly selective" trout using this size 8 monster fly. I have no idea how many fish came to the UFO that afternoon, but it was a lot. They took it dead drifted, they took it swinging at the end of the drift, and they took it when we skittered it across the surface. Some things just can't be explained.

It's funny, but when I describe something like this to other fly anglers, I frequently hear the comment "Oh well, it's just something they haven't seen before." My answer to this is "bull feathers." I think that many of these patterns have a terrific appeal because they look like food, big food. Let's assume you were really hungry and at a dinner party. There is a platter with some of those little bitty fancy cucumber and bread squares, and every now and then you sneak over and get one. Then the butler comes in and plops a fillet and baked potato down in front of you. Are you going to continue to sneak a little sandwich every so often, or are you going to go for the steak and potato? Maybe trout act the same way. When that UFO (or maybe any other big terrestrial) smacks down in front of them, I think it represents meat and potatoes, and they jump all over it!

While I'm at it, I've got to get something else out of my system. There are many patterns that trout see all the time, and they never seem to tire of them, so this bit about "they haven't seen that pattern before" just doesn't make any sense to me. Take the Adams, the PT Nymph, and the Elk Hair Caddis, for example. Trout see these all the time on certain rivers, and they never seem to lose their effectiveness. My buddies and I have fished the Firefly pattern for years on Virginia's Smith River, and it works as well today as it did when it was first conceived. I imagine that the majority of fish in certain sections of the river have seen this pattern many times, but it always produces. So much for that old saw about a pattern being effective because fish haven't seen it before. ■

Bumblebee

Hook:	Tiemco 8089, size 12, or equivalent.
Thread:	Gudebrod 6/0 or equivalent, black.
Underbody:	A 3/8-inch-wide foam strip, yellow, cut from 1/8-inch-thick "manufactured" sheet foam. The strip should be about 1/2 inch long.
Overbody:	A 1/4- to 5/16-inch-wide strip cut from Northern Lights Locofoam or standard 1/16-inch-thick black sheet foam.
Body wrap:	Kreinik Micro Ice Chenille, citron.
Wings:	White Ultra Hair (Super Hair), striped with a black permanent marker.
Head:	Triangle cut from Northern Lights Locofoam or standard 1/16-inch-thick black sheet foam. The triangle should be about 3/8 inch wide at the base and 1 inch long. After cutting the triangle, trim the tip so it is only 5/8 inch long.
Underhead wrap:	Kreinik Micro Ice Chenille, peacock or black.
Eyes:	A 1/8-inch-diameter foam cylinder, red, yellow, or gray.
Legs:	Round rubber legs, black, medium or small size.

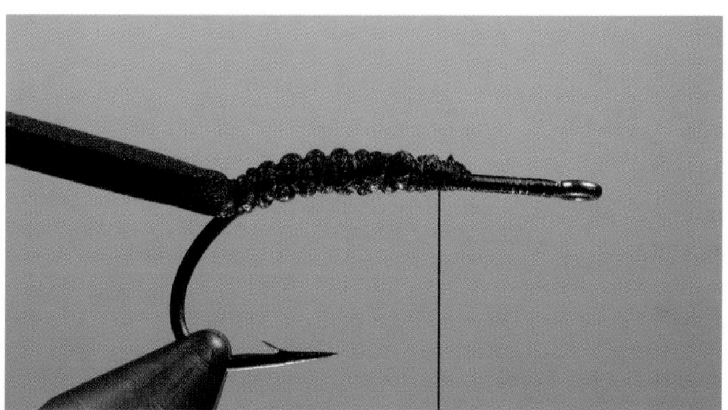

1. Wrap the shank of the hook with thread rearward to the bend of the hook. Wrap the tying thread forward approximately two-thirds the length of the hook shank. Trim the overbody material to a point, tie it down, and continue tying it down to the rear of the hook shank. Tie it in with the metallic surface of the Locofoam strip facing down.

2. Wrap the tying thread forward approximately two-thirds the length of the hook shank. Place the underbody foam strip on top of the hook shank so that the rear of

the foam strip is just forward of the rear of the fly. Tie in the front of the underbody foam strip with a few tight turns of the tying thread. Then wrap the tying thread rearward *loosely* over the underbody foam strip until you reach the rear of the strip. Tie down the rear of the underbody strip tightly. Wrap the thread forward loosely again and then back to the rear of the underbody.

3. Tie in the Micro Ice Chenille just behind the underbody foam strip. Wrap the thread forward loosely over the underbody and then to a point about $^{1}/_{16}$ inch past the front of the underbody. Using a needle, apply Zap-A-Gap cement to the top of the formed underbody.

4. Wrap the Micro Ice Chenille forward to the front of the underbody strip, tie it down, and trim the excess.

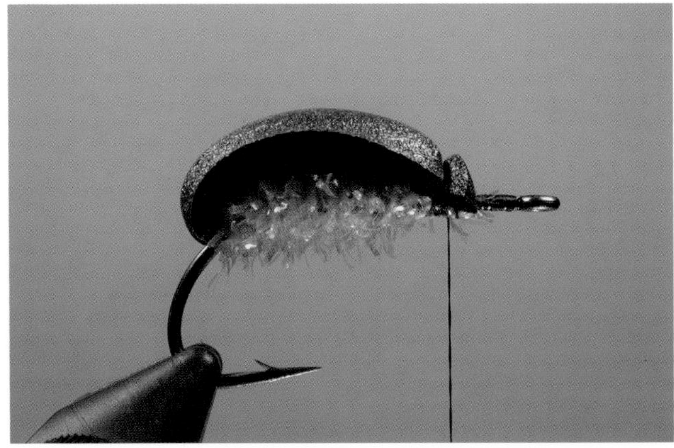

5. Fold the overbody foam strip forward, tie it off directly in front of the wrapped underbody, and trim the excess.

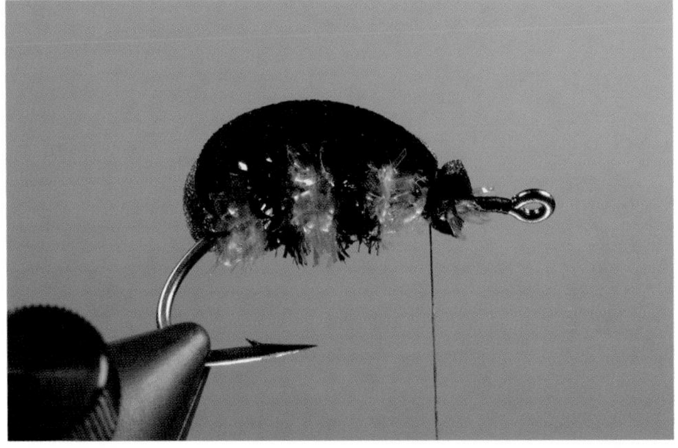

6. Rotate the fly upside down in the vise, and apply two or three stripes to the underbody with a black permanent marker.

7. Tie in the winging material in front of the formed body, and separate it into two equal portions on either side of the body. Trim the wings so that they are no longer than the length of the hook.

8. The triangle used to form the head is then tied in by the tip. The tip of the triangle is placed even with the point where the wings were tied down and is then tied down by wrapping the thread forward to the eye of the hook. Trim away any excess foam.

9. Wrap the thread backward, halfway between the eye of the hook and the front of the body. Tie in the eye cylinder with a few figure-eight thread wraps so that equal portions are on both sides of the hook shank. Wrap the thread rearward to the front of the body.

10. Tie in the Micro Ice Chenille.

11. Wrap the Micro Ice Chenille forward and around the eyes using a figure-eight wrap and then back behind the eyes. Tie it down, and trim the excess.

12. Fold the head triangle rearward over the eyes, and tie it down. Trim the points off the base of the head triangle. Using a sharp razor blade or scissors, trim the eyes flush with the formed head.

13. Tie in two unseparated rubber legs on opposite sides of the body at the point where the head material was tied down. Trim them to the desired length and then separate them. Place a small amount of Zap-A-Gap cement on the thread wraps under the head of the fly. ■

Mud Dauber

Hook:	Tiemco 5212, size 12, or equivalent.
Thread:	Gudebrod 6/0 or equivalent, black.
Abdomen:	A 7/32-inch-diameter foam cylinder, black, 1/2 to 5/8 inch long.
Body:	Thread wrap treated with either Zap-A-Gap cement or head cement.
Legs:	Black, round rubber, fine.
Wing:	White Ultra Hair (Super Hair).
Wing support:	A 3/16-inch-diameter disc cut from 1/16-inch-thick foam. Color at the option of the tier. I use red, yellow, or orange foam for the wing-support disc.
Head underwrap:	Three or four strands of peacock herl.
Head:	A 1/4-inch-diameter disc cut from a 1/16-inch-thick sheet of black foam.

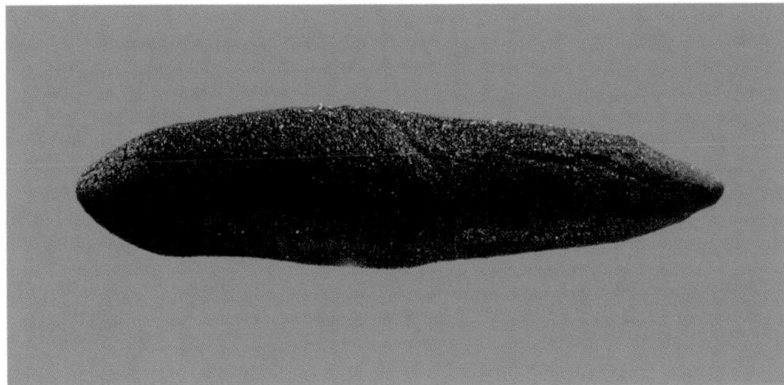

1. The abdomen of this fly must be prepared and shaped before it is tied in. The easiest way to do this is to use a heat gun (very hot air, but similar to a hair dryer). The foam abdomen material is heated and then rolled between the fingers to taper it at both ends. The front should be much more severely tapered than the rear, which should be bluntly tapered. This same procedure may be accomplished using an alcohol lamp, butane lighter, or any high-heat source, but the heat gun is the easiest way to accomplish this step. I have not tried a hair dryer, so I don't know if this would work or not.

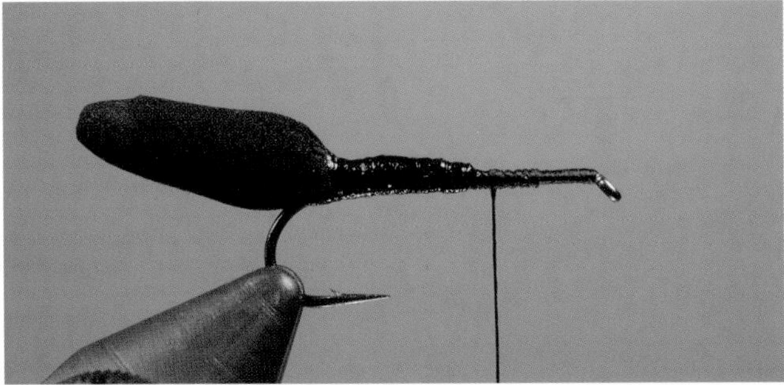

2. Wrap the shank of hook with tying thread to the bend of the hook and then forward about half the length of the hook shank. Place the prepared abdomen in position, and tie in the front portion rearward to the bend of the hook. Completely cover the tied-down region with thread wraps so that no foam is visible. Whip-finish, and remove the thread. Coat the thread-covered portion of the abdomen with either head cement or Zap-A-Gap cement, and allow it to dry. After the thread wraps have dried, reattach the thread at the front of the treated body.

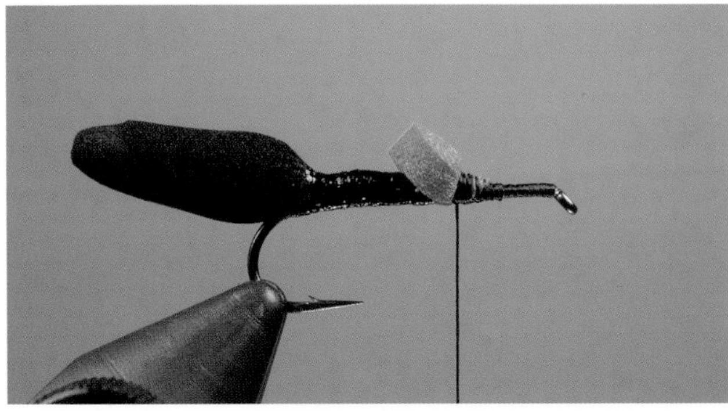

3. Tie in the front portion of the wing-support disc so that the rear of the disc extends over the coated thread portion of the abdomen.

4. Tie in a clump of winging material in front of the wing-support disc. Separate the winging material into two equal portions, and tie down the divided wings on opposite sides of the wing-support disc.

5. Tie in three or four strands of peacock herl in front of the wing-support disc, and wrap the tying thread to the eye of the hook.

6. Wrap the peacock herl to the eye of the hook, tie it off, and trim the excess. Wrap the tying thread rearward to a point about halfway between the front of the wing-support disc and the eye of the hook.

7. Tie in the head disc so that the front third extends to the rear of the eye of the hook and the rear two-thirds extend well over the wing-support disc. Fold the rear of the head disc forward, and place a small amount of Zap-A-Gap cement on the top of the wing-support disc. Press the rear of the head disc down on the wing-support disc so that the two bond together. This will keep the wings separated and on opposite sides of the fly.

8. Tie in a single rubber leg on opposite sides of the head disc, and trim the legs to the desired length. Place a small amount of head cement or Zap-A-Gap cement on the thread wraps under the head disc. If desired, the wings may be striped with a black permanent marker (see the Paper Wasp). ■

Paper Wasp

The Paper Wasp is tied using exactly the same procedure as that outlined for the Mud Dauber. The differences between the two patterns are as follows:

The abdomen is formed from a cylinder of yellow foam and is striped with a permanent black marker. The wing-support disc is cut from black foam. The head disc is cut from yellow foam, and the top of the head disc is colored with a black permanent marker. ■

Turbo Wasp

Hook:	Tiemco 5212, size 14, or equivalent.
Thread:	Gudebrod 6/0 or equivalent, fluorescent yellow.
Body:	A $^{3}/_{16}$-inch-wide strip cut from $^{1}/_{8}$-inch-thick black Evasote or Fly Foam.
Wing:	A $^{3}/_{16}$-inch-wide section of a mallard wing quill sprayed with artist's spray fixative.
Legs:	Six moose body hairs.
Thorax:	Fine black dubbing.

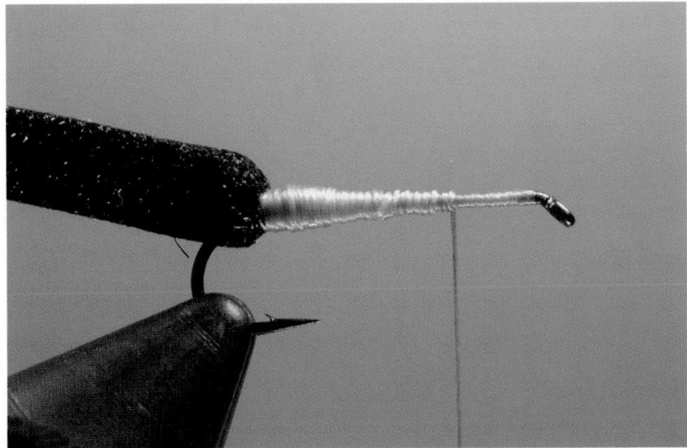

1. Wrap the shank of the hook with tying thread to a point just behind the barb of the hook. Tie in the body foam material at this point, and wrap the tied-in foam with thread until it is completely covered. This should form a slight enlargement at the rear of the hook shank. Wrap the thread forward about two-thirds the length of the hook shank. The thread wraps should cover the shank completely to give the underbody color.

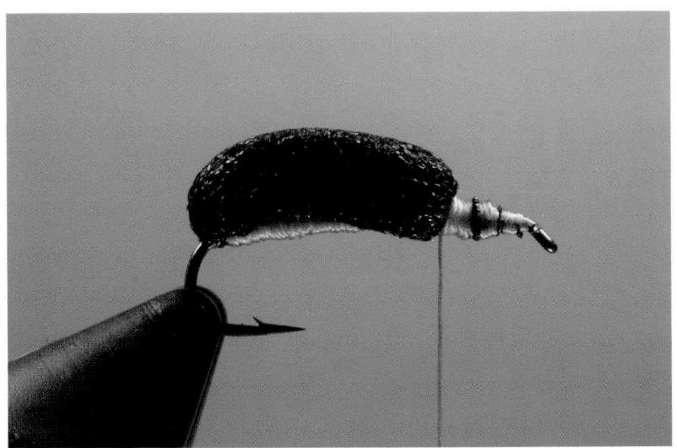

2. Fold the foam body material forward, and tie it down. Trim the excess.

3. Tie in six moose body fibers so that three lie along each side of the abdomen and extend well past the abdomen. Trim away the forward-projecting portion of the hairs, and tie down the butts.

4. Tie in the duck quill wing so that it extends well past the end of the abdomen. Trim away the forward-projecting portion, and cut the rear portion on each side of the wing at an angle.

5. Wax the tying thread, apply fine black dubbing, and build up a dubbed thorax region in front of the body. Form the head with tying thread, whip-finish, and remove the thread.

This little fly may not look like much, but over the years it has proved to be one of the most effective patterns in my fly box. I don't know why, but it seems to have some sort of universal appeal, much like the Firefly pattern. Does it really look like a wasp? Maybe it does, but it could resemble a caddisfly, a beetle, or some sort of winged ant as well. Whatever trout take it for, the important thing is that they take it. From the Smith River in Virginia (where it was first tested; see *Terrestrials* by Harrison Steeves and Ed Koch) to New York's Delaware River, the Henry's Fork in Idaho, and the Gunnison in Colorado, this pattern has consistently produced.

I remember one day in particular, on Henry's Fork, when it seemed to be the only pattern the rainbows would even look at. The unfortunate thing about that day was that the afternoon came to an abrupt end in one of the most horrific thunderstorms I have ever encountered. Miller Williams, Doug Hudgins, and I sat huddled in a depression on the bank, rain streaming down our jackets and lightening cracking all around us, wishing we were anywhere but there. Our rods had been placed upstream from us about 50 yards or so, and we expected to see them disappear in a puff of smoke any minute.

When the storm finally moved on, we retrieved our rods and waited hopefully for another hour. But there was not a rise to be seen. We called it a day, thanked the Turbo Wasp for our earlier success, and hiked back to the car. You can't win all the time. ■

Deer Fly

Hook:	Tiemco 100, size 12 and 14, or equivalent.
Thread:	Gudebrod 6/0 or equivalent, black.
Body:	A 3/16-inch-wide strip cut from 1/8-inch-thick sheet foam (Evasote or Fly Foam), color at the tier's discretion. I tie this pattern using black, yellow, orange, and tan foam for the body.
Underbody:	Three or four strands of peacock herl.
Quick-sight tag:	Fluorescent Orange Antron Yarn (I tie this only on the black-body Deer Fly).
Wings:	Kreinik 1/8-inch-wide flat ribbon, mallard, #850.
Thorax:	Two or three strands of peacock herl and one strand of black ostrich herl, twisted together.

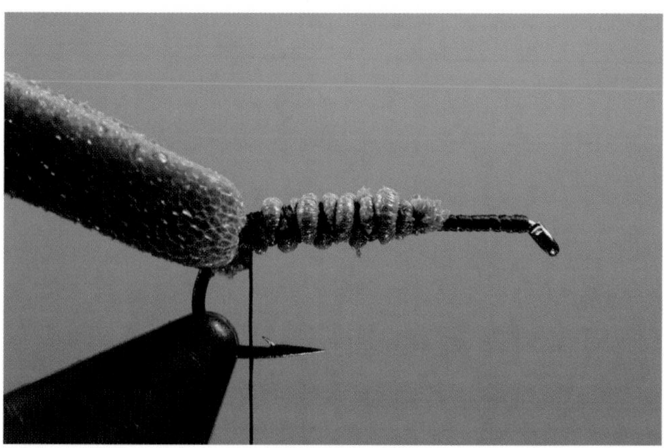

1. Wrap the thread on the hook shank to the rear of the hook, and then wrap it forward to a point just slightly ahead of the middle of the hook shank. Tie in the foam body piece. Continue tying it down rearward to the bend of the hook.

2. Wrap the thread forward slightly, and tie in three or four strands of peacock herl. Wrap the thread forward to just slightly ahead of the middle of the hook shank. Wrap the peacock herl underbody material forward just past the middle of the hook shank, tie it down, and trim the excess. Wrap the thread back and then forward through the herl to strengthen it.

3. Fold the foam body material forward, over the underbody. Tie it down with half a dozen or more tight thread wraps. Pull the foam toward the eye of the hook (stretch it), and cut it so that a minimum of foam is left ahead of the point where it is tied down. Wrap the thread over the remaining foam and forward about $^{1}/_{16}$ inch.

4. Tie in a piece of Kreinik winging material, and cut the winging material so that the wings will be shorter than the body of the fly. Trim away any excess material projecting forward.

5. Separate the winging material into two equal portions on either side of the foam body, and tie them in rearward to the front of the body.

6. Tie in two or three strands of peacock herl and one strand of black ostrich herl by the tips. Cut the butts off evenly so they are all about 2 inches long. Grasp the butt ends together with a pair of hackle pliers or a circuit tester, and twist them together.

7. Wrap the twisted herl forward, three to five wraps, to form the thorax. Trim away any excess material. Wrap the head, and whip-finish.

I have fished this pattern on numerous occasions, and it has always produced well, but one day in particular stands out. I was fishing the Gallatin River a number of years ago, and the deer flies were out in force. It was so bad that I had to resort to rubber gloves, a head net, and about a gallon of assorted insect repellants, none of which seemed to do a bit of good. At any rate, in the middle of my misery, I figured that if there were that many of these pests swarming around me that many of them just might end up in the water as fish food. I tied on a tan Deer Fly imitation, and after a few casts I was into a pretty good rainbow. There was no hatch going on at the time, so I simply fished the pattern to the bank and to what appeared to be good holding lies. It was great! There I was, swatting at deer flies, sweating, cursing, and catching enough decent fish to almost make me forget about the pests that were making me miserable. I had never done very well on the Gallatin before, at least in the sections that I was familiar with, so this was a unique experience. I was also amazed at the size of some of these fish, the largest of which was a touch larger than 18 inches.

Well, you can't have fun forever, particularly when deer flies are swarming all over you, and the deer flies won that afternoon. I took it for a couple of hours and then had to retreat to the car. That night, while nursing some nasty bites, I realized how dearly I was paying for my few hours of fun. Would I do it again? You bet! I went back the next afternoon dressed like a beekeeper.

Others have had similar experiences with this pattern without the accompanying annoyance of clouds of swarming deer flies. From what I hear from friends out west, it is a particularly effective pattern for high mountain lakes, mountain streams, and western spring creeks (particularly when no hatch is going on). Back here in the east, it seems to work just about everywhere. ■

Bluebottle and Greenbottle Flies

Hook:	Tiemco 102Y, size 13, or Tiemco 100, size 14, or equivalent. I prefer the TMC 102Y, size 13, for this pattern.
Thread:	Gudebrod 6/0 or equivalent, black.
Body:	Either Tiger Beetle Green or Frogskin Locofoam for the Greenbottle Fly and Dragonfly Blue or Blue Swirl Locofoam for the Bluebottle Fly. To prepare the bodies for these flies, use a sharp razor blade, and cut a 3/8-inch-wide, 6-inch-long strip of Locofoam. This strip is then cut into 1-inch-long pieces. Treat about half of each piece with a small amount of Zap-A-Gap cement (I use a sewing needle chucked into a pin vise for this step). The cement should be spread thinly and evenly on the nonmetallic side of the foam. The foam-body piece is then folded over on itself to form the finished body. When done correctly, the bond between halves of the foam-body piece is almost instantaneous.
Legs and antennae:	Black nylon paintbrush bristles.
Wing:	Natural CDC.
Head:	A 1/4-inch-diameter disc cut from Locofoam. Color to match that of the body.
Eyes:	Scribbles brand fabric paint, either Iridescent Copper or Ginger Snap.

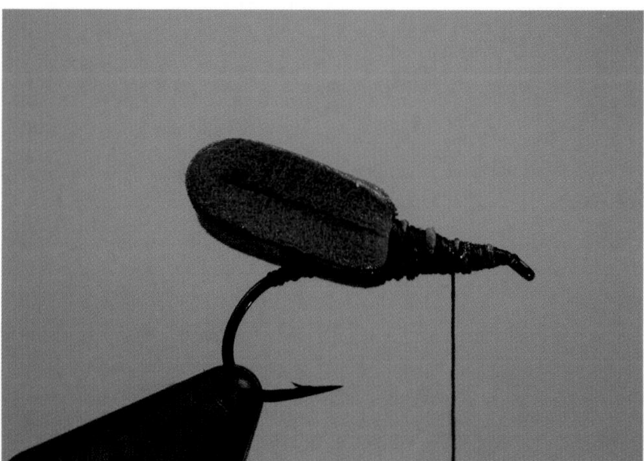

1. Wrap the shank of the hook with thread to the bend of the hook and then forward again to a point about halfway up the hook shank. The body is tied in at this point so that the rear of the body extends slightly over the bend of the hook. Trim away most of the forward-projecting body foam, and wrap the remainder down tightly.

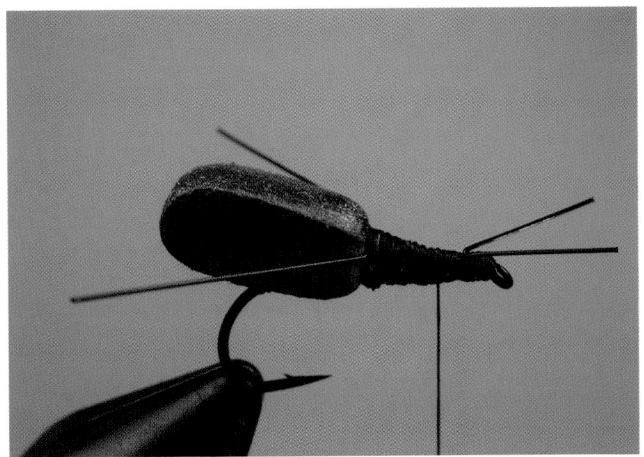

2. Wrap the thread to the eye of the hook, and form a small ball of thread immediately behind the eye. This will allow the antennae to spread apart when they are tied in. Tie in two nylon paintbrush bristles behind the ball of thread at the eye of the hook. They should spread apart evenly with no trouble. Tie down the paintbrush bristles rearward to the point where the body was tied in. Separate them just in front of the body with a couple of figure-eight wraps, and then tie them down tightly, on either side of the body. Trim the legs and antennae to the desired length.

3. Tie in the CDC winging material just in front of the body. Two or three CDC feathers is all that is necessary. Trim the CDC wings so that they are slightly longer than the body of the fly. Trim the forward-projecting CDC, and wrap the thread so that no remaining CDC butts are visible.

4. Tie in the head disc so that the front third of the disc extends to or slightly behind the eye of the hook. The rear two-thirds of the head disc should extend well over the base of the wings and the front of the body.

5. Turn the fly upside down in the vise, and using a fine needle, apply a small amount of Zap-A-Gap to the thread wraps directly under the head. Add the fabric paint eyes on either side of the head.

I have had some incredible days fishing this pattern all over the East Coast and in the western states as well. Next to the Firefly, it is probably my favorite small "go to" pattern and has accounted for innumerable trout, quite a few of which have been bragging size. Rather than recount my own stories about this pattern, I will simply include the following from a friend of mine, Tom Lawson, who was kind enough to send me this account of the Bluebottle Fly and a big brown on Virginia's Jackson River.

Who'd have ever thought it? The common house fly—and there it was among Harry's new collection of terrestrials. Makes sense in a certain way. One can never get rid of them. Maybe they are always around the fish, too. Anyway, it worked for Harry one November day on the Jackson River in the Virginia mountains. Typically, in this water, we fish only to rising fish, but when things were slow, Harry could just chuck that house fly out there, and the trout would race to get to it. Or at least that's the way it seemed to me.

Later in the day, Harry and I had shinnied down a steep bank with the aid of a rope, put there years ago before the construction upstream of Gathright Dam. The water was not so marvelously cold in those days. That is a thing attainable in Virginia in big water, even in the mountains, only by artifice, and, of course, it is the sine qua non for trout. The rope access had been contrived back when the river was warmer so that kids could get to the long pool just above us to play in it. Harry and I were standing at the bank in 4 or 5 inches of water, getting ready to move up to the pool, when there occurred a great ruckus just above us. We moved stealthily forward to see what was up. Harry, who knows his fish and has an eye for such things, quickly diagnosed trout on a redd. Soon I too could make out a hen trout finning out her spot and the would-be father excitedly working back and forth in her vicinity. Then came the commotion again, completely out of context with this domestic scene, but this time we were right on top of it. The back of a great fish broke the surface as he pushed a V-shaped wave right past us. We could only stand motionless in wonder. Finally, the usually imperturbable Harry gasped, "It's a pike!" I laughed. "Harry, there are no pike in this river." We decided it must be a trout, but its size and actions were decidedly out of the ordinary. We respectfully inspected the redd at a distance and headed off up river.

The fishing before us immediately took up our thoughts, and the incident left my mind entirely until a week later, when I found myself in the same spot, having again availed myself of the rope. Immediately the scene was reenacted in my mind's eye. Peering up the shallow river's edge, I picked out, somewhat to my surprise, the same two fish on the redd. Harry had been reluctant to disturb them, but I murmured to myself, "What the hell, there are too many fish in this river anyway." I tried to get a cast to the male, which was of decent size and still moving nervously about, but the fly came up short. That's right, it was a fly in both senses of the word. Having observed Harry's success the week before, I had put on one of his house flies. Actually, Harry had a technical name for the insect he had artfully mimicked, and it was supposed to be slightly different from what buzzes around us in the kitchen, but it was a house fly to me. Suddenly another eruption occurred, just below the cast. It was the big fish again, and I had innocently but—so it seemed to me—irrevocably spooked him. He rushed away from the fall of my line upon the thin water and back toward me, then swerved suddenly under a fallen tree limb. All sign of him disappeared as his wake slapped against the bank.

It took me two casts to get the fly to the male at the redd. I thought the presentation was OK, but there was no take. I was lifting my rod tip for another try, with the house fly drifting back toward me, when things became decidedly unstuck at the bank. Far from being disturbed, or in any case deterred, the big fish had seen the house fly from under his log and was making for it in a startlingly determined way. Maybe I was too astonished to move at all in the time it took the wake to surge a couple of yards out from the log and obliterate all sign of the house fly. In any case, I somehow avoided overreacting in setting the hook, assuming this was this fish's version of a rise, and so did not, as is easy to do with a big fish, jerk it out of his mouth, or, worse, demolish the 6X tippet in a panicked response. And, lo and behold, he was on, and so was the battle. After his initial runs, the trout settled into a steady, determined resistance, marking him as a brown. The sun was high, and the fish was plainly visible to me as our tug-of-war played itself out, ever downstream, just as fighter planes in a dogfight always end up "on the deck." I finally maneuvered the trout into the shallows by the far bank and slipped my all but inadequate net over his head.

It was a male. See, I haven't failed, after all, of gender-neutral language in giving this account. I had a chance to observe him closely after I released and resuscitated him, my hand over his eyes to keep him still, all 24 inches of him. He continued to lie, panting, in the transparent water at the stream's edge. He stayed there the whole time it took me, sitting on the bank, to recover myself and gain the presence of mind to put on a fresh tippet. A beautiful creature he was too, to have been seduced by something as ugly as a house fly. That is, something I *used* to think was ugly.

—Tom Lawson

Tom is right about this pattern. It does resemble a house fly. I got the idea for this pattern on Falling Spring Creek in Pennsylvania. Why there? It so happens that there used to be a dairy adjacent to the stream, and the house flies (face flies, bluebottle flies, etc.) in this section were thick as fleas on a dog's back. It stood to reason that many of them would eventually wind up in the stream, and taking a page from one of Marinaro's books, I decided that I would try to come up with a pattern to mimic these insects. It only took a short time at the vise to design this pattern, and it rapidly became one of my favorites. I tie them in both the green and the blue version and honestly cannot say that either of the two colors is more effective than the other. I do believe, however, that the metallic coating on the Locofoam used to tie this pattern really increases its effectiveness. ■

Horse Fly

Hook:	Tiemco 531, size 12, or equivalent. I prefer to use this hook when tying this fly because it is a 2X short hook. I can therefore tie a smaller fly with a wide hook gape.
Thread:	Gudebrod 8/0 or equivalent, yellow.
Underbody:	One brown and one yellow ostrich herl.
Body:	A 3/16-inch-wide strip of brown foam cut from a 1/16-inch-thick sheet of closed-cell foam. The strip is then cut into pieces 1/2 inch long, and each piece is shaped. The front of the piece is cut to form a short tapered triangle, and the rear is trimmed to a round or oval shape.
Wings:	A 7/16-inch-diameter circle cut from iridescent wrapping material and trimmed to shape.
Eyes:	A 1/8-inch-diameter foam cylinder punched from bright green foam (obtained from flip-flops or beach shoes).
Head:	A triangle cut from a 1/16-inch-thick sheet of brown foam. If an adjustable template is used (see chapter 2) to cut the triangle, the triangle should be about 1 inch long and 1/4 inch wide at the base.
Underhead wrap:	Two strands of peacock herl.
Legs:	Nylon paintbrush bristles, black.

1. Wrap the thread on the hook shank to the bend of the hook, and then wrap it forward about 1/8 inch. Tie in the two ostrich herl fibers rearward to the bend of the hook.

2. Wrap the thread forward about two-thirds the length of the hook shank. Twist the herls together, wrap them forward, and tie them off. Trim the excess. Trim the top of the wrapped herl so that it is flat.

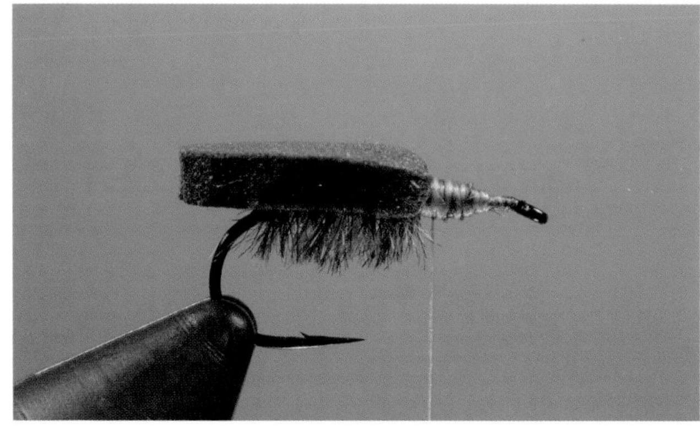

3. Tie in the shaped foam body piece so that the rounded rear portion extends just over the bend of the hook. Place a small amount of Zap-A-Gap on the top of the trimmed herl, and press the body piece down so that it bonds to the wrapped herl. Trim the herl under the body of the fly so that it is fairly short.

4. Tie in the point of the trimmed wing piece. The wings should *not* extend over the rear of the body and should be evenly spaced on either side of the body. Wrap the thread to the eye of the hook.

5. Place the tip of the head triangle even with the front of the body, and tie it down by wrapping the tying thread rearward. Tie it down to a point halfway between the front of the body and the eye of the hook. Trim away any excess foam.

6. Tie in the foam eye cylinder with a series of figure-eight thread wraps.

7. Tie in the peacock herl underhead wrap behind the eye cylinder.

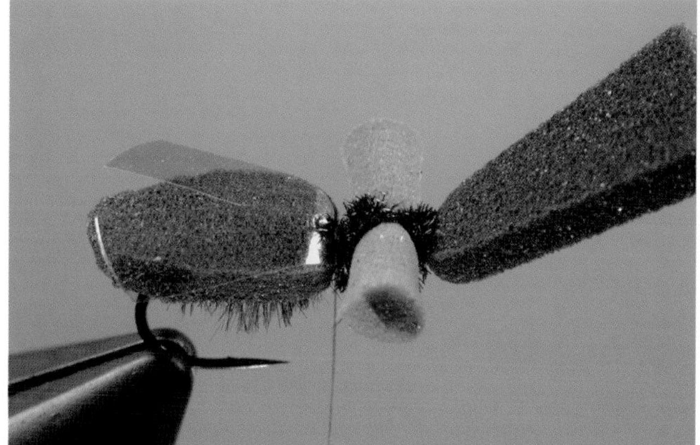

8. Wrap the peacock herl over the eye cylinder with a series of figure-eight wraps, in front of the eye cylinder, and then behind the eye cylinder. Tie it down behind the eye cylinder, and trim the excess.

9. Fold the foam head triangle over the eye cylinder, and tie it down. Trim the rear portion of the head triangle so that it extends just over the wings and the front of the body.

10. Using a sharp razor blade or a sharp pair of scissors, trim the eyes flush with the head.

11. Tie in two paintbrush bristles on either side of the fly. Rotate the fly upside down in the vise, and apply a small amount of Zap-A-Gap cement to the thread over the point where the legs were tied in. This will lock the legs firmly in place, and they will not slip when you trim them. Trim the rear legs even with the rear of the body. The front legs should be trimmed somewhat shorter than the rear legs. Cut off one of the front legs on either side of the fly so that the fly now has six legs, three on each side. Treat the thread wraps under the head with a small amount of Zap-A-Gap.

I need to explain just a bit about the eye cylinder used for this fly. So far no one (at least to my knowledge) produces the correct color of foam for the bright green eyes, nor do they produce it in a cylinder of the correct diameter. The only way to obtain the eye cylinder for this fly is to make your own, but it's easy to do. Simply visit one of the large retail stores (WalMart, for example) that stocks an abundant supply of flip-flops (foam beach shoes), and find a pair of bright green ones. These will supply you with more foam than you will probably ever need, and the cost is minimal. The best way I have found to form a foam cylinder of the correct length and diameter is to start by cutting off a piece of one of the flip-flops with a sharp knife (I use a fish-filleting knife with a razor edge). This piece is then split, using the fillet knife, and the foam cylinder is punched out from one of the halves using a set of small leather punches available from Tandy Leather Company. This set of punches comes with removal punch heads in different sizes that are relatively thin, but fairly short. When splitting the foam from the flip-flop, I measure just how thick it should be so that the punch will pass through it and split the foam from the flip-flop accordingly. It works beautifully.

If you don't want to go to all the trouble of buying and preparing the foam from a pair of flip-flops, you can use a sheet of bright green 1/16-inch-thick foam to form the eyes. This foam is available from most craft shops as well as WalMart. You simply cut a 1/16-inch-wide strip from the foam sheet and use this for the eyes. You will, of course, wind up with square eyes on the fly, but I doubt if the fish will notice this little detail.

Tying the wings on this fly also needs a little elaboration. The material I use is quite slick and difficult to tie in unless you learn the following tricks. Make sure that you have wound the thread back to the front of the body before you try to tie down the wings. Place the wings in position. Then, if you are right-handed, hold them in place with the thumb of your right hand. Using your left hand, make a couple of tight thread wraps in front of the tip of your thumb. You can then tie the wings down tightly with no slippage at all.

To form the wings for the fly, I use a 7/16-inch gasket punch to cut a circle out of the winging material. The circle is then folded in half, and the wings are cut as illustrated. This technique assures that the wings will be symmetrical in shape.

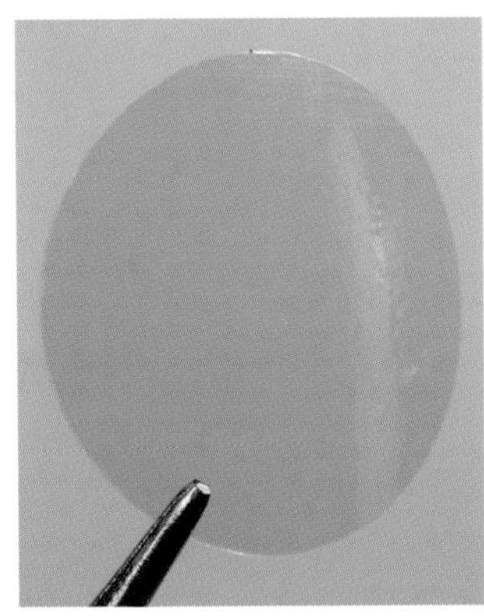

The idea for this pattern presented itself one day when I was sitting by the side of a river with the van doors wide open. There were at least a dozen of these green-eyed horseflies buzzing around in the van. I collected a few, put them in a jar of alcohol, and brought them home with me. I reasoned that if a dozen or more had invaded my vehicle, there must be hundreds of the things along the river, and many of them would certainly fall into the water.

Now I have a confession to make. I have not fished this pattern yet, but I have high hopes for it. It just looks too good for any self-respecting trout to turn down. We'll have to wait and see. ■

Salmonfly

Hook:	Tiemco 5263, size 2, or equivalent.
Thread:	Gudebrod 6/0 or equivalent, black.
Tail:	Dyed black elk body hair.
Underbody:	A 1/8-inch-wide strip cut from a 1/8-inch-thick sheet of orange foam. The foam is stretched between the fingers before tying it in so that it becomes thinner and shiny.
Body:	A 5/16- to 1/4-inch-wide strip cut from 1/8-inch-thick black sheet foam (Evasote or Fly Foam).
Ribbing thread:	Gudebrod size G, black.
Underwing:	Pearl Krystal Flash.
Middle wing:	Bleached white deer hair.
Overwing:	Natural elk body hair.
Underhead wrap:	Orange ostrich herl.
Head:	A 1/2-inch-diameter disc cut from 1/8-inch-thick black sheet foam (Evasote or Fly Foam).
Legs:	Medium-size round rubber legs, black.

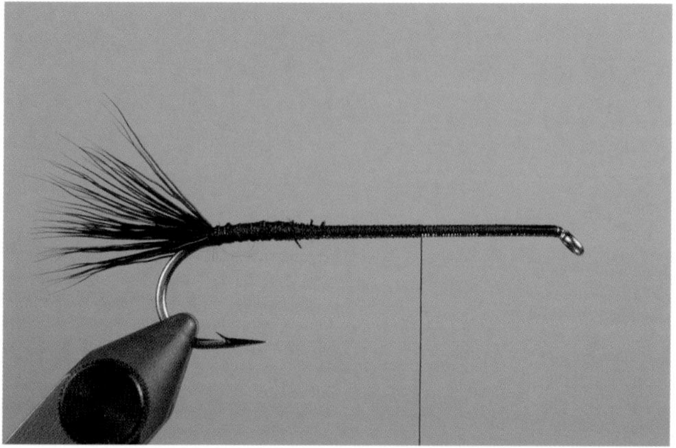

1. Wrap the shank of the hook with the tying thread to the bend of the hook, and tie in the elk hair tail.

2. Wrap the tying thread forward about two-thirds the length of the hook shank, and tie in the strip of foam that will be used to form the body. Tie the foam strip down tightly all the way back to the bend of the hook. Tie in an 8- to 10-inch piece of the ribbing thread in front of the foam strip.

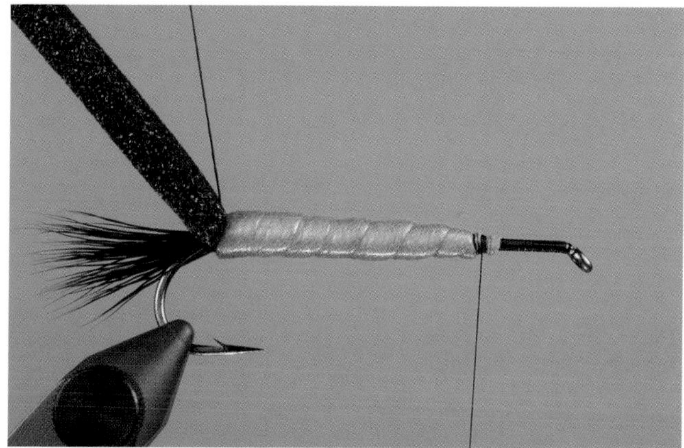

3. Tie in the stretched piece of orange foam, and wrap the thread forward two-thirds the length of the hook shank. Wrap the orange underbody foam forward two-thirds the length of the hook shank, tie it off, and trim the excess.

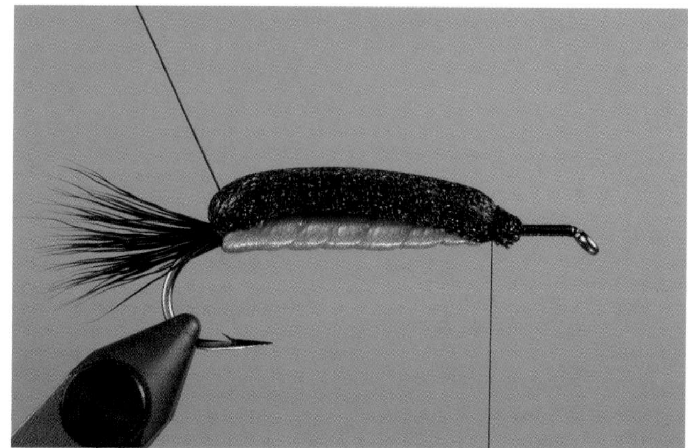

4. Fold the body foam over the hook shank, tie it off, and trim the excess. Tie down the trimmed front of the body foam tightly.

5. Rib the body with about seven or eight turns of the ribbing thread, tie off the ribbing thread, and trim the excess.

6. Tie in four unseparated rubber legs tightly, and trim them to the desired length.

7. Separate the legs (split them in the middle), and tie down the separated legs rearward to the front of the body so that two unseparated legs lie on opposite sides of the body.

8. Tie in a small bunch of Krystal Flash fibers (sixteen to eighteen). Trim them so that they extend to about the middle of the elk hair tail.

9. Tie in a good clump of bleached white deer hair so that the tips of the hair are even with the end of the Krystal Flash underwings. Trim the butts, and tie them in neatly.

10. Tie in a clump of natural elk hair. The tips of the elk hair should extend back about two-thirds the length of the other wings. Trim the butts, and tie them down neatly.

11. Tie in two or three orange ostrich herl fibers directly in front of the wings, and wrap the thread to the eye of the hook.

12. Wrap the ostrich herl fibers to the eye of the hook, tie them off, and trim the excess. Wrap the tying thread backward to a point halfway between the eye of the hook and the base of the wings.

13. Tie in the head disc at this point so that the front third of the disc extends to or slightly over the eye of the hook and the rear two-thirds extend back over the base of the wings. Separate the rubber legs, turn the fly upside down, and apply a small amount of Zap-A-Gap cement to the thread wraps under the head.

I have been lucky enough to encounter a few salmonfly hatches while fishing out west. I believe that anything big, orange, and buggy looking will catch fish during this hatch, but this pattern has been very successful. It floats forever without dressing, it is extremely durable, and it is a pretty accurate imitation of the natural. I've caught a lot of big trout with this fly, and I never travel out west without a couple dozen of these things tucked away somewhere in the van. You never know what is going to happen! ■

Chapter 8

Flies for Warm Water

Sometimes it takes me a while to catch on to the obvious, but if it's put in front of me enough times, then I might begin to figure it out. At a fly-fishing show in New Jersey last year, quite a few of the people that stopped by the tying table commented that the patterns I was doing in foam would be fantastic for panfish. After a dozen or more comments to this effect, something clicked in the cerebrum, and I remembered that I had heard this exact comment many times in the past. Another comment that was made on occasion was that if I tied them in larger sizes, they would be outstanding flies for bass. There was another click in the frontal lobe. I recalled that a couple of friends of mine had started tying patterns like the UFO and the Disc Head Cicada in large sizes and using them on smallmouth bass.

The smaller foam flies really did seem to be ideal for panfish, and the more I looked at them, the more determined I became to try them out on these scrappy little warm-water fish. All sorts of memories suddenly came flooding back. Having been born in Alabama, I grew up fishing for bluegills, sunfish, and shellcrackers on many of the streams and farm ponds around Birmingham. What a delightful time that was. These little beauties had a great deal to do with my lifelong love affair with the fly rod and are to my way of thinking some of the toughest fighters (for their size) of any species. I spent many afternoons fishing for "sunnies" using the old rubber cricket pattern that is still marketed. It was one of my favorite patterns for bluegills, as was a small yellow or white popping bug with a sinking black ant or black gnat as a point fly. When a big bluegill grabbed the popper, we used to let it swim around for a while, and nine times out of ten another one would latch on to the dropper fly. Boy, that was a ton of fun, and if bluegills and their kin regularly reached 4 or 5 pounds, I would probably fish for them exclusively.

These memories haunted me during the winter months, and I vowed that when warm weather arrived I would make a point of heading to a bluegill pond. I did just that not long ago.

Torrential rains made the rivers rise out of their banks, so trout fishing was out of the question, but I figured that this was the perfect time to try some of the foam "trout" patterns on bluegills. I loaded the canoe on top of the van and headed toward Hot Springs, Virginia, where I knew of three ponds that held plenty of bluegill and largemouth bass. When I arrived, there was only one other boat on the upper pond. "Perfect," I thought to myself as I unloaded the canoe, put the gear into it, and shoved off.

There was a gentle breeze blowing, which made conditions ideal for letting the sculling paddle and the breeze gently move me down the bank to the end of the lake. I was fishing a 9-foot, 5-weight fly rod with a 9 1/2-foot leader tapered to 5X, and I had tied a size 14 UFO to the tippet. I figured that this fly was large enough to keep the small stuff off but had enough bulk to attract the attention of some of the bass in the pond. It turned out that I was both right and wrong. I actually caught quite a few of the smaller bluegills and red-breasted sunfish, but anyone who has ever fished for these little guys knows that even the smallest ones will attack a large lure. I've frequently had them charge a bass plug that was larger than they were and hook themselves.

I drifted down the shoreline, sculling with one hand, casting to the bank with the other, and taking one bluegill after another. I was as happy as if I were sixteen again and floating one of the slow bluegill-infested Alabama creeks. I had almost reached the end of the lake when all hell broke loose. What I thought was the gentle take of another bluegill turned into a shoving match with a 3-pound largemouth. I had forgotten what fighters these fish are and was totally unprepared for the shattering leaps and head-shaking bulldog tactics of the fish. By the time I managed to get the fish to the side of the canoe, all the memories of past run-ins with largemouths had surfaced, and I wondered why I had stopped fishing for them. I vowed then and there to renew my acquaintance with this heavyweight of the panfish world.

By the end of the afternoon, I had lost count of the number of bluegills and sunfish I had taken. There had been so many that there was just no way to keep track of the number. Thirty, forty, fifty—it was impossible to say. But I *can* say that they had managed to suck the finish off the foam (Locofoam and Locoskin) that I had used to tie the fly with. I had never had this happen when using this fly for trout, even after a dozen or more fish. In the process of hooking all these bluegills, I did take another half dozen largemouths, but none were as large as the initial 3-pounder.

As I loaded the canoe onto the van and put the fly rod away, I realized that in my single-minded quest for trout I had been missing out on some of the greatest fishing in the world. I can assure you that will change.

Sometimes I believe that I am a total idiot. I live a stone's throw from the New River, one of the world's oldest rivers (if not *the* oldest) and one of the best in the country for smallmouth bass and muskies. It is also loaded with rock bass (red-eyes), bluegills, sunfish, crappie, carp, and catfish. When I moved back to Virginia in 1966, I took on the New River with a vengeance and fished it steadily for many years. Pete Bromley and I had some wonderful times on that river. One day, we arrived back at my house with a cooler full of huge bluegills we had taken. It took us the rest of the evening to fillet these fish, but it was worth the time and effort. There is nothing that can compare with a platter of bluegill fillets rolled in seasoned flour and fried in bacon grease, cholesterol be damned.

I would like to say that we took all these lovely bluegills on one of my foam fly creations, but that was not the case. Most of them were caught on either a brown Woolly Bugger or a popping bug. All this took place back in about 1985, and foam-bodied flies were not well known at the time. I had just begun designing flies and had no idea that foam was available for fly tying. A few years later, all that would change.

Over the past few years, I have taken up fly fishing for smallmouth bass with a vengeance and have developed a number of foam patterns that have worked very well. One of my favorites is nothing more than the Los Alamos Ant pattern, originally developed as a trout pattern, tied on a size 10 stinger hook. Although I have tied this pattern in a number of different color combinations, my favorite is tied with a yellow belly, green back, and chartreuse rubber legs. There have been many days on the James River when this is the only pattern I have fished and caught just as many or more fish as my partners. It has also become one of the favorite patterns of Cliff Rexrode, a fishing buddy of mine.

I remember one day when Cliff, Urbie Nash, and I were floating the James River and having a field day on smallmouth with the green and yellow LA Ant. At one point, I dragged my pontoon boat up on a gravel bar and walked downstream to fish a particularly promising bit of water. After about fifteen minutes, I caught movement out of the corner of my eye and saw Cliff sneaking down toward my boat. He unzipped one of the compartments, rummaged around, found what he was looking for, and then disappeared around the far side of the gravel bar. A little while later he came walking around the tip of the gravel bar and down toward me.

"I don't know what's wrong," he said. "I've had four good fish on and can't seem to get a good hookup. I've lost every one of them."

I looked over sideways at him and asked, "What are you using?"

"The green-and-yellow LA Ant," he answered.

"Where did you get it?" I asked. I knew he had broken off the one I had given him earlier.

"Aw, I sneaked over to your boat and took one out of the fly box," he confessed.

"That's your problem," I grinned. "You stole it."

"No, I didn't," he said. "I was going to give it back to you."

"Doesn't matter," I said. "You stole it. On top of that, you stole the wrong one."

"What do you mean I stole the wrong one?" said Cliff.

"Just that. You stole the wrong one. You got the one that had the point of the hook broken off just behind the barb. It happened when I was mashing the barb down earlier. That's what I get for using a twenty-year-old stinger hook, and that's what *you* get for being a thief."

Cliff took the fly out of the hookkeeper and looked at it. "It's broken," he said.

"Sure is," I grinned. "Honesty is the best policy."

"Not around you it isn't," said Cliff.

"Sure it is," I said. "Next time, just ask for one."

"No," said Cliff. "Next time I'll just look more carefully."

Then he walked back up to my boat, grabbed the LA Ant box, and walked off with three of them.

Although the green-and-yellow Los Alamos Ant is one of my favorite smallmouth bass patterns during most of the day, I will frequently switch to an all-white version during the late afternoon and early evening. For some reason, the white pattern is the one the bass seem to favor at this time day.

Most of the foam fly patterns for panfish were originally developed using different colors of either 1/16- or 1/8-inch-thick standard closed-cell foam. The advent of Locofoam and Locoskin opened a whole new avenue for experimentation. The shiny metallic colors on these two foam products really seem to bring out the aggressive nature of panfish of all species. As a result, most of my recently designed panfish patterns have revolved around the use of these two types of foam.

Besides the Los Alamos Ant, there are a number of other patterns included in this section that were originally designed for trout. It is a simple matter to modify the size of these patterns, and their effectiveness for bass makes it well worthwhile to tie them in these larger sizes.

At this point I have to confess that most of the following patterns are so new that I have not had the opportunity to test them out. I have high hopes for them, though, and feel that given the aggressive nature of the smallmouth bass, they should do very well. ■

Black Widow (Bass)

Hook:	Tiemco 8089, size 12, or equivalent.
Thread:	Gudebrod 6/0 or equivalent, black.
Tag (butt):	A 1/4-inch-diameter disc cut from Metallic Red Locofoam.
Spinning loop:	Gudebrod size G thread, black.
Underbody:	Black elk hair, spun in a dubbing loop and trimmed to shape.
Body:	A 5/8-inch-diameter disc cut from Northern Lights Locofoam or 1/16-inch-thick black closed-cell foam.
Underhead wrap:	Kreinik Micro Ice Chenille, either mallard or peacock.
Head:	A 3/8-inch-diameter disc cut from Northern Lights Locofoam or 1/16-inch-thick black closed-cell foam.
Legs:	Fine round rubber legs, four on each side (group of two tied in and then divided to give two front and two rear legs on each side).

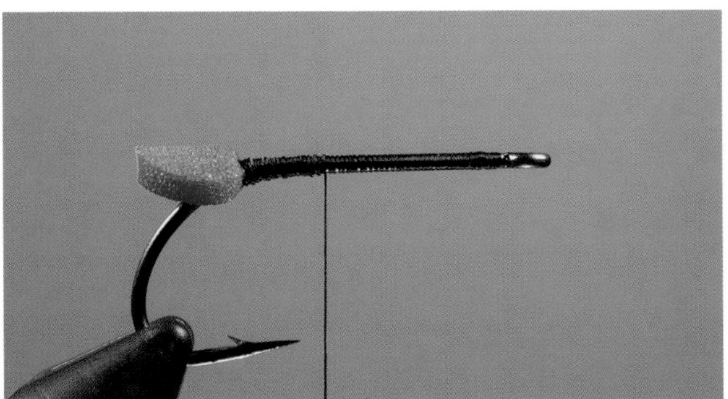

1. Wrap the shank of the hook with tying thread to a point behind the barb of the hook. Wrap the thread forward, and tie in the tag with the metallic surface facing down. The tag should extend rearward to a point even with the bend of the hook.

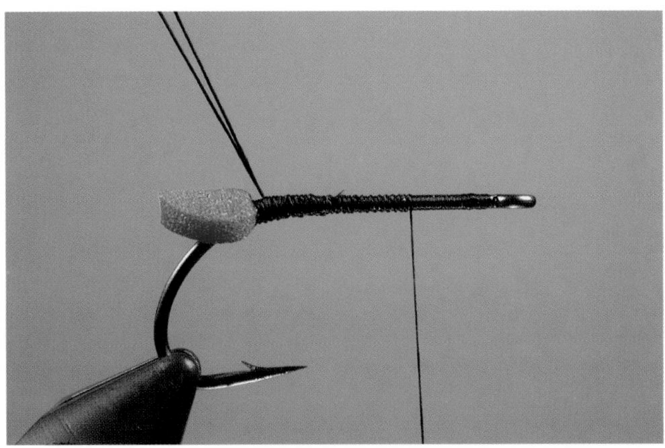

2. Wrap the tying thread forward to a point about two-thirds the length of the hook shank. Form a dubbing loop about 6 inches long with the Gudebrod G thread, tie it down at this point, and then continue to tie it down rearward to the tag. Wrap the tying thread forward again to a point about two-thirds the length of the hook shank.

3. Cut a generous clump of died black elk hair, even the tips in a hair stacker, and then trim the tips from the clump. Place the clump of elk hair in the dubbing loop, spread the hair evenly, and spin the loop to form a "hair hackle."

4. Wrap the hair hackle forward about two-thirds the length of the hook shank, tie it down, and trim the excess.

5. Trim the elk hair flat on the top of the fly using a pair of serrated scissors.

6. Tie in the front of the body disc at the point where the elk hair was tied off. If the elk hair body was formed properly, the disc should extend rearward to a point even with the end of the disc used to form the tag.

7. Apply Zap-A-Gap cement to the elk hair and the top of the disc used to form the tag. Press the body disc down firmly onto the trimmed elk hair and the top of the tag disc. Bonding should take only a few seconds.

8. Trim the elk hair underbody to the desired shape.

9. Tie in the Micro Ice Chenille in front of the body, and wrap the tying thread forward to the eye of the hook.

10. Wrap the Micro Ice Chenille to the eye of the hook, and tie it off. Trim the excess.

11. Wrap the tying thread rearward a short distance, and tie in the head disc so that the front of the head disc is even with the eye of the hook. About one-third of the disc should extend forward, and the remainder should extend rearward over the body. Apply a small amount of Zap-A-Gap cement to the underside of the head disc, and press it down firmly on the body disc.

12. Tie in two unseparated rubber legs on either side of the head. Once they are tied in, separate them. Whip-finish, turn the fly upside down, and apply a small amount of Zap-A-Gap cement to the thread wraps under the head. ■

Humpbacks

Hook:	Tiemco 8089, size 6, or equivalent.
Thread:	Gudebrod 6/0 or equivalent, color of choice.
Tail:	Marabou with a few strands of Flashabou or Kreinik Flash in a Tube, color of choice.
Underbody:	A 3/4-inch-diameter disc cut from 1/16-inch-thick foam (any color).
Back:	3/8-inch-wide strip of double-sided Locoskin, color of choice.
Body covering:	A 1-inch square of single-sided Locoskin, color of choice. Leave the protective covering on the Locoskin until the body is ready to be formed.
Wings:	White Ultra Hair (Super Hair).
Underhead wrap:	Kreinik Micro Ice Chenille, black, mallard, or peacock.
Head:	A 9/16-inch-diameter disc cut from 1/16-inch-thick Locofoam, color of choice.
Legs:	Fine or medium round rubber legs, color of choice.

1. Wrap the shank of the hook with tying thread to a point behind the barb of the hook. Wrap the thread forward about 1/4 inch, and tie in the marabou tail. Tie the marabou down to a point behind the barb of the hook, and then wrap the thread forward.

2. Tie in a few strands of either Flashabou or Kreinik Flash in a Tube, and wrap the thread forward about half the length of the hook shank. Trim the Flashabou so that it is about 1/2 to 3/4 inch longer than the marabou tail.

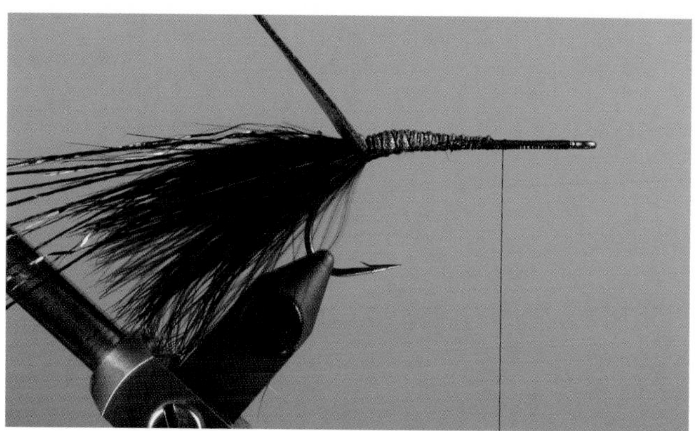

3. Trim the piece of Locoskin used to form the back of the fly to a point, and tie it in to the rear of the fly.

4. Wrap the thread forward to a point about two-thirds the length of the hook shank. Turn the fly upside down in the vise. Place the underbody disc on the underside of the hook shank, and tie down a small portion of the front of the disc.

5. Turn the fly right side up in the vise, and using a needle, apply Zap-A-Gap lightly to one side of the disc. Pinch the disc together so that it bonds along its entire length. A space should be left between the rear of the disc and the rear of the fly to accommodate the Locoskin body covering used in the next step. Wrap the thread forward to a point well in front of the disc.

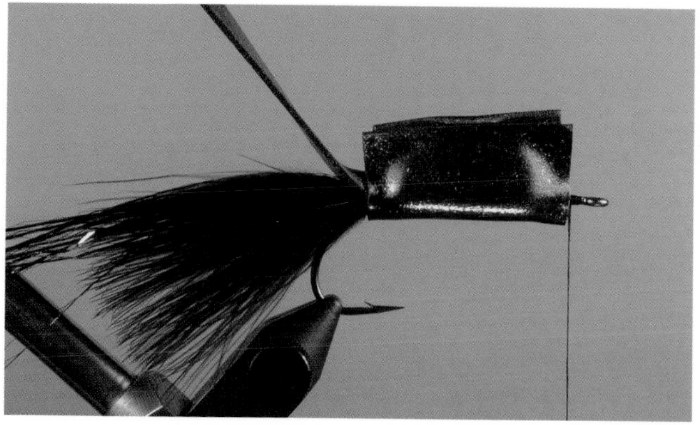

6. Remove the protective backing from the 1-inch square of Locoskin. Slide it under the fly, and bring it up evenly on both sides of the disc used to form the underbody. Pinch it together so that it bonds to itself.

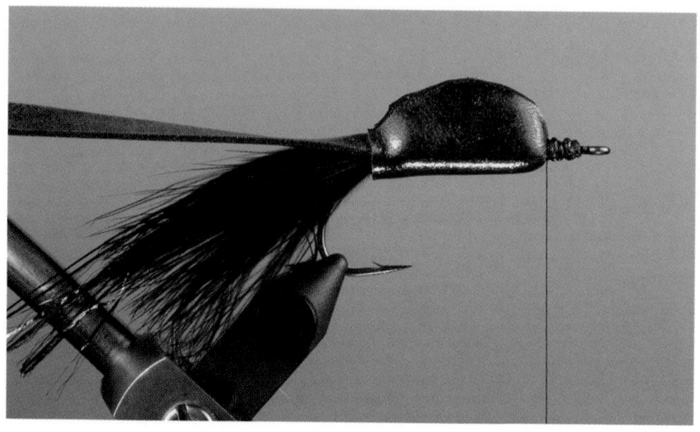

7. Trim the top of the Locoskin body covering to conform to the contours of the underbody disc, and tie down the front of the Locoskin body covering.

8. Using a fine needle, coat the Locoskin back piece with a small amount of Zap-A-Gap cement. Bring the back piece over the top of the body, and press it firmly into place. It should bond almost immediately to the body of the fly. Tie it off in front of the body, and trim the excess.

9. Tie in the wings where the body covering was tied down. A single bunch of winging material can be tied in on one side of the fly and then brought under the hook shank and up the opposite side. It is then held in place and tied down. Trim the wings slightly longer than the length of the hook.

10. Tie in a piece of the Kreinik Micro Ice Chenille, and wrap the tying thread to the eye of the hook.

11. Wrap the Micro Ice Chenille to the eye of the hook, tie it off, and trim the excess. Wrap the tying thread rearward to a point halfway between the front of the body and the eye of the hook.

12. Tie in the disc used to form the head so that the front portion of the disc extends just to the eye of the hook. When done correctly, about a third of the disc should extend forward, and the rear two-thirds should extend rearward over the body of the fly. Place a small amount of Zap-A-Gap on the underside of the head disc, and press it down on top of the body. It should bond almost immediately. Whip-finish, and remove the thread.

13. Thread a single piece of rubber legging material through the eye of a needle, and push the needle through the body of the fly just under the wings and even with the rear of the head disc. Cut the legs at the eye of the needle, and trim them to the desired length. Treat the thread wraps under the head of the fly with a small amount of either head cement or Zap-A-Gap. ■

Frawg

Hook:	Tiemco 8089, size 10, or equivalent.
Thread:	Gudebrod 6/0 or equivalent, yellow.
Butt disc:	A 1/4-inch-diameter disc cut from Pearl Yellow Locofoam.
Underbody:	Spun yellow deer hair.
Spinning loop:	Gudebrod size G thread, yellow.
Body:	A 3/4-inch-diameter disc cut from Frogskin Locofoam and trimmed to shape.
Head:	A 7/16-inch-diameter disc cut from Frogskin Locofoam.
Underhead wrap:	Kreinik Micro Ice Chenille, yellow.
Legs:	Green, round rubber leg material. The rear legs are formed from three strands of medium, round rubber legging material. The front legs are formed from two strands of the legging material. In both cases, a knot is tied in the legging material.
Eyes:	Black E-Z Shape Sparkle Body.

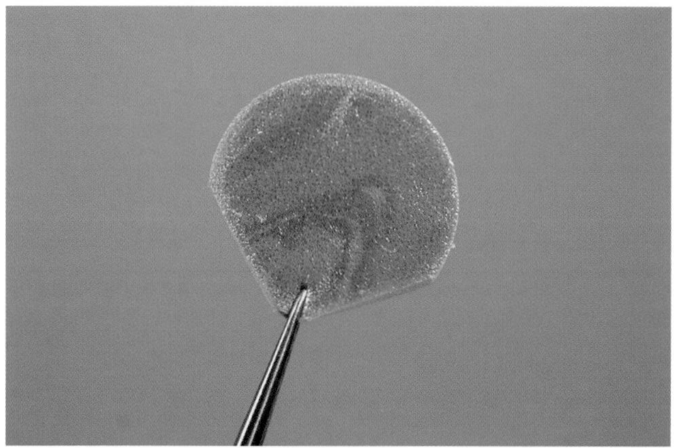

Trimmed body disc for Frawg.

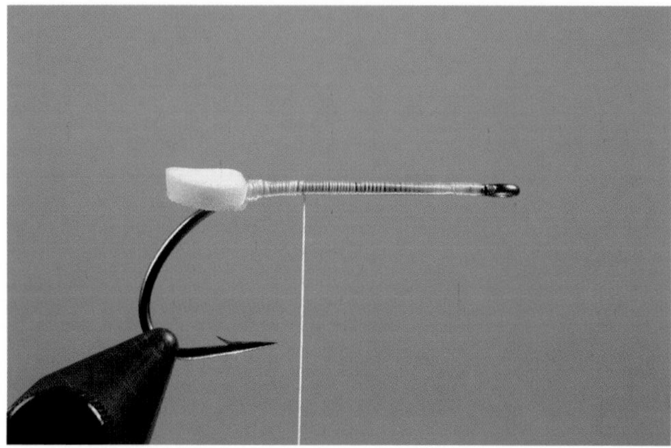

1. Wrap the thread to the rear of the hook shank, and tie in the butt disc. It is only necessary to tie in a small portion of the front of the butt disc.

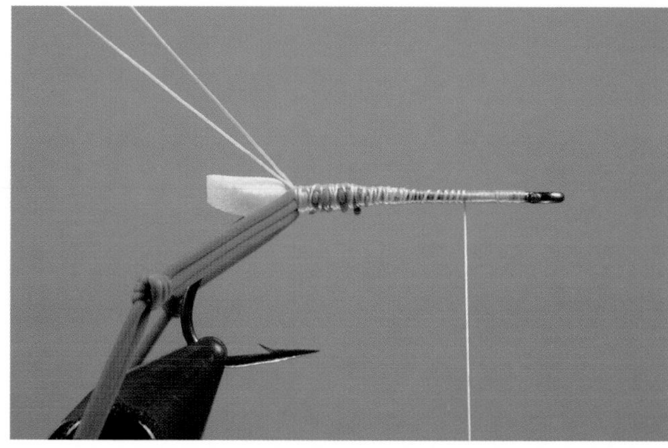

2. Wrap the tying thread forward a short distance, and tie in the two rear legs on opposite sides of the hook shank. Tie them down all the way back to the point at which the butt disc was tied in. Wrap the thread forward, and tie in a doubled strand of Gudebrod G thread to form the spinning loop. Wrap the thread forward about two-thirds the length of the hook shank.

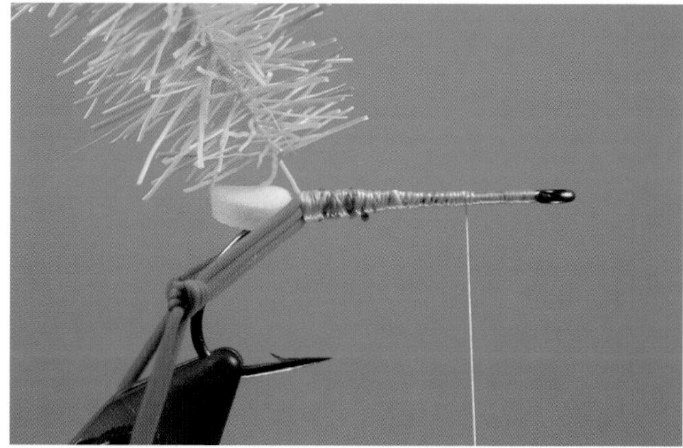

3. Cut a clump of yellow deer hair, even the tips in a hair stacker, trim the tips, and place the deer hair in the spinning loop. Distribute the hair evenly in the spinning loop. Spin the loop to form a "hair hackle."

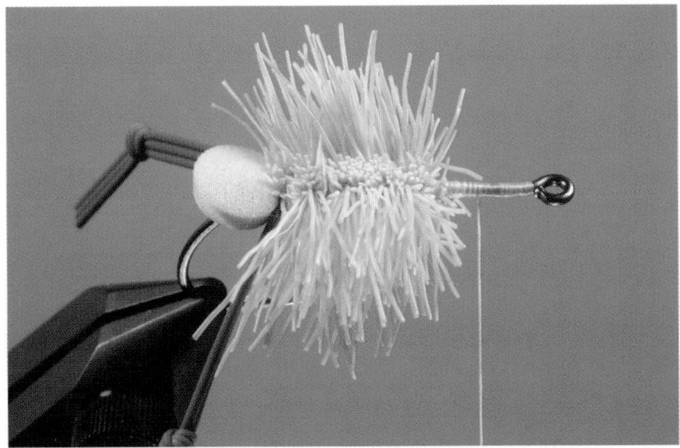

4. Wrap the spun deer hair forward about half the length of the hook shank, tie it off, and trim the excess. Trim the spun deer hair flat on top.

5. Trim the body disc to shape, and tie in the front of the body disc at the point where the spun hair was tied down.

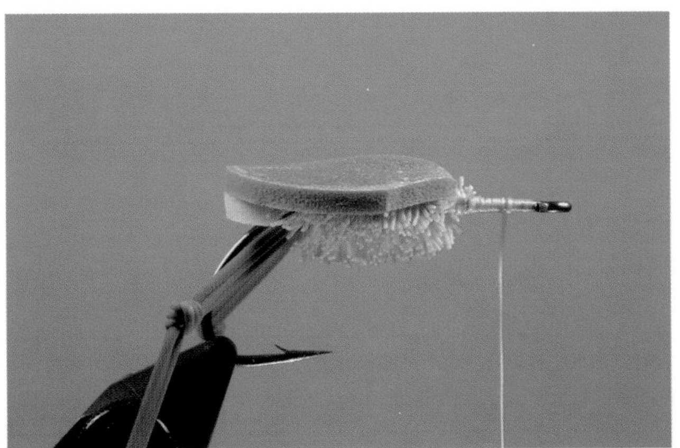

6. Apply Zap-A-Gap cement to the trimmed hair and the top of the butt disc. Press the body disc down firmly. It should bond almost immediately to the top of the body and the butt disc. Rotate the fly in the vise, and trim the deer-hair underbody to the desired shape.

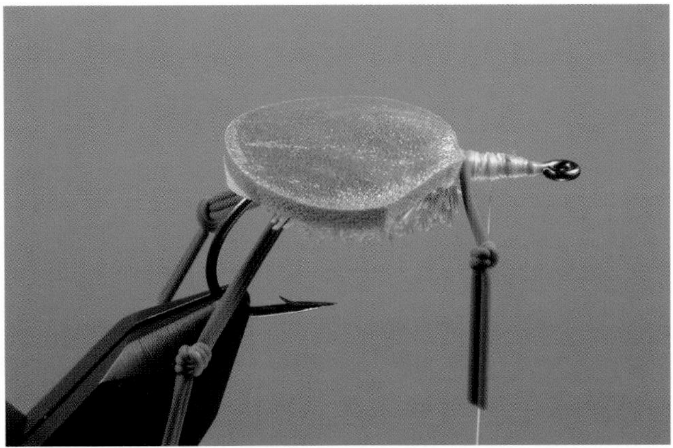

7. Tie in the front legs directly in front of the body disc and on opposite sides of the hook shank.

8. Tie in the Micro Ice Chenille, and wrap the tying thread to the eye of the hook.

9. Wrap the Micro Ice Chenille to the eye of the hook, tie it off, and trim the excess.

10. Wrap the thread rearward a short distance, tie in a small portion of the front of the head disc, and then wrap a thread "head" behind the eye of the hook. Whip-finish, and remove the tying thread. Fold the head disc forward, apply a small amount of Zap-A-Gap cement evenly to the underside of the head disc, and press it down on the foam body disc. It should bond almost immediately to the top of the body. Rotate the fly in the vise, and apply Zap-A-Gap or head cement to the thread wraps.

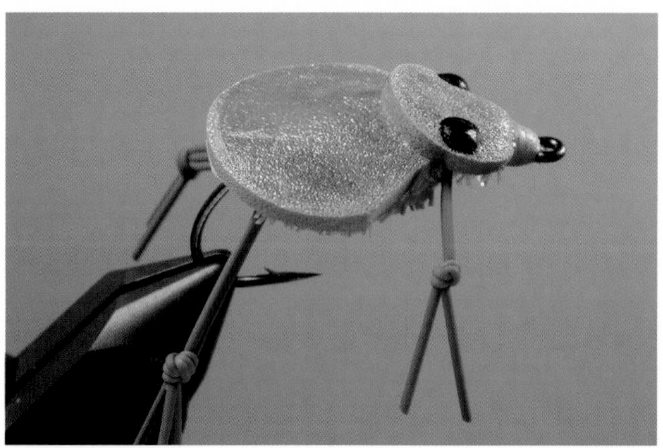

11. Add the eyes by placing a small drop of black E-Z Shape Sparkle Body on the sides of the head. Separate the rubber legging material to form the "hands" and "feet" of the fly. ■

Megabug

Hook:	Tiemco 5263, size 4, or equivalent.
Thread:	Gudebrod 6/0 or equivalent, black.
Back:	A 1/4-inch-wide strip cut from Green Swirl or Northern Lights Locofoam.
Underbody:	A 1/4-inch-wide strip cut from 1/8-inch-thick "manufactured" foam. The strip should be approximately 7/8 inch long, and any color will do.
Body:	A 1-inch square cut from single-sided Green Swirl or Northern Lights Locoskin.
Wings:	White Ultra Hair (Super Hair).
Head:	Triangle cut from Green Swirl or Northern Lights Locofoam. The triangle should be approximately 1 1/2 inches long and 1/2 inch wide at the base. Cut the tip off the triangle to give a final length of 7/8 inch.
Eyes:	A 3/16-inch-diameter foam cylinder. Use yellow, red, or gray cylinders for the eyes.
Underhead wrap:	Kreinik Micro Ice Chenille, peacock.
Legs:	Fine or medium, round rubber legs, black.

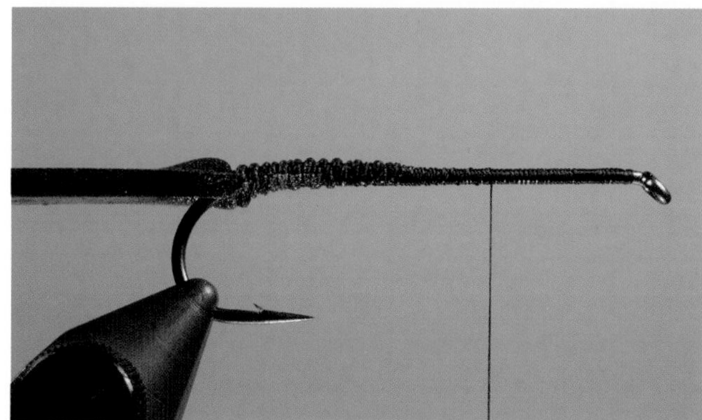

1. Wrap the hook shank with tying thread to the bend of the hook and then forward about one-third the length of the hook shank. Trim the Locofoam back piece to a point, and tie it in rearward to the bend of the hook. Tie it in with the metallic surface facing down.

2. Wrap the tying thread forward about three-fourths the length of the hook shank. Tie in the front of the underbody foam with a few tight thread wraps, and then wind the thread loosely over the underbody material back to the rear of the fly. Tie in the rear of the underbody

material with a few tight thread wraps, and then wind the tying thread forward loosely over the underbody and to the eye of the hook. Apply Zap-A-Gap cement to the bottom of the fly over the thread wraps.

3. Remove the backing paper from the square of Locoskin, place it under the hook shank, and fold it up and over the foam underbody.

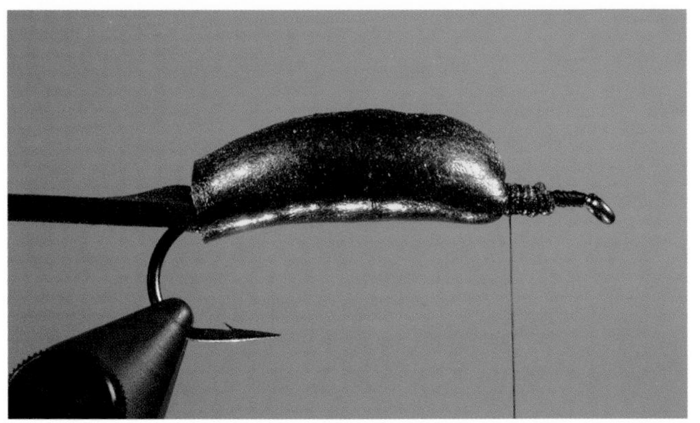

4. Pinch the Locoskin together tightly along the upper portion, and then trim it to the contours of the underbody foam. Tie down the remaining Locoskin at the front of the body. Spread a small amount of Zap-A-Gap cement on the piece of Locofoam used to form the back of the fly (I use a sewing needle chucked into a pin vise for this step).

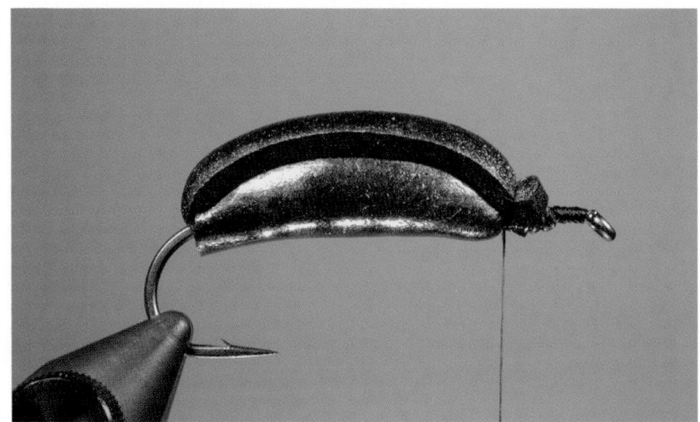

5. Fold the Locofoam back strip over the top of the body, and press it down firmly in place. Wrap the tying thread rearward, and tie down the front of the back material. Trim away any excess material.

6. Tie in a clump of winging material, and separate it into two equal portions on either side of the formed body. Trim the wings so that they are slightly longer than the body of the fly.

7. Place the trimmed tip of the triangle that will be used to form the head even with the front of the body, and tie it down all the way to the eye of the hook. Trim away any excess foam. Wrap the tying thread back to a point halfway between the eye of the hook and the front of the body.

8. Tie in the "eye" foam at this point with a few tight figure-eight thread wraps. Make sure that the eyes extend evenly on either side of the hook shank.

9. Wrap the tying thread rearward to the front of the body, and tie in the Micro Ice Chenille.

10. Wrap the Micro Ice Chenille forward around the eyes with a couple of figure-eight wraps, and then tie it off behind the eyes.

11. Fold the foam triangle over the eyes and rearward. Tie it down behind the eyes with about a dozen tight thread wraps. Trim off the corners at the base of the triangle. Using a sharp razor blade or scissors, trim the eyes flush with the head.

12. Tie in two unseparated rubber legs on each side of the head. Whip-finish, and remove the thread. Trim the legs to the desired length, and separate them. Turn the fly upside down, and place a small amount of Zap-A-Gap cement on the thread wraps under the head. ■

Steeves' Mouse

Hook:	Tiemco 8089, size 6, or equivalent.
Thread:	Gudebrod 6/0 or equivalent, brown or tan.
Tail:	A 1/16-inch-wide strip cut from tan suede leather.
Underbody:	Natural elk hair, spun in a dubbing loop, wrapped, and trimmed to shape.
Spinning loop:	Gudebrod size G thread, tan or brown.
Body:	A 3/4-inch-diameter disc cut from Tan Opal Locofoam and trimmed to shape.
Ears:	A 5/8-inch-diameter disc cut from Tan Opal Locofoam and trimmed to shape.
Beard:	A clump of natural elk hair.
Head:	A 1/2-inch-diameter disc cut from Tan Opal Locofoam.
Whiskers:	Four to six black nylon paintbrush bristles.
Eyes:	Black E-Z Shape Sparkle Body.

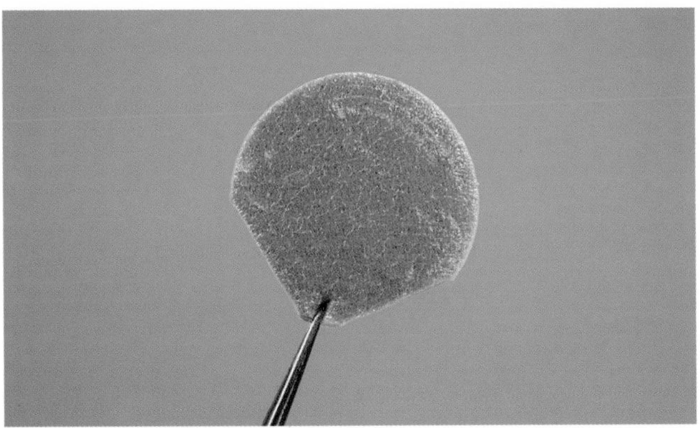

Foam disc trimmed to form the body of the mouse.

Foam disc trimmed to form the ears of the mouse.

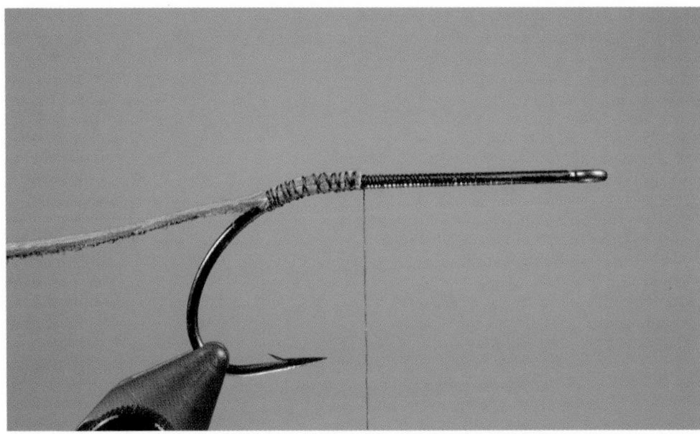

1. Wrap the hook shank with tying thread to a point behind the hook barb and then forward about 1/4 inch. Tie in the tail, and wrap the thread rearward so that the tail is firmly tied down. Trim the tail to the desired length.

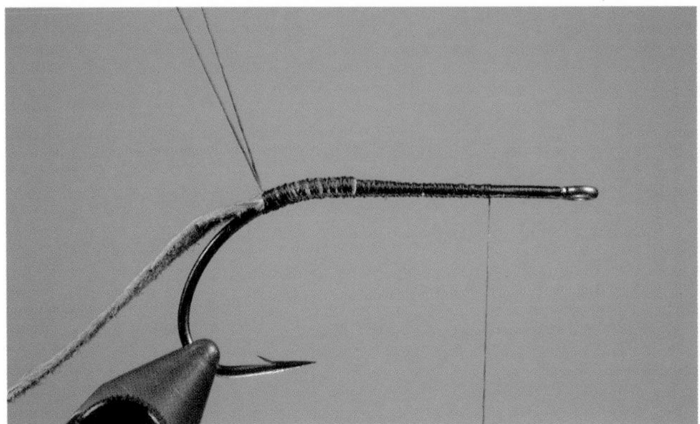

2. Wrap the tying thread forward a short distance, and tie in a doubled strand of Gudebrod G thread. Tie down the spinning thread loop to the rear of the hook, and wrap the tying thread forward about two-thirds the length of the hook shank.

3. Cut a good bunch of natural elk hair, and even the tips in a hair stacker. Trim the tips, and place the hair in the spinning loop. Adjust the hair evenly in the loop, and spin it to form a "hair hackle."

4. Wrap the spun elk hair forward about two-thirds the length of the hook shank, tie it off, and trim the excess.

5. Trim the spun elk hair flat on the top.

6. Tie in the trimmed foam-body piece at the same point at which the spun elk hair body was tied down. The foam-body disc should extend rearward to a point just over the base of the tail.

7. Apply Zap-A-Gap cement to the trimmed elk hair on top of the fly and a small amount to the top of the base of the tail. Press the body disc down firmly on the top of the fly and base of the tail. It should bond very quickly.

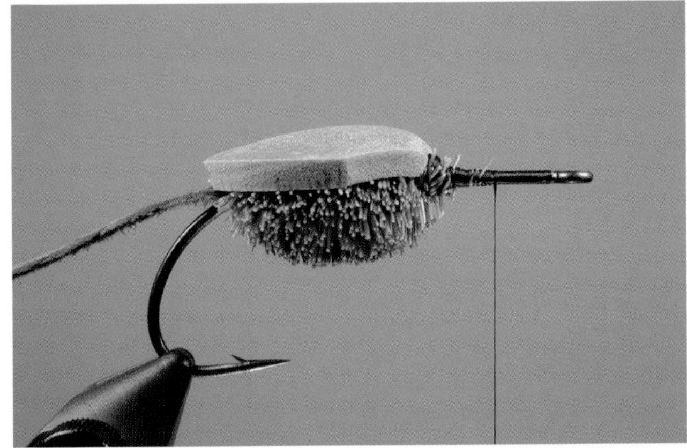

8. Trim the elk hair body of the fly to the desired shape.

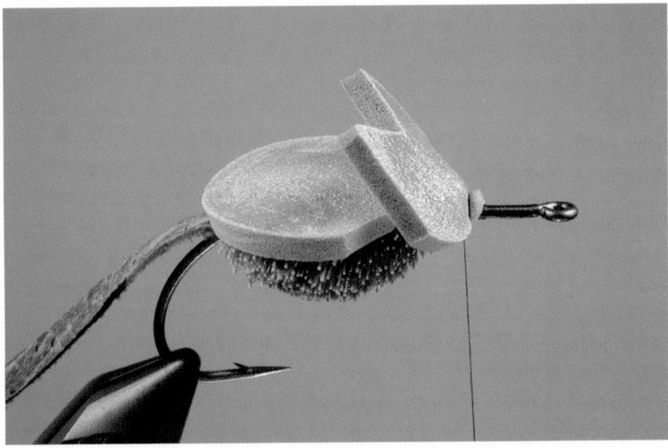

9. Tie in the trimmed ear disc directly in front of the body disc.

10. Fold the ears forward, and apply a small amount of Zap-A-Gap cement to the top of the body disc. Press the ear disc down on the body disc. The cement should be applied so that only the base of the ear disc will be cemented in place. The tips of the ears should be free of the body disc and stand up a little.

11. Tie in the elk hair beard under the hook shank.

12. Trim the elk hair beard to match the contours of the trimmed elk hair body.

13. Tie in the front of the head disc directly in front of the ear disc.

14. After five or six tight thread wraps, tie in the whiskers between the head disc and the small forward-projecting piece of foam of the head disc. A few figure-eight wraps are all that are needed. Trim the whiskers to the desired length. Apply a small amount of Zap-A-Gap cement evenly to the underside of the head disc, and push it down onto the top of the ear disc. It should bond almost immediately. Wrap the thread forward, and tie down any forward-projecting foam. This will effectively form a "nose" for the fly, with the whiskers at the base of the nose. Rotate the fly in the vise, and apply Zap-A-Gap cement to all thread wraps under the fly and on the nose.

15. Add eyes on the sides of the head using black E-Z Shape Sparkle Body. Allow the eyes to dry for at least twelve hours before fishing the fly. ■

Torpedo

Hook:	Tiemco 5263, size 2, or equivalent.
Thread:	Gudebrod 6/0 or equivalent, color at tier's option.
Tail:	Marabou with a few strands of Flashabou, color at the option of the tier.
Back:	A 1/4-inch-wide strip cut from either 1/16-inch-thick Locofoam or regular foam, color at option of the tier.
Underbody:	3/8- to 1/4-inch-wide strip of 1/8-inch-thick "manufactured" foam, any color. The underbody should be about 7/8 inch long.
Body covering:	A 1-inch square of single-sided Locoskin, color is the option of the tier. Leave the protective backing on the square of Locoskin until you are ready to form the body.
Wings:	White Ultra Hair (Super Hair).
Head:	*Top*—A 5/8-inch-diameter disc cut from Locofoam or regular 1/16-inch-thick foam. *Bottom*—A 9/16-inch-diameter disc cut from Locofoam or 1/16-inch-thick regular foam. The color of the discs is the option of the tier.
Legs:	Round rubber legs, medium size, color at option of tier.
Eyes:	3-D molded eyes.

1. Attach the thread to the shank of the hook, and wrap the thread rearward to a point behind the barb of the hook. Wrap the thread forward about one-fourth the length of the hook shank, and tie in the marabou tail.

2. Add a few strands of Flashabou on top of the marabou tail, and trim the Flashabou so that it extends well past the end of the marabou tail.

3. Wrap the thread forward about two-thirds the length of the hook shank. Trim the piece of Locofoam used for the back to a point, and tie it in. Tie in the Locofoam back material rearward to a point just behind the barb of the hook.

4. Wrap the thread forward to a point approximately 1/4 inch behind the eye of the hook. Tie in the front of the underbody foam strip about 1/4 inch behind the eye of the hook. The rear portion of the strip should extend to a point about 1/8 inch forward of the point where the tail was tied in. In other words, leave a little space at the rear. Wrap the thread rearward *loosely* over the foam underbody material, and then tie down the rear of the underbody material tightly. Then wrap the thread loosely forward again to the front of the underbody material. If the foam underbody material is tied in correctly, it will be tapered at the front and rear and barely tied down over most of its length. Rotate the fly upside down in the vise, and apply Zap-A-Gap to the underside of the fly. Using a bodkin or large needle, spread the Zap-A-Gap evenly on the underside of the fly.

5. Remove the protective backing from the Locoskin square, and bring it up underneath the hook shank and around the sides of the underbody. Pinch it together firmly along its entire length on the top of the fly.

6. Trim the excess Locofoam on top of the fly to conform to the shape of the underbody. A small amount of the Locoskin should extend forward of the underbody. Tie this down firmly.

7. Apply a small amount of Zap-A-Gap to the middle of the Locofoam back strip. Spread it evenly with a needle or bodkin, bring the Locofoam strip over the top of the fly, and tie it off at the same point at which the Locoskin body covering was tied down. Trim away the forward-projecting piece of Locofoam. Press down on the Locofoam back strip; it should bond almost immediately to the top of the Locoskin body. Apply pressure to the sides of the Locofoam back strip so that it bonds to the rest of the top. Trim away the forward-projecting piece of Locofoam back material.

8. Tie in the winging material in front of the formed body, separate it into two equal portions, and tie the wings in on the sides of the body. Trim the wings so that they extend past the rear of the body.

9. Wrap the thread forward to a point about 1/8 inch behind the eye of the hook. Rotate the fly in the vise so that it is upside down, and tie in the bottom disc used to form the head. Apply a small amount of Zap-A-Gap to the entire undersurface of the disc, and press it down on the underside of the body. Bonding should take only a few seconds. Pinch the sides of the disc inward so that it bonds to the sides of the body.

10. Rotate the fly upright in the vise, and tie in the top disc. Apply Zap-A-Gap to the entire underside of the top disc, and press it down firmly on the top of the body. Once the disc has bonded to the top of the body, pinch the sides of the top disc inward so that it bonds to the bottom disc. Form a neat thread wrap in front of the head, whip-finish, and remove the thread.

11. Add eyes by placing a small drop of Zap-A-Gap at the desired point on the top of the head and pressing the eye firmly into place.

12. Thread a single piece of rubber leg material through the eye of a large needle. Push the needle through the foam body at a point halfway up the body and just behind the bottom disc used to form the head. Cut the rubber legs at the eye of the needle, and trim them to the desired length. Cover the thread wraps of the head with either head cement or Zap-A-Gap cement. ■

Snakey Jake

Hook:	Tiemco 5263, size 2, or equivalent.
Tail:	A $1/8$-inch-wide, 4- to 5-inch-long strip of double-sided Locoskin. Color is tier's option. If desired, a few strands of Flashabou can be tied in above the Locoskin tail.
Back strip:	A $1/4$-inch-wide strip of Locofoam, color is tier's option.
Underbody:	A $3/8$- to $1/4$-inch-wide strip of $1/8$-inch-thick "manufactured" foam. Any color can be used because this will be hidden when the body is completed. The underbody should be about $7/8$ inch long.
Body covering:	A 1-inch-square piece of single-sided Locoskin. Leave the protective coating on the Locoskin until the body is ready to be formed. The color of the Locoskin is the tier's option.
Head:	*Top*—A $5/8$-inch-diameter disc cut from Locofoam or $1/16$-inch-thick regular foam, color is the tier's option. *Bottom*—A $9/16$-inch-diameter disc cut from Locofoam or $1/16$-inch-thick regular foam, color is the tier's option.
Legs:	Medium round rubber legs, color is optional.
Eyes:	3-D molded eyes.

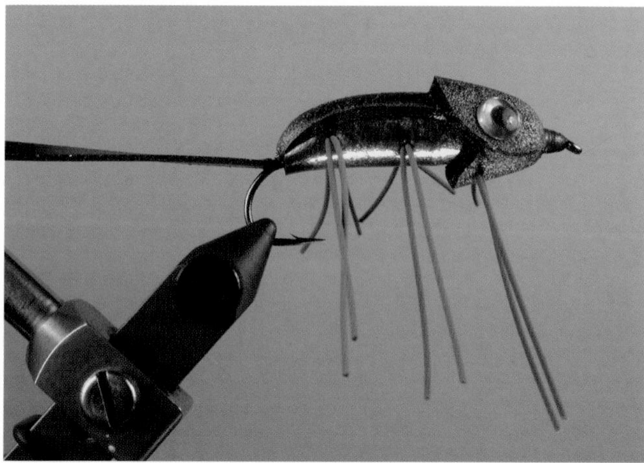

The Snakey Jake is tied using the same procedure as that for the Torpedo. The only differences are a strip of Locoskin is tied in for the tail, and three sets of legs are threaded through the body instead of one. ■

Ultimate Cicada

Hook:	Tiemco 8089, size 10, or equivalent.
Thread:	Gudebrod 6/0 or equivalent, fluorescent orange.
Underbody:	A 1/4-inch-wide strip of 1/8-inch-thick "manufactured" foam, 5/8 inch long.
Underbody wrap:	Orange Estaz.
Back:	A 5/16-inch-wide strip of Northern Lights Locofoam.
Wings:	Orange Kinky Fiber.
Head:	A triangle cut from Northern Lights Locofoam. The triangle should be about 1/2 inch wide at the base and 1 1/2 inches long. Trim the top of the triangle so that the final length is 7/8 inch.
Underhead wrap:	Kreinik Micro Ice Chenille, peacock or mallard.
Eyes:	A 3/16-inch-diameter foam cylinder, yellow, red, or orange.
Legs:	Round rubber legs, medium size, black.

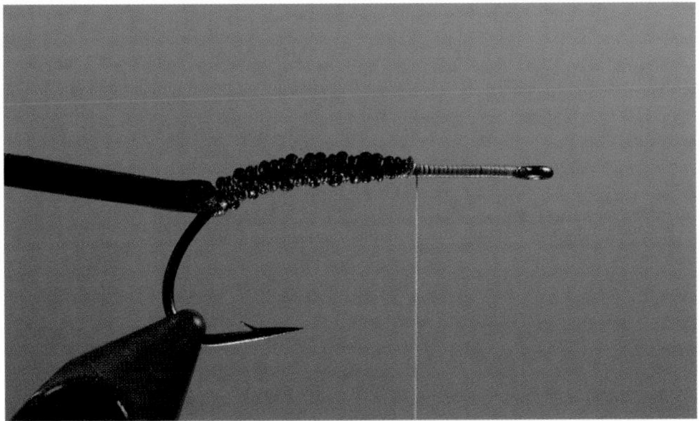

1. Wrap the shank of the hook with thread to a point past the barb of the hook. Tie in the back material with the iridescent (metallic) side down.

2. Wrap the thread forward about two-thirds the length of the hook shank, and tie in the front of the underbody strip with a few tight thread wraps. Wrap the tying thread rearward, loosely, over the underbody foam. Tie down the rear of the underbody foam with a few tight thread wraps. Wrap the tying thread forward, loosely, to the front of the underbody and then back to the rear.

3. Tie in the Estaz at the rear of the fly, and wrap the tying thread forward loosely to a point about 1/8 inch in front of the underbody. Rotate the fly upside down in the vise, and use a fine needle to apply Zap-A-Gap cement to the bottom of the underbody foam and the thread on the hook shank. Turn the fly right side up, and apply Zap-A-Gap to the top of the underbody foam.

4. Wrap the Estaz forward, and tie it off. Trim the excess.

5. Trim the Estaz fibers so that they are shorter than on the original piece.

6. Fold the back foam over the formed body, tie it off, and trim the excess.

7. Tie in the winging material on opposite sides of the body, and trim the length so that the wings extend slightly past the bend of the hook.

8. Wrap the tying thread to the eye of the hook.

9. Place the tip of the trimmed triangle even with the front of the body, and tie in the triangle by wrapping the thread rearward toward the body. Remember to tie the triangle in with the iridescent side down. Trim and tie down the foam extending rearward.

10. Cut a 3/4-inch-long piece of the foam cylinder used for the eyes, and using a series of figure-eight wraps, tie it down halfway between the eye of the hook and the front of the body.

11. Tie in the Micro Ice Chenille behind the eye cylinder.

12. Wrap the Micro Ice Chenille over the eye cylinder with a couple of figure-eight wraps and behind and in front of the eye cylinder. Tie it off behind the eye cylinder, and trim the excess.

13. Fold the head triangle rearward over the eyes, and tie it down. If it appears to be a little long, it can be trimmed. It should extend rearward about $^3/_{16}$ to $^1/_4$ inch from the point where it was tied down behind the eyes. Place a small amount of Zap-A-Gap cement on the top of the body, and press the rear-projecting portion of the head triangle down to cement it in place. Trim the corners of the head triangle.

14. Using a sharp razor blade or scissors, trim the eyes flush with the head.

15. Tie in two unseparated legs on either side of the head of the fly, and trim them to the desired length. Separate the legs after they are tied in. Rotate the fly upside down in the vise, and apply a small amount of Zap-A-Gap cement to the thread wraps under the head. ■

Afterword

Since this book is primarily devoted to terrestrial patterns, I believe I should limit my closing remarks to those wonderful land dwelling bugs that make up an important component of the diet of all trout. I am so hooked on terrestrial insects that I seem to fish terrestrial patterns in preference to everything else, even during a major hatch of aquatic insects. There is something oddly satisfying and rewarding about catching trout on a tiny beetle or ant pattern during a hatch of caddisflies or mayflies. I might add, not just catching a trout, but actually catching more than those around you who are using imitations or the hatching aquatic insect. When this happens I take almost perverse pleasure in answering the question "What were you using?" with "A size 19 Firefly."

Does this happen often? Yes, it does. Last summer I took seventeen browns on a terrestrial pattern during a hatch of sulfurs on the west branch of New York's Delaware River. That's just one example of many. What is difficult to understand is that it is almost impossible to convince most anglers that they too can do the same. I routinely fish a beetle during a Trico hatch. I will often fish a fluorescent orange ant during a midge hatch, a hatch of sulfurs, or a hatch of blue-winged olives. I have fished the UFO during a blizzard hatch of pale morning duns with incredible results. Most of the guys I fish with have experienced the same results using different terrestrial patterns. In this respect, terrestrials seem to have a universal appeal as a choice food item. The problem is convincing others that this really works.

I fish terrestrials all year long, or at least I used to. I now no longer fish during the winter months, but a decade ago I would stand in 40-degree water with the air temperature well below freezing and fish tiny terrestrials to midging fish. If nothing was hatching on tailwater fisheries in the middle of January, I could always bring up a few good fish with a terrestrial pattern. Those days are over. I no longer derive any pleasure from standing in a river in the middle of winter and freezing to death. I no longer fight ice buildup in the guides of the rod. I no longer hope that a fish will get off before I can bring it to net just because I don't want my hands to get wet. I no longer walk back to the car on feet that have turned to wooden stumps. But when I used to put myself through this torture, I caught plenty of fish on terrestrial patters during the coldest months of the year.

So there you have it. I used to fish terrestrials all year long. Others still do. If you read the anecdotal material carefully, I hope you were intrigued by two of the anecdotes that were sent to me. One from Pat Devney told about his success with the Crystal Butt Cricket on a December day. The other was the account Tom Lawson sent to me about taking a 24-inch brown with the Bluebottle Fly in November. What this tells me is that a few others have discovered the effectiveness of terrestrial patterns during the winter months.

Terrestrial patterns will produce for you from early spring, through the summer and fall, and on into the winter. You should take advantage of their universal appeal, their tremendous effectiveness, and their ability to bring up big fish throughout the year. After all, a few of us have discovered that a good terrestrial pattern is truly a fly for all seasons.